D0638643

SONG AND SYSTEM

SONG AND SYSTEM

The Making of American Pop Music

Harvey Rachlin

ROWMAN & LITTLEFIELD
Lanham • Boulder • New York • London

Published by Rowman & Littlefield
An imprint of The Rowman & Littlefield Publishing Group, Inc.
4501 Forbes Boulevard, Suite 200, Lanham, Maryland 20706
www.rowman.com

6 Tinworth Street, London SE11 5AL, United Kingdom

Copyright © 2020 by The Rowman & Littlefield Publishing Group, Inc.

All rights reserved. No part of this book may be reproduced in any form or by any electronic or mechanical means, including information storage and retrieval systems, without written permission from the publisher, except by a reviewer who may quote passages in a review.

British Library Cataloguing in Publication Information Available

Library of Congress Cataloging-in-Publication Data

Names: Rachlin, Harvey, author.
Title: Song and system : the making of American pop music / Harvey Rachlin.
Description: Lanham : Rowman & Littlefield Publishing Group, 2020. | Includes bibliographical
    references and index. | Summary: "Growing in tandem with each other, pop music and the
    business of creating and distributing it have become a relationship that defines modern cultu-
    ral history. This book not only charts the music that we all know and love but also reveals our
    active participation in its development throughout generations."—Provided by publisher.
Identifiers: LCCN 2019038978 (print) | LCCN 2019038979 (ebook) | ISBN 9781538112120
    (cloth) | ISBN 9781538112137 (epub)
Subjects: LCSH: Popular music—United States—History and criticism. | Sound recording indus-
    try—United States—History.
Classification: LCC ML3477 .R35 2020 (print) | LCC ML3477 (ebook) | DDC 781.640973—dc23
LC record available at https://lccn.loc.gov/2019038978
LC ebook record available at https://lccn.loc.gov/2019038979

♾ ™ The paper used in this publication meets the minimum requirements of American National Standard for Information Sciences Permanence of Paper for Printed Library Materials, ANSI/NISO Z39.48-1992.

For Alysa

CONTENTS

ACKNOWLEDGMENTS

First and foremost, I would like to thank Natalie Mandziuk, the music book acquisitions editor at Rowman & Littlefield. I came to her with an idea that in retrospect was somewhat vague, and she diligently and expertly shaped it into something more concrete. Her excellent critiques and editorial guidance made this book far better than what I delivered to her, and so I am very grateful to her and cannot lavish enough praise on her. Natalie is truly an "editor's editor."

I would also like to lavish praise on assistant editor Michael Tan for his great work in helping shepherd this work toward publication and to express my utmost appreciation to production editor Lara Hahn and everyone else at Rowman & Littlefield who was involved in the process of helping transform my manuscript into the book you are now holding. In book publishing, there are many unheralded people behind the scenes, and I am happy to enthusiastically salute those who were involved with this book.

I am grateful to my daughter-in-law Rebecca Rachlin, who provided perspicacious insights into the music of the 1980s and beyond that helped shape my chapter on "A New Age of Pop Stars." Her keen knowledge of the modern pop era was of great advantage to the chapter.

I have run the music business program at Manhattanville College in Purchase, New York, for many years and owe a great debt to many people I have interacted with there over the years, ranging from faculty to administration to students. I will attempt to list some people, but undoubtedly there will be many whose names I have omitted, and to those I apologize. I owe a great debt to Jerry Kerlin, who is the present chair of the Music Department. Dr. Kerlin is one of the finest music educators I have ever known, and his great teaching talents and administrative capabilities are matched only by his geniality and kind-heartedness. Former Music Department chair Tony LaMagra hired me many years ago, and to him I will always be grateful. Other Music Department faculty I would like to thank (with apologies for not heaping praise on each) are Geoffrey Kidde, Mel Comberiati, Mark Cherry, Olivier Fluchaire, Beverly Meyer, James Lorusso, Diane Guernsey, Ronald Cappon, and Jeongeun Yom, as well as our invaluable Music Department coordinator, Kathryn DiBernardo, and retired professors Mary Ann Joyce and Francis Brancaleone. I appreciate the wonderful assistance I received from the Manhattanville College Library staff, and in particular I would like to thank Jeff Rosedale and Susan Majdak. Also at the college I am grateful to the president, Dr. Michael E. Geisler; the interim provost, Dr. Louise H. Feroe; and the dean of the School of Arts and Sciences, Christine Dehne.

For more than two decades I have learned much from students who have sat in my classroom at Manhattanville, and among them I would like to thank Richard Sica, Colleen Calabro Dahlstrom, Kerry Kaleja, Jamar Chess, Raina Mullen, Violet Foulk, Kimberly Spataro, Bobby Gasparakis, Terelina Cruz, Nicole Meyers, Thomas Solari, Julianna Ross, Richard Schertzer, Mariana Trodella, John Calicchia, Jarrett Dellaquilla, Jaime Ortega, Dan Hosannah, Tori Macchi, Quincy Primus, Francis Cardona, Isabella Passaretta, Natalia Veras, Kelsey Lora, and Serena Smacchia. For those I have left out, I offer my sincere apologies. I would also like to acknowledge musicologist Judith Finell, who accepted many of my students as interns and helped set them off into wonderful careers in the music business, and Stefanie May, the marketing director of the Capitol Theatre in Port Chester, New York, who has taken many of my students as interns and trained them well in all sorts of areas related to concert management.

I would like to thank my longtime friend Michael Kerker, who runs the Musical Theatre Department at ASCAP, for all the kindnesses he has bestowed on me over the years. Among his many generosities was helping me put together a "Charles Strouse Day" at Manhattanville College, getting stars associated with Strouse's musicals such as *Bye*

Bye Birdie and *Annie* to come pay tribute to and perform with the renowned Broadway composer (original *Annie* star Andrea McArdle singing the Edith Bunker part and Strouse singing the Archie Bunker part on Strouse's theme song "Those Were the Days" from *All in the Family* was precious, hilarious, and unforgettable). Michael is a legend at ASCAP and has worked with many of the greatest composers in musical theater history from Jerry Herman to Stephen Sondheim.

Many years ago when I aspired to write about music, two publishers saw potential in me, I suppose, and published my articles. To them I shall always be grateful. They are Syde Berman, publisher of *The Songwriter's Review*, and James D. Liddane, publisher of *Songwriter*, a division of Songwriters International Association. I would also like to thank Mike Lawson, the editor of *School Band & Orchestra* and *Choral Director*, who has given me the opportunity to write for these magazines, which have also broadened my horizons with respect to pop songs. Mike is a super-talented editor who is as nice as he is talented.

Others who offered valuable input include Jeff Jastrow, Jeff Burke, Jesse Berensci, Richard W. Lewis, Jaime Babbitt, and Bonnie Schachter Barchichat. I'd like to especially single out Jean Bennett, who helped launch the iconic group The Platters with Buck Ram, and who has been a dear friend and inspiration through the years. A prime force in the 1950s of making the Platters the super-sensation they were, and fighting hard for the group to enjoy the same civil rights as any white act, she is a true legend in the music business. She has affectionately been referred to as "The Grandmother of Rock and Roll."

I would also like to offer special thanks to Glenn Rachlin, Steven Rachlin, Barry Sasson, Danielle Sasson, and Alex Rotker. Most of all, I would like to thank Alysa Sasson, my "better half," who endured the oft-mentioned loneliness and frustration of being an "author's spouse," but who was always patient and supportive (or at least most of the time). It is with much love that I dedicate this book to her.

INTRODUCTION

The music industry is now immersed in the digital era, a form that would have been virtually inconceivable only a handful of decades ago. Over the years, its recorded product was disseminated in a multitude of physical forms: wax cylinders, 78 rpm discs, 33 1/3 rpm albums, 45 rpm singles, cassette tapes, eight-track cartridges, and CDs. These various offerings showed that consumers adapt well to technological changes that enhance or expand the listening experience. But while consumers readily embraced format changes (even with their shortcomings), it would have been hard for them to comprehend a day not too far off into the future when they wouldn't have to purchase physical records at all.

Contemporary fans in the heyday, say, of the rock and roll, folk rock, heavy metal, disco, and punk rock eras would have been flabbergasted at the notion—something out of science fiction, they might say—that they could have virtually any recording ever made at any time and anywhere, instantly and for free, by a mere click on a device. No more running to the nearest record shop, no more riffling through album bins, no more clinking of cash registers and waiting for your change. Just a press of your finger and—ta-da!—any music you want (and more music than you ever dreamed of)—from antediluvian melodies to the most current tracks and even tunes being recorded in live time—is there for your picking and enjoyment. Modern technology has indeed made this wondrous expedience possible, but even with all the dazzling computer code/microchips/cloud technological wizardry fueling the anytime-anywhere accessibility of music, it should be remembered that the goal of the music business today is essentially the same as it was back in its quaint earliest days of the late nineteenth century—to bring music to the public as efficiently and affordably as possible.

While the public today may be pleased with the bounteous offering of recorded music and its expeditious delivery, the digital transformation of the industry has not yet eliminated the myriad kinds of complexities and problems that have always beset the music industry. Indeed, with technology, business practices, and laws constantly changing, it seems the music business has always suffered from growing pains, with numerous issues causing economic and emotional distress such as piracy, entities that resist taking out licenses or fighting for lower-than-fair-market licensing rates, outdated laws, and lack of transparency regarding the payment of royalties. One would think that advanced technology would minimize all that, and while there has been some mitigation, modernization has also given rise to new sets of problems.

Today, a litany of problems draws the attention of the industry: low royalties paid by streaming services that make it difficult for songwriters who are not performers to earn a livelihood off their craft; streaming services lacking the proper data on all the rights holders of a musical composition, making it difficult to identify who the royalty recipients are and how to pay royalties accurately; unauthorized uploading of songs and sound recordings on content-sharing websites that is abetted by the Safe Harbor provision of the Digital Millennium Copyright Act; no performance royalty for artists and labels when their recordings are broadcast on terrestrial radio (as opposed to songwriters and music publishers who do earn a performance royalty for terrestrial radio airplay); the rampant illegal sampling of songs and sound recordings; the ability of scalpers to use technology to purchase bundles of concert tickets upon their being offered for sale, and a secondary online market in which scalpers can sell tickets for highly inflated prices.

Along with such contemporary problems, evolving cultural and social perspectives have torn down the pillars of longstanding traditions in the music business and given rise to confusion. With the habits of music listeners being scrupulously tracked with all sorts of data, who decides which artists get signed to labels—A&R scouts or data systems? What role do fans and social media have in the creation of an album? With albums released of excessive varying lengths, how long should an album be? When is an album completed and released? Are albums even necessary when the bigger money is in touring? Indeed, is there a future for albums when album sales have plummeted and a flow of singles, in our world of streaming where a smash song can rack up hundreds of millions or even billions of views, may be more lucrative?

Welcome to the new digital music industry, which evolves on almost a daily basis with floods of ideas constantly springing forth, creating new opportunities and challenging established practices.

With such a radical shift in the delivery and consumption of music today, as Nobel Prize–winning songwriter Bob Dylan famously said in his 1964-released song, "The Times, They Are a-Changin'." Despite some format spikes like we've seen with vinyl records, sales of recordings may never recover to their previous levels, even with downloads, whose sales have been decreasing in recent years, in the retail mix. Ditto for sheet music and other forms of printed music. And with sampling enjoying huge popularity among young generations of music makers and music fans, songs may not be written and recorded en masse like they used to be—that is, all original choruses, bridges, verses, and other elements without the interpolation of preexisting music and sounds.

Still, with the digital era of music now upon us, the possibilities for new kinds of music, new forms of delivery, and new musical experiences are at once exciting and intriguing. The music industry is in an ever-constant state of flux, but today it's in a wonderful state of flux as more music becomes more readily available and with technology ever-transmogrifying, but who knows what the future will bring? Technology is taking the music industry to heights never thought achievable, and it's anyone's guess as to what the industry will look like twenty or forty or a hundred years down the line. Will there one day be hologram technology that enables us to sit in a chair and experience in front of us a live concert of any artist who ever lived? Will we one day have chips implanted within us that enable us to hear any song we want come resoundingly alive in our heads? Will there one day be live mass-audience concerts in floating stadiums in outer space or on exotic heavenly bodies? It seems anything we imagine of what is to come is within our grasp, and the very fact that that is a possibility in itself signals an exciting future.

For now, streaming seems the way of the future. People can stream interactively or non-interactively and choose the songs they want or from curated lists or have music programmed for them according to their tastes. Streaming services are the new big content-deliverers, ubiquitous any-song-you-want song suppliers that are open twenty-four hours a day, seven days a week. They all vie for consumer participation, hoping to draw them with their own unique offerings and convert those who opt on for free to become premium customers (or ad-free paying subscribers). It may have taken people a while to get used to the idea of paying to hear music, with older segments of the public used to getting music for free after lifetimes of listening to gratis terrestrial radio, but sometimes progress comes with a price tag that takes times to accept. Indeed, the streaming service Spotify by the end of 2018 (after it had become a publicly traded company) had 96 million paying subscribers and 207 million monthly active users from around the world, although in February 2019 Apple Music reportedly surpassed Spotify's 26 million U.S. subscribers by 2 million. And if people wish, they can still purchase music, in either physical or digital form. It's all there, giving people many options on how they can choose to receive music.

Streaming is now the fastest-growing segment of the multi-billion-dollar recorded music business. The International Federation of the Phonographic Industry reported that in 2017 revenue from streaming for the first time was greater than that from physical product—but it comes hinged with expensive licensing rights, with low royalty rates, with the challenge of getting people to subscribe to the services that provide it, and with the challenge of becoming profitable. Artists complain that labels don't fairly share the income they receive and there is a lack of transparency when it comes to accounting for royalties. With songwriters and music publishers likewise complaining about the low streaming royalties, it seems everyone in the content-licensing arena is fighting for those micro-pennies. But revenue is there. Sony Corporation reported that for the year 2017 earnings of its music division increased 5.9 percent to almost $4 billion. Other music companies, too, such as concert promoter Live Nation, reported their best year in 2017.

The doom-and-gloom forecasts of the music business that began in the 1990s with epidemic illegal peer-to-peer file sharing have given way to a prosperous digital music industry in which innovators are constantly coming up with new ways to enhance the music experience for the public as well as to improve behind-the-scenes business activities such as the administration of song rights. With more music than ever before being produced (it can be done facilely and cheaply on home recording devices, enabling anyone to put out a professional record) and new cutting-edge management methods to help the industry on the horizon such as blockchain technology and cryptocurrency, there has perhaps never been a better time for the music business and its fans.

From multi-day music festivals to the latest smartphones, from streaming services always trying to be competitive to the vast array of social media, music in the digital age is more exciting than ever. *But, one may ask, how does it all work, and how did we get to where we are today?*

This book focuses on the evolution of the pop music industry and how it works today. Indeed, behind the simple streaming of a song or the broadcast of a record or the purchase of an album is a long and complex tale that stretches back centuries ago and involves numerous grand themes that, when you get down to it, are nothing less than the story of humankind—the right to be free from oppression, the creation of democracy and inalienable rights, the human quest for exploration, the human desire for creative expression and entrepreneurship. Yes, all these themes and more in one way or another got us to where we are today with regard to the music that has evolved and the people who create it, the technology that has developed from which we receive music, the laws that govern the business of music, the culture that has emerged that is both the spark and the setting for all the music. Though we may not think about it, a myriad of events in the story of civilization is really behind a stream or broadcast or purchase of music.

This book attempts to frame the evolution of the music business with the evolution of the popular song. There is truly a symbiotic relationship between songs and the music business, as songs shape the business and the music business shapes songs. Songwriters, who are often artists today, supply the songs, and the music publishers go out and exploit the songs to maximize their income. Both creator and entrepreneur need each other to keep the supply of popular songs going to the commercial marketplace and sating the public appetite for music, a process that has indeed been going on for a long time.

Popular music was born, nurtured, coddled, and cultivated on numerous diverse and well-known stages:

- In mid-eighteenth-century New Orleans, the seeds of jazz were planted in Congo Square, where slaves gathered to dance to African rhythms.
- In nineteenth-century American towns, infectious new songs (antecedents to later popular songs) were introduced in revues, skits, walk-arounds, and performances by touring minstrel shows.
- In the antebellum cotton fields of the American South, blues were wailed out by slaves as they toiled under the hot, beating sun and their master's whip.
- In the brothels and saloons of the Storyville sector of New Orleans in the late nineteenth century, a new kind of toe-tapping music with syncopated rhythmic patterns called ragtime was thumped out by pianists who couldn't read a note of music.
- In early twentieth-century New Orleans and then spreading north to Chicago around the time of World War I, combos of piano, trumpet, guitar, trombone, clarinet, banjo, and drums improvised in two- and four-beat rhythms called Dixieland.
- In the theater districts of late nineteenth-century and early twentieth-century New York City, professional tunesmiths cranked out catchy popular songs (precursors of later pop tunes) intended to charm the public with their commercial appeal.
- In Manhattan's northern neighborhood of Harlem, African American musicians played jazz and other forms of music in the Cotton Club in the 1920s and 1930s.
- In Nashville's Grand Ole Opry, beginning in the mid-1920s, country music twanged out to warm the hearts of loyal fans.
- On Beale Street in Memphis in the mid-twentieth century, rockabilly and blues influenced the development of popular music.
- In early 1950s Cleveland, WJW disc jockey Alan Freed became the midwife of a new youthful rebellious music called rock and roll.
- In 1950s Los Angeles, producer Buck Ram working with the Platters, and in Detroit Berry Gordy Jr. launching a hit factory record label, brought African American groups not just into the pop mainstream but to its forefront.
- On 52nd Street in Manhattan in the 1950s, bebop circulated and swing found a new haven to propagate itself in jazz clubs.

- In 1950s Philadelphia, Dick Clark's *American Bandstand* TV show featuring high school students dancing at his studio after school let out brought rock and roll into the living rooms of American homes and launched the careers of many a pop teen idol.
- In the Brill Building in New York City in the 1950s and 1960s, some of rock and roll's greatest tunesmiths penned songs for the puppy-love-and-blemishes set in cubicles in Tin Pan Alley fashion.
- In southern California in the early 1960s, surf songs became an ebullient new component of pop music.
- In Nashville again the future king of rock and roll, otherwise known as Elvis, was launched on Sun Records.
- In 1950s and 1960s Liverpool, England, four young mop-top British lads formed a band that would cause a worldwide sensation and revolutionize popular music.
- In the streets of the Bronx in the 1970s, rap and hip hop germinated and would eventually become the reigning genre of pop.

From these and other seminal settings, pop music in its sundry varieties blossomed and diffused around the world, attracting legions of fans and causing music industries to crop up in cities large and small, and in America, eventually centralizing in Los Angeles, New York City, and Nashville, which are among the most prominent music business capitals of the world. Indeed, when you get down to it, it was not just these settings but also the history that gave rise to these settings, all the human interactions of people carving out their worlds, of nations acting out as they saw fit, that are all responsible for the pop music we have today, this ubiquitous music that paves the cultural landscape of the daily lives of people around the world.

The story of pop music has been told in innumerable books, and everyone from Stephen Foster and Irving Berlin to Elvis and the Beatles and beyond are well known as indelible constituents of the tapestry of pop music, but what was happening behind the scenes that facilitated the development of the music business and the rise of popular music as well as what was transpiring in society and the world is the subject of this book. From America's earliest music publishing companies to today's Universal Music Group, Sony, and Warner; from Alexander Graham Bell and Thomas Edison to Apple and Spotify; from the 1710 Statute of Anne to the current copyright law—these and other segments are all part of the story of the music business, and consequently are part of the story behind a stream or radio broadcast or sale of a recording. Indeed, so much has changed over time with culture, technology, and laws shepherding in new forms of music, new ways to access music, and new ways to govern how music is commercially regulated, but what hasn't changed over time is people's steadfast and fervent love of music and the industry's mission to satisfy that love, which, at the risk of repetition, is the same as it was back in the modern music industry's quaint earliest days of the late nineteenth century—to bring music to the public as efficiently and affordably as possible.

The music business is renowned for its glitz and glamour, from red-carpet awards shows to dazzling concerts, from sensational music videos to splashy album covers, but like any industry it is foremost a business, in the music industry's case one guided not only by economic principles but also by legal, technological, social, and cultural factors as well. The economic and legal factors are usually not of consequence to consumers; they only want to get the music they like as well as to discover new music they can enjoy. Contractual terms, revenue splits, licensing arrangements, physical and digital chains of distribution, concert riders, entertainment-related laws, and all the other intricacies that make the industry run are of little concern to consumers as long as the music they want keeps on coming. But for those who earn their livelihood from an industry in which songs are created, recorded, publicly performed, distributed, printed, marketed, synchronized, broadcast, and streamed, it is not only an industry that fuels the music appetite of consumers and entrepreneurially caters to it in myriad creative ways, but also one that demands much effort and a perspicacious understanding of the operations that make the music industry work.

One might say it all starts with a song. There can be no singles or albums, no concerts or tours, no radio spins or streams, and probably no merchandise, brands, or platforms of musicians without the song. It is the bedrock of the entire industry. It is the impetus to all that glitz and glamour. It is what launches music aficionados into flights of joy. Songs have been around for ages, bringing great pleasure to people, but today the breadth of popular music is more varied than ever before.

Popular music is an umbrella term for a multitude of genres, sub-genres, hybrids, and styles of songs that, as its very words imply, denotes music that has mass appeal or is intended for appreciation by large audiences. The origin of *popular music* is uncertain, although it was in use no later than just after the end of the American Civil War, as indicated by a brief item in the July 15, 1866, edition of the *New York Times* titled "Popular Music," whose opening testified to the growing public appreciation of this type of music: "The taste for popular music is increasing in this country with great rapidity. The vast number of people that flock to the Central Park on Saturday afternoons 'to hear the music' is proof of this."

Whether it was intended or not, the term *popular music* has a capitalistic bent about it since it suggests mass consumption or the potential for such economic activity concerning songs; even if its coining was to differentiate a certain type of music from classical, serious, educational, and religious music, it still implies that it is a general, lighter, simpler form of music intended for the enjoyment of the masses. When the term blossomed into full economic maturity in the early days of Tin Pan Alley, a song's main source of income was from sheet music sales (piano rolls were a subsidiary source of income at the time), but even this essentially solitary source of income for songs could make its writers and publishers (the copyright owners and purveyors of songs) wealthy, as hit songs, not infrequently at the time, sold over a million copies of sheet music and some tunesmiths racked up numerous hits. Over the years the revenue streams for popular music (or any other kind of music) have increased and songs have had even greater earning potential than ever, although in recent years, with the advent of the Internet, piracy found a new domain to ply itself, and music publishers and songwriters have complained that their royalties for streamed songs are minuscule.

Out of the term *popular music* came the shortened form *pop music*, which is used and discerned in many different ways. As an abbreviation for *popular music*, it may refer to essentially all music outside of classical, serious, and certain other types of music that are intended to have mass appeal. Thus a plethora of genres may be deemed to be "pop" such as hip hop, R&B, Latin, country, rock, gospel, metal, ska, and grunge. In a narrower purview, pop music may be deemed to have multiple meanings. It could refer to the new youth music that developed after Tin Pan Alley popular music, that is, rock and roll, and *all* the youth-oriented music that followed. It could refer just to the popular music that descended from rock and roll, that is, songs by such artists as the Beach Boys, Herman's Hermits, the Hollies, Simon and Garfunkle, the Bee Gees, and The Carpenters and the music that followed these artists but only in their ilk. Pop music of the 1960s gave rise to numerous different genres or subgenres such as rock, glam, glitter, and punk, and artists who performed in some of these styles such as rock groups were sometimes referred to as pop groups, and vice versa. (Were the Beatles a pop group or a rock group?) Indeed, *pop* is used in so many different ways in music that its currency is linguistically interchangeable. Although some pop music purists may object to the term *pop* being applied to styles outside of what they specifically deem to be pop, *pop*'s definition may be deemed to be determined by popular usage, and therefore it is a fluid term.

Billboard is today the reigning popular music industry publication and is renowned for its charts. Over the years there were other industry publications such as *Cash Box* and *Record World* that also published charts of the bestselling and most-listened-to (on radio) records. All had charts of the top 100 singles, which were commonly referred to as the "singles pop chart," even though there might be crossover singles from other genres such as R&B and country. In a strict sense, such a chart couldn't accurately be called a "pop chart" since it could comprise multiple popular music genres.

For many years now *Billboard* has called its mainstream singles chart the "Hot 100," which is essentially a heterogeneous ranking of songs from any genre with the highest sales, radio spins, and streams, and its general title absolves the publication from labeling songs. Singles from a variety of genres may land on this chart, and in recent years it has been dominated by genres outside of the traditional mainstream such as hip hop and rap. In this sense, it may be said that if enough people buy or listen to a song, it doesn't matter what genre it's in or what chart position it's reached—it's a popular, or *pop* song, period. It's a liberal definition to be sure, but such has the breadth of popular music become that pop songs may be regarded as what's popular for the masses. A point in case would be Marvin Hamlisch's recording of Scott Joplin's ragtime composition "The Entertainer." This rag would probably not be regarded by many people as a pop tune, yet it landed at the number 3 position on *Billboard*'s Hot 100 in 1974 thanks to it being included in the score of the Academy Award–winning movie *The Sting*, showing that pop culture can, in a quirky way, make pop songs out of non-pop songs if they resonate with enough of the public (not to mention it can resurrect interest in old or unusual styles of music).

Still, in its commentaries that accompany its Hot 100, *Billboard* will distinguish between pop and rap and other genres, usually identifying a genre that dominates the top of the chart by the artist rather than the song. There may also be considered to be an ethnic bent to the term *pop music* generally referring to music produced by white artists. *Billboard* has referred to the music of Maroon 5 and Ariana Grande as pop, for instance. Of course, this may be considered a general overview, as there are many artists who are identified with a genre of music outside their ethnicity, such as Eminem, who is often identified as a hip hop artist.

Essentially, a particular style of performance and arrangement of a song can make it a pop song. Songs from, say, before 1940, for example, would generally not be considered pop songs. They were typically performed by larger ensembles consisting of string players and musicians who played acoustic instruments such as clarinet, trumpet, trombone, saxophone, banjo, and piano, all led by a conductor or bandleader. However, numerous songs from early decades of the 1900s became pop hits in later eras when they would otherwise be considered outdated or corny or "your parents' music." Many Tin Pan Alley, or vintage, popular tunes, for example, spawned later pop bestsellers. For example, "Ain't She Sweet" (Milton Ager and Jack Yellen, 1927) was a 1964 hit for The Beatles; "Dream a Little Dream of Me" (Gus Kahn, W. Schwandt, and F. Andre, 1931) was a 1968 hit for Mama Cass with the Mamas and the Papas; "I Only Have Eyes for You" (Harry Warren and Al Dubin, 1934) was a 1975 hit for Art Garfunkle, and "Just a Gigolo" (Irving Caesar, Leonello Casucci, and Julius Brammer, 1930) was a 1985 hit for David Lee Roth.

We can even go back further, say, to the American Civil War, from which came the sentimental ballad "Aura Lee," whose melody was extracted for "Love Me Tender," which became a number 1 pop hit for Elvis Presley in 1956, or to the War of 1812, whose alleged Southern fiddle tune (its origin is uncertain) "The 8th of January," had its melody lifted for the 1959 number 1 Johnny Horton pop hit (and 1959 Grammy

Award winner for Best Country and Western Performance) "The Battle of New Orleans." Even Beethoven's famous four-note theme from his *Symphony No. 5 in C minor* became the basis of a modern-day hit when it was adapted by Walter Murphy to become a disco hit in 1976 called "A Fifth of Beethoven."

The list could go on and on, but the point is that virtually any tune from any era could be a pop song with the right instrumentation, arrangement, production, and vocal delivery. And it's all to say that as music is flexible and malleable and lyrics can be used to express any emotion or tell any story, pop songs are rich in their diversity. The forces that creatively put music out there—songwriters, producers, artists, and musicians—are like puppeteers, pulling the strings of the public's emotions by buoying and wrenching and inspiriting them with the compact art form of pop songs.

When rock and roll launched around the 1950s, it arose out of an eclectic stew of popular music consisting of such genres as vintage pop, jazz, ragtime, blues, country and western, western swing, and rhythm and blues, all with their own antecedents. The practitioners of these popular music genres included such artists as Bing Crosby, Louis Armstrong, Eubie Blake, Billie Holliday, Hank Williams, Bob Wills and the Texas Playboys, and Etta James. Rock and roll music did not seek to eradicate these other genres and their artists; it was just a natural evolution musically and culturally, and it had its own audience it wished to attract. Rock and roll groups had different manifestations but often went like four young fellows playing electric guitars and drums and singing youth-oriented songs aimed at white teenage audiences. The bandmates were possessed of raw energy and mod looks, if not a hint of lechery, and teenage girls swooned over them. Over time, the relative tameness of this primordial modern pop music and its artists would unleash itself to deeper, darker, wilder, and more penetrating, rebellious, and salacious forms.

Pop music is generally designed to appeal to youths with its relatable subject matter or generally up-tempo (and danceable) beat and lyrics that speak to youthful concerns and pastimes. Romantic pursuits, pledges of fidelity, heartbreak, loneliness, insecurity, anxiety, sexual passion, despair, jealousy, romantic warnings, messing with someone's head—these are the kinds of soul-touching themes for which pop songs are known. But pop, with its catchy hooks and basically universal lyrics, is really not just the province of teenagers but is for people of all ages, ranging from tots to seniors. Even when their language is coarse and their content graphic, pop songs can cross all age barriers in their appeal, although some parents shield their young ones from them and some older people find them repugnant.

Our current frame of reference of equating the pop song to a form adapted for the commercial marketplace was shaped first by Tin Pan Alley, the original modern music industry, and later by the charts of the bestselling records. But Tin Pan Alley didn't invent the so-called popular tune. It had been around for long before that, or at least its DNA was. We may find the seeds or roots, the pith or heart of pop music, for example, in the suffocating cargo holds of slave ships by shackled Africans whose beats and chants were heartfelt expressions of their unbearable anguish; in mountain cabins of the Appalachians by pioneers who passed down to their children frolicsome tunes that parodied barnyard cries or poignant ballads about life in the backwoods; on whaling vessels whose sailors sung sea chanteys as a diversion from hoisting sails and pulling ropes; at campfires on cold nights on the plains of the American west by cowboys who were lonely and tired from herding cattle all day; in army camps of the American Civil War by soldiers who were weary from long days of fierce fighting; in forests where lumberjacks sang to help ease the burden of their strenuous work of chopping down giant trees; in mid-nineteenth-century red-brick schoolhouses where children's ditties and farm songs were sung by earnest young students; in the catchy tunes introduced by black-faced minstrel troupes in their skits and walk-arounds in American cities; in cities, tidewater towns, and settlements in early America where immigrants brought folk tunes from their far-away homelands; in towns and villages of medieval Europe and Asia, and, it might even, if we are *really* liberal in tracing its origins, be found in biblical times and before as musical instruments have been found that go back more than 40,000 years showing humans have a musical soul and spurring us to imagine long-ago people playing or singing a motif that they liked. Indeed, while people today tend to think of a pop song as music that is played on Top 40 or other contemporary-format radio stations, its purview actually extends way beyond what is commercially successful and includes tunes of the distant past as well as those of the present that may not necessarily fit into commercial music radio formats.

Songs are such an indelible part of culture that they permeate the public mind. What true-blue music fan today couldn't sing a bevy of pop tunes that are currently riding the charts or that were chart hits from his or her youth? What self-respecting pop music aficionado couldn't dip into the standard catalog of rock and roll and recite, sing, or hum a few lines from such legendary hitmakers such as Elvis, the Beatles, the Rolling Stones, Stevie Wonder, the Supremes, and Michael Jackson? Pop tunes, ubiquitous in society from radio, streaming, movies, television shows, and advertisements to shopping malls, elevators, buses, doctor office waiting rooms, and telephone holds, are in our psyche almost as much as knowing the days of the week or numbers. We are all weaned on songs to the point that even lines from songs of the nineteenth century and earlier are often recognized—which when we know the words we just don't say them but sing or think of them with the tune that's ingrained in our heads—such as "Jingle Bells" ("Dashing through the snow"); "America the Beautiful" ("O beautiful for spacious skies"); "Yankee Doodle" ("Fath'r and I went down to camp along with Captain Gooding"); "The Battle Hymn of the Republic," also known as "Glory, Glory Hallelujah!" ("Mine eyes have seen the glory of the coming of the Lord"); "The Star-Spangled Banner" ("Oh, say can you see?"); "America" ("My country 'tis of thee"); "Swing Low, Sweet Chariot" ("Comin fo' to carry me home"); "Loch Lomond" ("Oh, ye'll take the high road and I'll take the low road and I'll be in Scotland a-fore ye"); "Oh! Susannah" ("I came to Alabama wid my banjo on my knee"); and "Auld Lang Syne" ("Should auld acquaintance be forgot"). These old ditties may not be pop songs as we regard pop songs today, but they were very much in their times popular songs and gems of culture just as well-known pop songs are in our own times.

Songs are so influential that they are used to brand everything from organizations to products. For the former they may traditionally be referred to as theme songs, but they are often so closely identified with groups that the message they impart is taken as the personality of the group. The U.S. armed forces, for example, have official or associated songs. For the Navy it is "Anchors Aweigh," for the Army it is "The Caisson Song" (also known as "The Army Goes Rolling Along"), for the Air Force it is "Off We Go into the Wild Blue Yonder" (or "The U.S. Air Force"), for the Marines it is "The Marines Hymn" (which is based on a melody by the French operetta composer Jacques Offenbach), and for the Coast Guard it is "Semper Paratus" ("Always Ready"). "Anchors Aweigh" was a sheet music bestseller in 1907 and was later recorded in a swing arrangement by Big Band leader Glenn Miller and his orchestra; the song's title was also the title of a 1945 movie starring Frank Sinatra and Gene Kelly with the song being sung by a chorus at the end of the film. Another Big Band leader, Shep Fields, recorded "The Caisson Song"; "Off We Go into the Wild Blue Yonder" was recorded by such popular artists as Bing Crosby and Gene Autry. A song commonly identified with baseball is "Take Me Out to the Ball Game," written in 1908 and a hit in vaudeville halls, although it is not the official song of professional baseball; even though the song was written over a century ago it is still so closely identified with baseball that it summons up images of watching games with "peanuts and crackerjacks" and root, root, rooting for the home team. In 1971 the song "I'd Like to Buy the World a Coke" was used in an ad and became a hugely popular musical vehicle for Coca-Cola, and was even turned into a chart-making pop song under the title "I'd Like to Teach the World to Sing." There are many other examples, and the point is that pop songs (or pop arrangements of what may be considered non-pop tunes) can be used to sell products, sports, military groups, and probably anything else. It just takes the right song to be matched to what's being sold.

Songs have been used as themes for presidential campaigns and military victories, as paeans to heroes and revered political and historical figures, as symbols of wondrous deeds and celebrations. We only have to look to previous centuries to see how poets and entertainers, as well as pastors, politicians, pioneers, and soldiers who felt the need to canonize people and happenings put quill to paper to immortalize celebrated people and events in song. There are many different types of songs but in their best sense pop songs are the poetry of slices of life set to music.

Pop songs are heard and recognized everywhere today—at schools and in homes, on the street and in the office, in countries of every stripe around the world. They are ubiquitous in entertainment and the media. They are sung by legions of performers and continue to enthrall audiences as the years pass on. Often timeless and universal, they become celebrated cultural gems and pass down from generation to generation, continuing to be recognized and beloved long after their creation.

The goal of the pop songwriter indeed is to write a *standard*, a song that lives on forever. The standard, also referred to as an "evergreen" or "chestnut," is passed on from one generation to another, each successive generation able to instantly recognize it and adore it and even able to sing along with performances of it. Like a great document of history or a celebrated work of art, the standard is beloved long after its creation, indubitably due to its catchy melody and meaningful words. Historically, ballads and torch songs such as "Over the Rainbow" and "Yesterday," respectively, have most facilely ascended to that lofty state of song immortality.

The general public may look at pop songs as artistic creations, even with their often-formulaic structures and bromidic lyrical themes, but the music industry professional alternatively regards them as product—commodities that the public might consume that have to be exploited and promoted to realize their full commercial potential. Of course, referring to songs as a "product" is not meant to disparage them, but the business essentially revolves around selling songs, so it's the industry's premier product. In many ways the music business is like any other business, like apples and oranges, one might say, bound by principles of economics and laws, but where it differs is in the special characteristics of songs and sound recordings, and the special promotions, legal arrangements, and forms of delivery needed to bring them to the marketplace.

Still, no matter in what mercantile terms pop songs are regarded, they are literally musical creations and as such may be viewed through an emotional lens: Why do we love songs? What makes them so aesthetically appealing? What makes them so artistically special?

A pop song is a magical thing. It can change forms like a chameleon and be adapted to any genre, style, era, or mood through new and creative arrangements and orchestrations. It can enjoy popularity in its original form or, long after its debut, in contemporary vogues and styles never even dreamed of when the song was written.

A pop song (using the term in a general sense) can transform the human soul, mind, or spirit—the psyche—by evoking emotional responses on behalf of the listener. It can brighten people's days or make them feel sad. It can soothe or inspire people, make them feel better about themselves, or move them sentimentally to tears. It can make people want to dance or tap their feet, or serve as relaxing background music as people go about their business at home or in the office.

A pop song can stoke memories of particular people, events, times, and places. As musical portals to the past, a deceased grandparent, erstwhile boyfriend or girlfriend, summer camp experience, or childhood vacation can all nostalgically materialize from the stirring words and music of an old tune.

A pop song can touch the hearts and souls of all people. It can reach across all barriers and appeal to people of all races, creeds, nationalities, and ages. Poor and rich alike are moved by these compact ditties. Pop songs are so emotionally powerful that they are impervious to intellect, wealth, status, age, or gender and can impact people from all walks of life.

Pop songs are generally meant to be catchy and to embed themselves stubbornly in listeners' heads. Indeed, the infectious pop earworm stays in the head, where its hook (or main melodic phrase) repeats itself incessantly, sometimes irritatingly, and refuses to leave. Only when the sundry distracting forces of life intervene does the catchy pop song finally lose its firm grip on the neurons and synapses of the brain and, alas, dissipate. To be sure, when a pop song ingrains itself in the head in that unshakable (if not, after a while, annoying) way, it has admirably done its job.

A good song creates a bond between the artist and the listener. In the best sense, the listener is swept away into the musical and lyrical richness of the song, of which the artist is the creative, stylistic, and skilled interpreter.

Pop songs are typically reflections of daily life and culture, of people's interactions with other people, and of the resultant sentiments or feelings. Some songs have lyrics that use the language and idioms of particular groups or that are currently in vogue; others have lyrics that are traditional and could be applicable to almost any time period. As so-called three-minute works of art, pop songs offer in brief spaces streams of memorable melodies and relatable lyrical themes that while often universal can create an insular world for the listener. A pop song will generally comprise different musical sections, and the melody and lyrics of a good pop song ideally complement each other so that they come across as a seamless whole.

A pop song is a singularly unique product in that in just a few minutes it can make an artistic statement and evoke an emotional response. That is why, for all its terseness, every lyrical line and every music phrase carries great weight and contributes to the overall emotion, experience, and artistic representation of the piece. A pop song's relative brevity belies its import. Although there are only a limited number of musical notes and music styles, a good song will have its own personality, distinct from other songs in its genre.

Songs not only come in a variety of genres and subgenres but also may be characterized in other diverse ways. They may be slow, fast, sad, happy, bouncy, upbeat, lethargic, danceable. Slow songs are commonly called ballads; fast songs are referred to as upbeat or up-tempo. No matter what form pop songs take, there is potentially a vast public audience for them because they may be not only personally meaningful but also fun.

With many genres and subgenres, pop songs have a multitude of characteristics and personalities. But they do have some common features. It may be said that pop songs:

- generally range in length from two to five minutes (and are most commonly between three and four minutes long);
- contain catchy (sing-along) hooks or verses;
- have repetition, whether a short hook, a long hook, or entire verses (bridges, too, may repeat);
- are simple enough so that they can be sung by the average person;
- contain lyrics that convey an emotion or feeling, or tell a story or contain a message or are just silly expositions;
- reflect to some degree the culture, social mores, and attitudes of society or a group of people; and
- lyrically embrace everyday themes such as love, broken-heartedness, relationships, dating, marriage, drugs, getting high, restlessness, unhappiness, melancholy, sorrow, redemption, destiny, rebellion, anarchy, materialism, self-expression, school, cars, celebrations, and other special events in a person's life.

Today's pop music may be regarded as a musical kingdom of songs that is a product of the evolving and melding and diverging of innumerable song genres over hundreds of years (and that is itself always further evolving as writers infuse their originality with existing styles). A plethora of genres and subgenres, hybrids and fusions of popular music exist as not only are there a multitude of distinct styles of music but also because any kind of music can essentially be mated with others through sounds, rhythms, harmonies, vocal styles, arrangement, and production. Popular music, in this way, is a living, breathing expression of song styles in the confines and forms of the art. Popular music may be deemed to include but is by no means limited to the genres, subgenres, hybrids, and fusions listed in table 0.1.

Songs become commercially successful today for a variety of reasons including the quality of the song, the performance of the artist who recorded it, the reputation and following of the artist who recorded it, the promotion efforts of the label that released the recording, social media efforts on behalf of the song, the timing of the song in terms of similar artists or competing songs at the time the song is released, the support of the song by the artist with respect to the artist performing it at concerts, the availability of the song as a product that is sold, and the availability of the song on streaming services. There are many more factors that go into the impact or success of a song, to be sure, but the point is, generally speaking, in today's market, successful songs don't just happen; they are made to happen.

A pop song can be powerful in terms of its effect on people, but what makes a pop song successful? A song's impact may be attributed to a number of factors including its:

- *aesthetics*: How catchy is the song?
- *message*: What is the song's intended message? Do the lyrics successfully convey that message, or could they be expressed in a better way? Do the words evoke the proper imagery? Is the economy of the lyrics satisfactory, or are there wasted words? Does the title summarize the lyrics appropriately? Are the lyrics relatable and universal? Is the song's language or jargon current or appropriate for its audience?
- *genre*: Is the song's genre currently in vogue, or does it have the potential to appeal to many people?
- *commerciality*: Is the song commercial? Is it the type of song the masses will like? Is it a "fun" song, a message song, a sing-along

Table 0.1.

acid rock	Afro-Cuban	airs
alternative	American folk	Americana
anthems	avante-garde rock	bachata
barbershop quartet	bluegrass	blues
bomba	boogie woogie	bop
bossa nova	British pop	Broadway
bubblegum	bugalú	cambien
campfire	Caribbean	carols
Celtic	Celtic rock	cha cha cha
chanteys	Christian	Christian rock
circus	classic rock	classic pop
college	comedy	cool jazz
country	country and western	country blues
country rock	courting	cowboy
Creole	dance	dance pop
death metal	dembow	dialogue songs
disco	Dixieland	doo-wop
drum and bass	dub	easy listening
electronic	electronic dance music (EDM)	electropop
ethnic	folk	folk rock
free-form jazz	funk	gangsta rap
garage rock	glam	glitter rock
go-go	gospel	grime rap
grindcore	grunge	hair metal
hard rock	heavy metal	hillbilly
hip hop	Hollywood	humor
hymns	indie rock	industrial rock

international folk	Jamaican	jazz
jazz-rock	Klezmer	K-Pop
Latin	Latin trap	lumbering
marches	mariachi	merengue
metal	Mexican	middle-of-the-road
military	minstrel	mountain
movie themes	Mozambique	Native American
neo-metal	New Age	New Wave
noise rock	norteno	novelty
nursery	parlor songs	parodies
party-game	patriotic	pioneer
plena	polka	pop
pop punk	progressive jazz	progressive rock
protest	psalms	psychedelic
punk	ragtime	railroad
ranchera	rap	rap-rock
reggae	reggaeton	rhythm and blues
rock	rock and roll	rockabilly
romantic soul	rounds	rumba
salsa	sentimental	silly
ska	soft rock	soul
spirituals	square dance	story ballads
surf	swing	synthpop
synthwave	tango	techno
Tejano	television themes	Tex-Mex
trance	trap	trip-hop
tropical	Western swing	work songs
world	World War I songs	World War II songs
zydeco		

song, or any other type that the public will react to? Does the song have international potential?

- *singability*: Is the song singable (in terms of range and simplicity) by the average person?
- *emotional effect*: What is the song's emotional effect on the listener? What kind of mood does it put the listener in? Does the song leave the listener satisfied when it is over?
- *physical effect*: Do listeners want to tap their feet or snap their fingers or dance to the song? If a ballad, does it make listeners want to sing along or just sit back and enjoy it?
- *long-term potential*: Does the song have the potential for longevity? Is it strong enough that it will stand the test of time? Why or why not will it be relevant in future times?
- *competition*: What other recordings is the song competing against at the time? Similar songs may result in it getting less airplay or attention on streaming services and take away from its potential success.
- *licensing potential*: Can the song be adapted for advertising? Could it be used in movies? Television? Videogames? Music boxes? A curated streaming playlist? As a selection for concert bands, orchestras, or choral groups? Does it have the potential to be used as a theme song for a particular purpose or organization?
- *artist specificity*: Is the song particular to one artist (who recorded the song), or can other artists easily cover it?

At the same time, the thing about popular music since the advent of recording technology is that it's not necessarily a great song that makes a great record but a great record that makes a great song. In other words, a song can be great, but a recording of it can make it not-so-great. The arrangement, production, musicianship, vocal delivery, and mix are all components that go into making a recording that contribute to its success, plus, if it may be said, that ineffable "magic" that happens in the studio when everything comes together just right. And when that happens, the result can be spellbinding, as a great record beckons you to enter another world for three minutes or so where the melody and words and performance immerse you in the artistry of the song.

As an art form, the pop song has its own intrinsic qualities. Unlike other great art forms like a book or television show or movie, you don't need a device or considerable chunk of time to experience it. It's in your head, and you can run it through your mind or sing it out loud anywhere. You can envision what a picture or painting or sculpture looks like when you're away from it, but appreciation for these works of art is best when actually seeing them. On the other hand, a pop song is a piece of art that may be distinguished from other art forms in that through its brevity, relative simplicity, easiness to memorize, and aesthetic appeal, it may be performed by anyone, anywhere, and at any time. This is perhaps because it has many singular qualities. A pop song is short and compact and within a relatively small amount of time can tell a story or render a message and have a powerful emotional impact, not to mention that it can get the body tapping its toes or moving in some other rhythmic way.

Like all art, pop songs are expressions of the human condition, which is why, with a universality of human conditions, so many pop songs express the same basic themes—"I'm lonely and heartbroken since you left me," "your love has brought me great happiness," "my world now shines like the bright sun since you came into it." It's the way songs are expressed with their different metaphors and clichés that give us different pop songs.

Indeed, like all art, pop songs are its own unique arena, with numerous forms, styles, genres, subgenres, and other methods of expression. Since the human condition is essentially timeless and universal, there are songs about almost every conceivable aspect of the human emotional experience. It's the idioms of the times that change, providing songwriters with new linguistic tools to breathe new life into popular songs for the same basic sentiments. And presumably, the well of language for finding new forms of expression will never run dry, as we are all unique human beings with our own inimitable perspectives and ways of looking at and reacting to situations and experiences. Consequently, there will never be a limit to the kinds of lyrics songwriters can write, as individual perspectives enable people to see things in different ways and find new forms of expression, yet at the same time those forms of expression, human forms of expression, will surely fit within the realm of universal human experience and consequently be relatable by the masses.

Art aside, a pop song is more than just a song; it is also a commercial product with numerous potential revenue streams, a business in and of itself, and it is in this way that professionals in the music business approach pop songs today just as they have going all the way back to the late nineteenth century when the production and distribution of pop songs first became a bona fide specialized industry. A pop song—indeed any musical work—is a curious artistic specimen in that it may be regarded as an intangible intellectual property that has no substance in and of itself but can be reproduced in a variety of objects including compact discs, video games, ringtones, audiovisual works, music boxes, sheet music, songbooks, and greeting cards. It can be disseminated over the radio, television, and Internet. It can be adapted for symphonic arrangements or advertising. It can be used to deliver messages or move stories forward in movies, television shows, and stage productions. It can be sung in the shower or in front of a live audience of 50,000 people. But its commercial aspects notwithstanding, a pop song is, in any or all of its permutations, a fun and enjoyable work of art with a long and distinguished heritage.

And so today we have this vast and magnificent catalog of popular music, diverse and rich as the people who are its adoring fans. But it didn't just come out of nothing; it evolved, as it will continue to evolve. Behind the marketing to the public of the vast array of pop songs is the adventurous and enterprising music business, whose very own story is a multi-layered tale.

I

THE DAWN OF POP

No one knows how far back the dream of recording sound goes, but perhaps the first written expression of it occurred in 1657 when the French novelist Savinien de Cyrano de Bergerac's futuristic novel *A Voyage to the Moon* was posthumously published. In his science fiction satire, de Bergerac described a journey to the moon and told how his namesake protagonist came upon

> a box—somewhat of metal. . . . It was a book, indeed, but a strange and wonderful book . . . made wholly for the ears and not the eyes, so that when anybody has a mind to read in it, he winds up the machine with a great many little springs . . . and straight, as from the mouth of man or a musical instrument, proceed all the distinct and different sounds.

That an object could capture and reproduce sound was, in the mid-seventeenth century, almost as fantastical a notion as man flying to the heavens and landing on a celestial body, but de Bergerac, who allegedly had no background in mechanical arts, as primitive as they were in those days, indeed foretold the audio book and the phonograph player. Music had not yet reached the alpine heights it would later achieve in compositional creativity and popularity with the public, what with the births of the First Viennese School of composers such as Mozart, Haydn, and Beethoven about a century away, so it was a testament to de Bergerac's rich and vivid imagination that he could forecast the invention of a device that played words and music for the pure enjoyment of the listener.

De Bergerac's chimerical conception came amid the medieval era emerging from the depths of long-standing traditions, stagnant thinking, and deep-rooted shibboleths with revolutionary discoveries and effulgent ingenuity changing the course of human history. By the dawn of the sixteenth century, Copernicus, Gutenberg, and da Vinci were changing the world with their progressive view of the heavens, mass dissemination of the printed word, and engineering experiments presaging new technologies to come, respectively. But the most spectacular discovery of the time was made by the mariner Christopher Columbus, who, in 1492, in search of a new trade route west to Asia, instead opened the other half of the planet for Europeans.

Columbus, on the Santa Maria, along with crews aboard the smaller vessels the Nina and the Pinta, ventured across an unknown and dangerous ocean and sailed into the Caribbean. More than two months into their journey, land was sighted early one October morning, and a gunshot from the Pinta pierced the silence of the day and signaled land ahead. After alighting on an island in what later became known as the Bahamas, the admiral kneeled and was joined by his men in chanting the hymn *Te Deum* ("We Praise Thee, O Lord"), probably the first tune of Europeans sung in the New World. But the white man's transient Latin liturgical performance notwithstanding, music was not unknown in this hemisphere, as indigenous peoples had their own forms of music with dances, chants, songs, and rhythms.

In the wake of Columbus, other explorers came, followed by adventurers, merchants, missionaries, and those seeking religious freedom or a better life, and music flowed onto the shores of the New World. Airs, ballads, hymns, folk songs, and ditties from European lands—Spain, England, France, Scotland, Ireland, the Netherlands, Germany, Norway—over time were planted like seeds in a garden that flourished and would eventually produce its own intrinsic flowers.

As settlements, villages, towns, and cities cropped up, America became a melting pot. Music was present and vibrant but largely inherited from countries across the ocean. At the same time the music of Native Americans, who were spread across the land, would influence white music as well as be influenced by white music.

Pizarro (Spain), Cortez (Spain), Vespucci (Italy), de Soto (Spain), Drake (England), and Cartier (France) were some of the explorers who sailed into the New World. Jamestown was settled in 1607, its settlers bringing with them airs and folk tunes, followed by the landing at Plymouth Rock by Pilgrims seeking religious freedom from England in 1620 who brought with them Puritan psalms. Following the formation of Virginia and Massachusetts, other colonies of England were founded: New York, Maryland, Rhode Island, New Jersey, Delaware, Maryland, Pennsylvania, Connecticut, North Carolina, South Carolina, and Georgia. In 1640, two decades after the Pilgrims reached Plymouth Rock, the first book in the New World was published. It was called *The Whole Booke of Psalmes Faithfully Translated into English Metre*, and had the subtitle "Whereunto is prefixed a discourse declaring not only the lawfulness, but also the necessity of the heavenly Ordinance of singing Scripture Psalmes in the Churches of God . . . Let the word of God dwell plenteously in you, in all wisdom, teaching and exhorting one another in Psalmses, Hymns, and Spiritual Songs, singing to the Lord with grace in your hearts . . . If any be afflicted let him pray, and if any be merry let him sing psalms." It became known as the *Bay Psalm Book*, and a third edition contained "hymns and spiritual songs of the Old and New Testament," and the ninth edition contained musical notation.

Over time, many songs from foreign lands came to America and enjoyed popularity, such as "Prayer of Thanksgiving," "The Little Dustman," and "Rosa," folk songs of the Netherlands; "Alouette," "Canadian Boat Song," and "Voyageur's Song," French-Canadian tunes; "Come, Good Wind" and "At Pierrot's Door," songs from France; "Barbara Allen," a folk song from Scotland; and "Believe Me, if All Those Endearing Young Charms," an air from Ireland.

Printing music goes all the way back to the Italian publisher Ottaviano Petrucci in the early sixteenth century, but in the early days of America there wasn't much manufacturing of printed music or song collections—lyrics were printed on long sheets called broadsides or in folios called songsters—and for tunes consumers looked to book emporia, which obtained printed material from English companies sent over by sea. A book printed by Thomas Harper and sold by the bookseller John Playford in England around the mid-seventeenth century called *The English Dancing Master* contained, as its subtitle indicates, "Plaine and easie Rules for the Dancing of Country Dances, with the

Tune to each Dance." It had the melodies and words to over a hundred songs, and no doubt the collection eventually made its way across the ocean to America, where some of the tunes became well known.

The popular music garden of early America, a mélange of secular, patriotic, and religious melodies, grew in many other ways, too. Numerous songs were written by denizens about political leaders and military heroes. There were songs about war and family, animals and nature, hardship and triumph, liberty and faith. And, of course, there were songs about that most universal and timeless of emotions, love. Just as the twenty-first-century lyrics of rock or hip hop reflect the vernacular of their culture, these old love songs were expressed in the language of the day. Yet in their essence, they were the same love songs as we have today, and presumably will have in the future. Take, for example, "The Token" by Charles Didbin, the eighteenth child of poor parents who was born in 1745 in Southampton, England, and wrote popular songs about the life of sailors. In "The Token," a mate takes solace by reading the words inscribed in his tobacco box, "If you loves me as I love you/ No knife shall cut our loves in two." Is this not the theme expressed in numerous modern pop songs like Sade's "Nothing Can Come between Us" or the Captain and Tennille's "Love Will Keep Us Together"? In another Old English song, "Oh, Dear! What Can the Matter Be?" the angst of young love is expressed when the lass laments that "Johnny's so long at the fair" even though he promised to buy her "a trinket to please me" and a "bunch of blue ribbons to tie my bonnie brown hair." Isn't that uncertainty or insecurity frequently echoed in such rock and roll songs as "Will You Love Me Tomorrow?" a number 1 1961 pop hit for The Shirelles, or "Don't Go Breaking My Heart," a UK number 1 pop 1976 hit for Elton John and Kiki Dee? In 1971 John Denver had a *Billboard* number 2 pop hit with "Take Me Home, Country Roads" (it reached the summit position in the *Cash Box* and *Record World* pop singles charts), in which he longs to be in the place where he belongs, West Virginia, with its heavenly mountains and Shenandoah River. The theme of love of home is a perennial one and can be found in such nineteenth-century tunes as "Home, Sweet Home," "My Old Kentucky Home," and "Home on the Range," a cowboy song in which the narrator longs to be "where the buffalo roam, where the deer and the antelope play." Different words, same theme. In the English folk song "O No, John," we see a harbinger of the male pining for a desired female that would be echoed in scads of songs of Tin Pan Alley and rock and roll: "O Madam in your face is beauty/On your lips red roses grow/Will you take me for your husband/Madam answer yes or no." A young man puts a young woman on a pedestal in another old English folk tune, "Sally in Our Alley": "Of all the girls that are so sweet/There's none like pretty Sally/She is the darling of my heart/And lives in our alley." Sentimental by our current standards, indeed, but how many songs are there from all of pop music where a boy idolizes a girl? That very notion is one of the cardinal themes of pop music!

Of course, there are countless old songs that are intrinsic only to their own times, as they are expressed in poetic or bombastic language or embrace themes that wouldn't travel well to future eras, but basically songs of any time are about the human experience, and if you strip them down to the bare themes, from airs to raps, spirituals to rock and roll, patriotic tunes to country, they are all almost all bonded by the commonality of the human condition and the range and outpouring of human emotions.

Songs through the mid-nineteenth century were structured in various ways. Some just had repeating stanzas, such as the 1832 patriotic ditty "America," also known as "My Country 'Tis of Thee," (its melody taken from the British "God Save the King"), which has repeating stanzas of fourteen bars. The work song "The Erie Canal" has sixteen-bar verses leading into an eight-bar refrain. Similarly, the beloved Civil War–era song "Listen to the Mockingbird" has eight-bar verses leading into a nine-bar chorus, and the Scottish airs "Loch Lomond" (which has been performed or recorded numerous times from the swing era to the rock era) and "Auld Lang Syne" (which is commonly referred to as the New Year's Eve song) have eight-bar verses leading into an eight-bar chorus. These olden song structures foreshadowed the structures of modern popular songs.

In the world of pop, it seems there's a precedent for everything (even in technological and business aspects, as we'll see later on in this book). If the notion of British musicians becoming the rage in America sounds familiar, one need only to look back way past the British invasion of the 1960s to the early nineteenth century, when such English troubadours as Thomas Haynes Bayly ("Gaily the Troubadour" and "Long Long Ago"), Henry Russell ("A Life on the Ocean Wave" and "Cheer, Boys, Cheer"), R. Bishop Buckley ("Wait for the Wagon"), and

Thomas Dunne English ("Ben Bolt") gave young America some of its best-known songs. And before this, in the late eighteenth century, numerous British songs came to America, where the melodies were kept and the words replaced by lyrics written by Americans reflecting their viewpoints. This proved to be especially ironic in times of war between the two countries when British lyrics were re-cast by the American colonists into rabble-rousing patriotic songs.

But while songs of many foreign lands seeped onto America's shores, home-grown music also made its way to the public. An early composer whose works were acclaimed was William Billings, a one-eyed, Boston-born music educator who wrote hymns and other sacred music, choral works, and patriotic tunes. Perhaps his most important work was "Chester," a song sung by American soldiers during the American Revolution that, with its inflammatory words, helped inspire the colonists to victory over the Redcoats. Samuel Woodworth, Samuel Francis Smith, Francis Hopkinson, and Dr. Samuel Arnold are also among the late-eighteenth-century and early nineteenth-century Americans whose works became popular songs.

Indeed, Americans of all ages learned patriotism from songs born from conflict and love of country, whether pre– or post–Revolutionary War, with their spirited verses. Consider these lyrical snippets of early American patriotic treasures:

- "America": "My country 'tis of the, Sweet land of liberty, Of thee I sing";
- "Hail, Columbia!": "Immortal patriots! rise once more, Defend your right, defend your shore";
- "Columbia, The Gem of the Ocean": "O Columbia, the gem of the ocean, The home of the brave and the free, The Shrine of each patriot's devotion, A world offers homage to thee."

These early tunes presaged the popularity of such works at later times, as patriotic songs—and records—would flourish in the twentieth century during the two world wars, which meant, at that time, that the music business could help fight a war while at the same time profiting from it.

More than two hundred years after Africans were captured and brought to the New World on slave ships, white people began to take the African spirit, speech, and experience and adapt them for songs and musical skits in which they would perform in blackface. This new form of entertainment was called minstrelsy, and although reviled in modern times as racist, it is regarded by some as the first authentic indigenous musical art form in America. It started out with individual singers performing in blackface, and a few decades later the practice was adopted by professional troupes. One of the first white men to sing and perform comedy in blackface was Gottlieb Graupner, a German who around the mid-1790s emigrated to America. Playing a Negro character in the play *Oroonko* in Boston at the Federal Street Theatre at Federal and Franklin streets on December 30, 1799, and accompanying himself on banjo, Graupner sang "The Gay Negro Boy" and previewed a black-imitation form of entertainment later to come.

Thomas (Daddy) Rice, a tall New York City–born white man, helped popularize the minstrel show. In a performance in Pittsburgh around 1829 or 1830, Rice, wearing the borrowed attire of an African American, sang "Jim Crow" as he danced in African style and brought the house down. Songwriters started writing minstrel songs, and minstrel companies formed to tour the country. On stages audiences would see white men and women in blackface recreating the experiences of Africans. But were they authentic? Did using some dialect of Africans in song and imitating the expressions or manners of Africans really make their songs Negro songs? The answers to these questions may be debated, but the popularity of whites performing black music in the first half of the nineteenth century surely foreshadowed white covers of black music that was to come in the mid-twentieth century as rock and roll covers.

A musical component of some minstrel shows was the so-called Negro dialect song in which the patois of African Americans was put into lyrics. One such popular song was "Ole Shady," written by Benjamin Russell Hanby, a white composer who wrote well-known Christmas songs in the nineteenth century as well as songs from a black perspective. Using the speech and patter of a particular group, Negro dialect songs foreshadowed the use of such language that would much later occur in rap and hip hop. To quote the verses in "Ole Shady": "Oh! Yah! Yah! Darkies laugh wid me, For de white folks say ole Shady's free, So don't you see dat jubilee is a coming, coming" and "Oh! Mass got scared and so did his lady, Dis chile breaks for ole Uncle's Aby, Open de gates out here's Ole Shady, coming, coming, Hail mighty day!"

White plucking of the black experience notwithstanding, African Americans from their days of slavery on contributed heavily to the rich palette of popular music. Out of black rhythm and blues and some other forms of popular music came rock and roll, but the torment and suffering they experienced as slaves gave the world many spirituals, which were the roots for later forms of music such as gospel and the blues. Famous Negro spirituals of yore include "Nobody Knows the Trouble I've Seen," "Down by the Riverside," and "Swing Low, Sweet Chariot."

America has always been a melting pot, with people of many lands coming to its shores and making the country their home. Early on its songs reflected that experience, being a heterogeneous mix of many styles, a practice that would continue all the way through the contemporary music scene. Immigrants poured into America from all over the world, bringing with them tunes of their native lands. Ironically, some of these songs became more popular in America before they achieved popularity in their homelands. The nineteenth-century German songs "Silent Night" and "O Tannenbaum" are two such examples. Upbeat songs such as "Funiculi, Funicula" from Italy and "Jacob, Drink" from Poland also became popular in America.

With American copyright law not applying to songs until 1831, there wasn't much money to be made from popular music in the country's early days. Some musical works were commissioned, but songs, more or less, were written as artistic or cultural expressions and not for commercial enterprise. That started changing around the time that songwriter Stephen Foster came on the scene in the 1840s. Foster plied his craft for commercial gain and wrote some of the nineteenth century's most popular songs, such as "O, Susanna," "I Dream of Jeannie with the Light Brown Hair," "De Camptown Races," and "Beautiful Dreamer."

Some insight to the practices of music publishers and songwriters can be gained from a September 12, 1849, letter to Foster from his publisher, Firth, Pond & Co., of New York:

> Your favor of 8th instant is received and we hasten to reply. We will accept the proposition therein made, viz., to allow you two cents upon every copy of your future publications issued by our house, after the expenses of publication are paid, and of course it is always our interest to push them as widely as possible. From your acquaintance with the proprietors or managers of different bands of "Min-

strels," and from your own reputation, you can undoubtedly arrange
with them to sing them and thus introduce them to the public in that
way, but in order to secure the copyright exclusively for our house, it
is safe to hand such persons printed copies only, of the pieces, for if
manuscript copies are issued, particularly by the author, the market
will be flooded with spurious interests in a short time.

It is also advisable to compose only such pieces as are likely both
in the sentiment and melody to take the public taste. Numerous
instances can be cited of composers whose reputation has greatly
depreciated from the fact of their music becoming too popular and
as a natural consequence they write too much and too fast and in a
short time others supersede them. (Milligan, 1920, p. 50)

From the letter the reader can take away the publisher's concern of
pirated copies of music being made (a concern still today of music
companies), that music companies depend on artists and writers to help
them promote their wares (another contemporary concern), and for
music to be profitable composers should write songs that will appeal to
the "public taste," that is, that are commercial (and yet another concern
today of music companies).

Not only are the business practices of all those years ago relevant
today, but also Foster's personal sad personal story is likewise relevant.
Before he was even in his mid-twenties, Foster achieved much commercial success with his songs, and when he was twenty-four, he married Jane Denny McDowell of Pittsburgh. Some of Foster's songs such
as "The Old Folks at Home" were enormously popular and made him
tidy sums, but his marriage was not a happy one, and his wife, perhaps
not approving of his chosen field, eventually left him, and for reasons
not entirely clear, Foster's life fell apart. His songwriting career suffered as the quality of his work diminished—he did not develop his
melodies sufficiently and in new creative directions—and he was cast
into poverty.

Harold Vincent Milligan, a Foster biographer, relates in his book
about America's arguably most brilliant nineteenth-century songwriter
an interview he had with Parkhurst Duer, a nineteenth-century employ-
ee of a New York City music publishing concern that was frequented by
professionals in music:

Every day I met teachers and composers, and was hoping that Stephen Foster would appear. I had heard that he was living in New York but had never known anything about his life; yet his songs had created within me a feeling of reverence for the man, and I longed to see him. One day I was speaking with the clerks when the door opened and a poorly dressed, very dejected looking man came in, and leaned against the counter near the door. I noticed he looked ill and weak. A clerk laughed and said:

"Steve looks down and out."

Then they all laughed and the poor man saw them laughing at him. I said to myself, "Who can Steve be?" It seemed to me, my heart stood still. I asked, "Who is that man?"

"Stephen Foster," the clerk replied. "He is only a vagabond, don't go near him."

I was terribly shocked. Forcing back the tears, I waited for that lump in the throat which prevents speech, to clear away. I walked over to him, put out my hand, and asked, "Is this Mr. Foster?"

He took my hand and replied: "Yes, the wreck of Stephen Collins Foster." (Milligan, 1920, p. 101)

Mrs. Duer spoke kindly to Foster that day and said it was an honor to hold his hand, which caused the composer to weep. She invited him to sit at her desk, and he told her he had no friends. Mrs. Duer asked if she could be his friend and said if he had no one to write down his songs, she would be happy to take his dictation. He came back to visit her on different occasions, and one day he brought her a new tune called "When Old Friends Were Here," saying it might be the last of his career. Mrs. Duer recalled:

As he prepared to leave the store it was growing dark and as he appeared weaker than usual I offered to go with him to the street. As I helped him into the stage he said very earnestly, "You are my only friend," and as the door closed he waved his hand and the last words I heard were "God bless you." I am sure they were his last words on earth. (Milligan, 1920, p. 102)

It is not known if the words Mrs. Duer mentioned were in fact the songwriter's last spoken words, but on January 10, 1864, Foster, thirty-seven years old, was admitted to Bellevue Hospital, where he died on January 13.

In the 1840s an American singing group came into prominence that was a harbinger of performing artists that would emerge in later eras. After hearing an Austrian minstrel group sing in Massachusetts, John Hutchinson formed a singing group with his brothers, and they called themselves the Hutchinson Family. The brothers sometimes collaborated in the writing of original songs, and some composed individually. The Hutchinson Family sung out against slavery, alcohol, and the lack of opportunity and rights for women in songs as well as other subjects they deemed needed support in such songs as "Slavery Is a Hard Foe to Battle," "Eight Dollars a Day," "Uncle Sam's Farm," and "The Batchelor's Lament." The group foreshadowed protest singers who would come to public attention in the twentieth century like Joe Hill in the early 1900s, who called for the uniting of workingmen everywhere; Woodie Guthrie, who called for labor-movement reform; and 1960s anti-war and civil rights activist-singers such as Pete Seeger, Bob Dylan, Joan Baez, Phil Ochs, and Peter, Paul and Mary.

The foreshadowing of popular music to come arrived not only in singing groups but also in a practice called "street cries" in which vendors would go out onto streets and sing musical chants or phrases to induce passersby to purchase goods they held or that were in their shops. The practice of "street cries" was used in old London and carried to the colonies, where food and goods such as oysters, milk, lettuce, spoons, and knives could be the subject of street cries. In the United States, vendors using street cries could be found in various cities such as New York or Charleston. However, this precursor to twentieth-century radio jingles and television advertisements didn't go over too well with everybody. This public hawking of goods, which George Gershwin parodied in his opera *Porgy and Bess*, got so out of hand with numerous hawkers simultaneously out on the streets pitching products in loud, shrill voices that it became a disturbance to the peace and was frequently assailed.

Broadsides and songsters were the first media on which songs were disseminated (the words only), and over time music publishers arose to satisfy the public need of music. A London-born composer and musician, Benjamin Carr, visited Philadelphia with his theatrical company and ended up establishing during the presidency of George Washington a music publishing company, perhaps the first such concern in the United States. His New York office was later sold to another English-born composer, James Hewitt, who published many compositions by British tunesmiths. Hewitt's son, John Hill Hewitt, wrote popular songs and operettas, with one tune, "The Minstrel's Return from the War," published in 1825, achieving great success not only in the states but also in Europe, but unfortunately for the composer losing much money in America because of lack of copyright protection. Other music publishers became established also, including Winner & Shuster, with an office in Philadelphia; White, Smith & Perry with an office in Boston; Firth, Pond and Company with an office in New York; Lee & Walker with an office in Philadelphia; S. Brainard's Sons with an office in Cleveland; and Balmer & Weber with an office in St. Louis. Music publishers were spread out across the country and actively published all kinds of music works, including religious works and educational materials.

Theaters sprouted up after the Civil War in cities across America. Various types of entertainment were presented including concerts and variety shows. In the small towns shows would be presented on weekend evenings in their town halls. Dance bands were popular, too. They appeared in different locales, often traveling in wagons, and some would have an advance man who would travel ahead of the band, booking it into local venues as they moved along. These dance bands played square dances and were comprised of fiddlers, bass players, wind instrument players, and a drummer.

As America was rebuilding from its Civil War, momentous technological achievements were shaping up that would usher in a new era in how people communicated and how music was disseminated to the public. In 1876 in Canada, Alexander Graham Bell uttered in discernibly transmitted words over a wire to his assistant in another room, "Come here Mr. Watson, I want you," and as a result became immortalized for inventing the telephone. A year later Thomas Alva Edison would recite a poem that he recorded for the invention of his phonograph player and would likewise become immortalized. Edison would come to be regarded as one of the greatest inventors of history, and with his phonograph player he ushered in a new means of bringing music to the public, although he was not the first person to dabble in inventing a mechanism to record and play back sound.

Edison's invention of the phonograph came out of efforts he was making to improve the telegraph and telephone. After the telephone was invented, it was envisioned that an operator in an office would receive messages from operators in remote locations and the messages would be transcribed and delivered to the designated recipients. Edison, like other inventors of his time, was constantly looking for ways to store messages relayed over the telegraph, and while trying to build an apparatus that could store such messages, he noticed that when a telegraph stylus made contact with inscriptions by moving over paper quickly, "light, musical, rhythmical sound" that mimicked human speech seemed to issue from the telegraph. Taking the idea that in a telephone its diaphragm's vibrations are converted into electricity and then back to audible sound, Edison surmised that by placing a stylus over a lead-based surface, he could record vibrations as impressions that could be converted back to their original sound. For Edison, this notion sparked the possibility of a phonograph player, although his vision for it at this stage was utilitarian: since at this time only the wealthy could afford the recently invented telephone, the phonograph player could be placed in offices where people could come in and record messages that could be transmitted over a telephone and be heard by recipients in remote offices.

Subsequent to an experiment conducted in July 1877, Edison drew pictures on paper of a person conveying air through a telephone tube, with the sounds of wind and hisses producing vibrations, causing the diaphragm to vibrate strongly. Pleased with the results, he wrote, "Just tried experiment with a diaphragm having an embossing point & held against paraffin paper moving rapidly the spkg vibrations are indented nicely & theres no doubt that I shall be able to store & reproduce automatically at any future time the human voice perfectly" (Rosenberg et al., 1995).

Edison quickly followed up the experiment with a British patent for a sound telegraph, in which he explained,

> The vibrations of the atmosphere, which result from the human voice or from any other musical instrument or otherwise, are made to act in increasing or lessening the electric force upon a line by opening or closing the circuit, or increasing or lessening the intimacy of contact between conducting surfaces placed in the circuit at the receiving station; the electric action on one or more electro magnets causes a vibration in a tympan, or other instrument similar to a drum, and produces a sound, but this sound is greatly augmented by mechanical action. I have discovered that the friction of a point or

surface that is in contact with a properly prepared and slowly moving surface, is very much increased or lessened by the strength of the electric wave passing at such point of contact, and from this variation in the friction a greater or less vibration is given to the mechanism or means that produce or develop the sound at the receiving station, thereby rendering clear and distinct the sound received that otherwise would not be audible. (Rosenberg et al., 1995)

While Edison continued to ponder transmitting sound vibrations with diaphragms, an article about the work of a French inventor, Charles Cros, appeared in a French publication in October 1877. Cros expanded on the work of a French printer, Édouard-Léon Scott de Martinville, who, in the 1850s, built a contraption that made indentations corresponding to sound vibrations called the phonautograph (a phonautogram recording of "Au clair de la lune," an eighteenth-century French folk song, is believed to be the first recording of a human voice singing). Cros's conception for a contraption put forth the idea that inscriptions can be made on a flat lamp-blacked glass that was caused to vibrate, with the inscriptions then used to reproduce the vibrations and reproduce the original sounds made. But Cros could not build a working apparatus to do what he conceived, showing that it's not always who thinks of an idea first but who makes that idea workable that gets credit for the invention. Edison drew a diagram of his conception for a recording device on November 29, 1877, and gave it to an assistant, John Kruesi, to build under his supervision. Carefully adhering to the diagram, Kruesi built the apparatus, and Edison then tried it out in his Menlo Park, New Jersey, laboratory. Into a horn Edison recited the words "Mary had a little lamb, its fleece was white as snow, and everywhere that Mary went, the lamb was sure to go," and turned a crank that put the apparatus in motion. A recording needle, responding to the air waves of his voice, moved and made indentations on a piece of tinfoil wrapped around a cylinder. Then Edison turned the crank in the opposite direction, which rewound the cylinder and brought the tinfoil back to its starting point. The needle was then reset down on the tinfoil, and the crank turned, and the poem Edison recited was heard.

News of Edison's newfangled invention spread quickly, causing great interest in and curiosity about the machine. Seeking to profit from it, he licensed the Edison Speaking Phonograph Company in 1878 to exploit the new machine. It was founded by a group of enterprising men including Alexander Hubbard, whose son-in-law, Alexander Graham Bell, invented the telephone. The so-called newfangled machine that could record and reproduce sound was considered a technological marvel, but what exactly was its purpose?

Edison's company manufactured hundreds of machines and had demonstrators all over the country show how it could record and play back sound. Excited crowds flocked to theaters and country fairs to hear the new talking machine. With a technician operating the phonograph on a stage, people would stand nearby and create all types of sounds—they would sing, recite poetry or monologues or Shakespeare, whistle, yodel, or dance. An enthusiastic Edison predicted his "baby" would be an important medium for exposing music and literature and be useful as a dictating machine. Ironically, Edison never fully enjoyed the technological advances in recorded sound, as he was hard of hearing.

Despite the sensation that resulted from the invention of the phonograph, public interest in it faded as the novelty of recording and reproducing sound wore off. The machine had no practical application at this time, as the sounds it played back were harsh, sibilants were missing, and the tin foil sheet on which sounds were recorded lasted no more than a handful of plays.

In 1880, Alexander Graham Bell, keenly following Edison's progress, hired two technicians to improve on the phonograph. In 1885 they had five patent applications for a machine somewhat different, replacing Edison's tin foil with a wax-coated cardboard tube. They called this machine the "graphophone." Edison, engrossed in his work on the electric light, renewed his attention to the phonograph. He improved his machine, and the two groups went into commercial battle. It was a contest of the phonograph versus the graphophone as a dictating machine. Bell's group sold their patents to a group of Washington businessmen, who formed the American Graphophone Corp. (the antecedent of Columbia Records). But neither Bell's or Edison's company gained a foothold. Machines installed in offices performed erratically; the parts were not interchangeable. The greatest reason for their defeat, however, was the enormous resistance of office stenographers (almost all men in those days), who feared technological displacement! The neophyte sound-recording industry seemed doomed.

In 1890 an enterprising businessman changed the destiny of the crippled business. Louis Glass, a manager of the Pacific Phonograph

Company, a subsidiary of the North American Phonograph Company, installed battery-powered models of Edison's phonograph in the Palais Royale Saloon in San Francisco. The machine had several listening tubes, and patrons paid a nickel to open a tube and hear recorded music. The machines—each with four sets of listening tubes—could earn 20 cents a play. Glass's idea caught on, and there were eager lines waiting to deposit five cents in the "nickel in the slot phonograph" (the antecedent to the jukebox). Hence was born the phonograph parlor, and it basically saved the enfeebled record industry.

Entrepreneurs across the nation began installing nickel-in-the-slot machines in locations. Manufacturers of coin-operated phonograph players such as the Automatic Phonograph Exhibition Company formed to meet the demand for such machines. The machines were made with different numbers of listening tubes; some were manufactured with eight, for example. What people wanted to hear most were vaudeville and musical comedy songs, band arrangements of marches, concert pieces, comic monologues, and virtuoso whistling solos.

The Columbia Phonograph Corp., with a franchise from the American Graphophone Corp., was growing strongly in the District of Columbia area, selling 300 cylinders (recordings) a day. Its profits enabled it to gain control of AGC, and since Columbia now owned the greater share of existing patents, it sued all its competitors, claiming copyright infringement. It wasn't long before all competition was eliminated except for Edison.

In 1894 Columbia introduced a $50 graphophone. Now many families could afford a "talking machine" in their own homes. In 1896 Edison formed the National Phonograph Company and sold phonographs for $50. The result of this competition was lower prices and new, higher quality.

Improvements in recordings were being made constantly. Emile Berliner, a German immigrant, was experimenting in acoustical research. He had developed the flat disc record by perfecting a method of cutting lateral grooves into the surfaces of wax-coated zinc discs, which were placed in chromic acid, forming grooves of required depth and width. From the zinc originals, he made negatives by an electrotyping process. These negatives were pressed into heat-softened "rubber biscuits," which when cooled became exact copies or "records" of the original.

Berliner's flat disc was a great improvement on the existing cylinder. Sound reproduction was better, it could be stored and transported easily, and it was readily mass-manufactured. He called the disc player for it the "gramophone" but because of legalities its name faded from use in America (although it continued to be used in Europe). Subsequently, the word *phonograph* became the accepted name for all types of record-playing machines.

In 1901 Berliner and a business associate, Eldridge Johnson, formed the Victor Talking Machine Co. and issued recordings by Russian stars on an appropriately named "red label." These recordings sold for $5 and, though costly, were very successful.

The quest to improve phonograph players and their fidelity was ongoing. In 1905 the Columbia Record Company came out with a two-sided disc. The company's ad for this innovation read:

> Columbia Double-Disc Records! Music on both sides! A different selection on each side! And both for 65 cents—practically the price of one—32 1/5 cents for each selection! They may be played on any disc machine, no matter what make, and they give you double value for your money, plain as daylight—better surface, better tone and for greater durability. If you have not heard a Columbia Record issued during the last year and a half, don't say that you know what your talking machine can do. The present Columbia process of recording produces a naturalness and roundness and perfection of tone that is positively unequalled in any other. Send 65 cents for a sample and a catalog and the name of our dealer. Columbia Double-Disc Records! Double discs, double quality, double value, double wear, double everything except price! Don't put your record into any other! (Rachlin, 1981, p. 258)

Soon to come along was the two-sided record introduced by the Odeon Record Co. of Europe. Price wars began. In 1906 Victor reduced its price of seven-inch records from fifty cents to thirty-five cents; ten-inch records from one dollar to sixty cents; and twelve-inch records from $1.50 to $1. Cylinder records soon became obsolete; Columbia halted its manufacturing in 1912, and Edison followed later.

Following World War I, the industry entered a so-called "golden age." Records were the most popular form of home entertainment (not enough people had radios yet). Singers Enrico Caruso and John

McCormack grew rich from record royalties. When the exclusive patents of Edison, Columbia, and Victor expired between 1915 and 1920, many new companies entered the industry. In the first couple decades of the twentieth century, the nascent record industry grew steadily as the equipment to play records and fidelity continually improved; new, exciting genres of music developed and caught on with the public; bands and singers continually came on the scene; the tunesmiths of Tin Pan Alley were prolific in churning out catchy tunes; and new independent record companies formed to release specialized genres and to fulfill the public appetite for new music. With more records being sold over the years, the Tin Pan Alley music publishers had a viable partner in bringing music to the public—record companies. But increased record sales meant decreasing sheet music sales. Whereas in sheet music sales the music publisher paid the songwriter a royalty and kept the rest of the profit for itself, in record sales, pursuant to the Copyright Act of 1909, which provided a compulsory (or mechanical) license for the reproduction of a song on records, both the publisher and songwriter made less per unit sold—the statutory royalty for the sale of a recording of a song was two cents paid by the label to the songwriter and music publisher, which they split. But it was an early lesson that while technological progress could result in a wider audience for music, the payoff for the creators and owners of music could lessen (as would be seen about a century later with streaming). The changing music scene was all within the context of a culture that was gradually moving away from the strict mores of the Victorian era to less constricted, freer society. In 1920, a couple of years after World War I, there was an economic slump that affected the music industry, and if the future seemed bleak, it was thought that the new free home entertainment medium of radio would hurt the industry even more.

Edison originally envisioned his newfangled machine as a dictation device and not for the recording and playing of music since it had fidelity shortcomings and the tinfoil wasn't very durable. With a utilitarian purpose in mind, little could he have imagined that his phonograph player would one day become the means for distributing music around the world, and be the prototype for a slew of other new devices, including CD players, iPods, and smartphones in the age of a multi-billion-dollar music business. But with his archetype tinfoil-playing machine, Edison brought to reality the longtime fantasy of recording and playing back sound, a concept once just a dream, a fantastical notion that the Frenchman Savinien de Cyrano de Bergerac wrote about in a science fiction novel about a voyage to the moon more than two centuries earlier.

2

POP IN THE ALLEY

The nineteenth century was a luminous bridge between the Old World and the New World, a golden gateway from stagnant and uninspired medieval practices to remarkable human achievements. At its dawn people traveled by horse-drawn carriages; used cool spaces, or ice, if they could afford it, to store or age certain foods; and heated their homes by lighting candles or fireplaces. By the century's sunset years, the world was bustling with trains, telephones, phonograph players, electric lights, professional cameras, motion pictures, and gasoline-powered automobiles, with air conditioners, airplanes, and refrigerators on the near horizon. Never before had the march of human technological progress been as steadfast and prodigious as it was in the nineteenth century.

In America there were other dramatic changes, too. Slavery was abolished with the ratification of the Thirteenth Amendment, setting free African Americans after centuries of bondage. Almost-instant communication of the East with the West was enabled with the implementation of the first transcontinental telegraph in 1861. Both halves of the country were physically connected by their rail lines eight years later with the completion of the transcontinental railroad. The country's population swelled, too, as immigrants from Ireland poured into the country to escape the potato famine in their homeland and Jews from eastern European countries fled pogroms in which they could be persecuted or slaughtered. In the aftermath of the calamitous Civil War, America was rebuilding itself and people were looking for new opportunities to make money in the recovering U.S. economy. People from small towns and rural areas flocked to cities where they could gain employment or, even better, find untapped areas where new businesses or industries could be established and fortunes could be made.

At the same time, with more spare time on their hands, people savored entertainment that was offered to them in myriad ways: minstrel shows, theater, concerts, circuses, square dancing, medicine shows, and boxing matches, among others. But from the country's earliest days, music was always one of Americans' most beloved pastimes, and the folk tunes, patriotic songs, sentimental tunes, and all other types of songs that came out of minstrelsy, the Civil War, and post–Civil War eras fueled the appetite of Americans for popular music.

It was a confluence of these and other factors that led to the country's first centralization of music publishers. Popular music publishing had long been a business in America but its companies were geographically scattered. It was an ideal time for a centralized music industry—and one that would adopt business practices more in tune with the times such as actively exploiting and marketing music—and for sundry reasons it cropped up in New York City.

With its large population and plethora of theaters, saloons, music halls, dance halls, vaudeville houses, and burlesque houses, New York City, by the early 1880s, was the entertainment capital of America. It was a vibrant music mecca where singers and minstrel troupes, vaudeville acts and song-and-dance teams, musicians and bandleaders came to earn a living and possibly stake their claim to fame.

As a burgeoning popular music industry began to take shape in the expansive metropolis, companies began sprouting up to supply songs for these performers and the public around the early 1880s. These new companies were to revolutionize the field of popular song publishing. Unlike the mostly laid-back music publishers that operated throughout the United States and didn't actively bring popular music to the public, they were aggressive in carving a commercial marketplace for popular songs and bringing them to the marketplace. They had a feel for the kinds of songs that would catch on with the public and manufactured those songs in the Tin Pan Alley publishing mills to feed the public appetite that they essentially created.

These fledgling publishers actively sought out and nurtured songwriters to turn out catchy songs that would appeal to the public. Then the companies' song pluggers went after singers, musicians, and bandleaders to get them to put their firms' musical wares in their repertoire. Once the singers and musicians were performing the new tunes in public, the publishers' song pluggers would go out to wherever their company's songs were being performed and use various promotional techniques to exploit them in spirited and enterprising ways with the public. Finally, with their songs in the public mind, they could even be found at the final leg of commercial exploitation—at stores promoting their tunes to potential buyers of their sheet music at the point of purchase. With these companies' nurturing of talent, exploitation of songs to performers, promotion of music to the public, distribution of product to retailers, and centralized location, this was the beginning of the modern music industry.

It was natural that these music publishers would follow the theater district because theaters were where music was performed, and publishers wanted to be near the acts to whom they plugged songs. In the 1880s several young and ambitious entrepreneurs began setting up music publishing offices around Union Square in New York City, where the theater district had moved from the Bowery downtown. Beginning in 1882 and over the next half century, among the dozens of well-known theaters in New York City where songs and plays were introduced to the public were Koster & Bial's at Twenty-Third Street west of Sixth Avenue; the Lyceum Theatre, Twenty-Fourth Street and Fourth Avenue; Hammerstein's Victoria, Forty-Second Street and Seventh Avenue; the Fifth Avenue Theatre, Broadway and Twenty-Eighth Street; People's Theatre, Bowery and Houston Street. One of the most famous theatrical venues was Tony Pastor's, at Fourteenth Street near Third Avenue, which put on variety acts for family entertainment—not just for men, who if they wanted more salacious entertainment could go to saloons, but for women and children as well. Bills would include singers, comedians, and magicians, and with no booze or obscenities allowed, Pastor's venue differentiated itself from the competition.

One of the first of this new enterprising lot of song-business entrepreneurs was M. Witmark and Sons, a company named for members of a Manhattan family but not one in which the father was an active participant; it was just that the three Witmark brothers, Isadore, Jay, and Julius, were too young to have a company in their name alone. A musical family whose talent was nurtured and encouraged by their father, their journey into the business world began after eleven-year-old Jay won a toy printing press as a prize in arithmetic (Miss Roy, his teacher, declined to give him the customary prize of a gold medal because his behavior wasn't meritorious enough for that award), and the brothers segued from printing cards to printing sheet music. The company began publishing successful songs in 1886, the year it formed, with such Victorian-titled tunes as "As I Sat upon My Dear Old Mother's Knee" and "Is Mother Thinking of Her Boy?"

Among other prominent companies in this primordial mix of late-nineteenth-century popular song music publishers in New York City was York Music, run by Albert Von Tilzer, a composer who would pen the melody for songs such as "Take Me out to the Ball Game" and "I'll Be With You in Apple Blossom Time"; Leo Feist Inc., an eponymous firm owned by an erstwhile corset vendor who would publish the works of the renowned Italian tenor Enrico Caruso, popular World War I and armed forces songs like "Over There," "Torpedo Jim," and "Good Morning, Mr. Zip-Zip-Zip," as well as general hits like "My Blue Heaven," "Peg O' My Heart," and "Hail! Hail! The Gang's All Here!"; Charles K. Harris, another eponymous firm named after the man who would compose in 1892 one of the era's first major hits, "After the Ball," with over 10 million copies of sheet music sold; Shapiro-Bernstein, which would have hits with songs like "Down by the Old Mill Stream" and "The Glory of Love"; and Jerome H. Remick, which would publish hits such as "Put on Your Old Grey Bonnet" and "September in the Rain." Other notable publishers of the time with writers on staff included T. B. Harms; Woodward & Co.; Howley, Haviland and Dresser; and F. A. Mills.

Budding songwriters from around the country flocked to New York City, America's rising popular music publishing hub, but many found it wasn't easy to get published. Some pitched songs to publishers for years without getting a song accepted; others finally got a song or two published after years, and some, after years of pitching, found great success with an avalanche of hit tunes. It was not unusual for songs to sell a hundred or two hundred thousand copies of sheet music, and many hit tunes in fact sold millions of copies. A hit song could earn a tidy sum for its writer and publisher, unlike earlier days when songwriters didn't make much money. Back then, tune scribes would commonly sell their songs for a small sum of money such as three or four or five dollars with no future royalties or sign them over to a publisher who would pay them a small royalty on sheet music sales.

The tunesmiths of this new era took their inspiration from everyday scenes, conversations, overheard remarks, trends, observations, stories from daily life they heard, newspaper headlines, personal experiences, and other sources and expressed their ideas in poetic words and catchy melodies and christened them with romantic, sentimental, heart-tugging, whimsical, and other types of titles (which were, of course, part of the song lyrics). There was, for example, "The Little Lost Child" which came about when its two writers, Joseph Stern and Edward B. Marks, meeting on a business trip talked about their hometown of New York City with Marks recalling a story in which a police officer found a little wandering girl with tears in her eyes and pledging to find her mother. At the stationhouse the little girl's mother walked in looking for her lost child and the officer recognized her as his long-lost wife who walked out on him one day after a fight, and then he realized the girl was his daughter. The hit tune "In the Good Old Summertime" came about when Ren Shields, dining at a restaurant near Coney Island on a wonderful warm day, was taken by a line exclaimed by his collaborator, George Evans, who said "There's nothing like the good old summertime." "The Picture That Is Turned toward the Wall" was written by Charles Graham, who was inspired to write the ditty after seeing a scene in the dramatic play *Blue Jeans* in which a father turns his daughter's picture around after she runs off with her beau against his wishes. "Twelve Months Ago To-Night" was written by John F. Mitchell as he lay gravely ill in a hospital from the White Plague and recalled sitting among good friends a year before and vowing eternal friendship (unfortunately, he didn't live to see his song become a hit after giving his publisher the lyrics, who had it set to music and promoted it to various singers). James Bland, a son of former slaves who couldn't get hired to perform in minstrel companies in which white performers blackened their faces to do impressions of African Americans because he was African American, wrote "In the Evening by the Moonlight" about how African Americans would gather after work to sing all night as old folks sat around enjoying the music, which ironically ended up being performed by the minstrel companies who wouldn't hire him as a singer or performer. "After the Ball," Charles K. Harris's aforementioned multimillion sheet music bestseller, was inspired by his seeing a pretty young woman alone on the street after a dance and, curious as to why, found out she had a spat with her beau and both individuals were too proud to offer conciliation. Unlike earlier songs whose words and music were often written by the same person, tunes of this era were tailored to fulfill the demand for songs in the commercial marketplace and were often written by two or more individuals who brought their individual expertise to their craft, with some notable exceptions such as George M. Cohan and Irving Berlin, who prolifically and proficiently wrote both words and music to numerous hit tunes.

Near the end of the nineteenth century, the theater district once again moved north and the music publishers followed them from Union Square. Many settled on 28th Street between Broadway and Sixth Avenue, the firms one on top of the other in three- and four-story brick buildings that stretched down the street, and it was here that the name "Tin Pan Alley" was minted.

As the story goes, one day a reporter named Monroe Rosenfeld was visiting the offices of Harry Von Tilzer (a composer and brother of songwriter Albert) for an article, and the air seemed to be filled with the tinny sounds of pianos reverberating in the building and around the street. Many composers in these days of ragtime and vaudeville favored taking off the baseboards of pianos and inserting strips of paper between the piano strings to give this distinctive sound effect. In his article Rosenfeld dubbed the street "Tin Pan Alley," although this story could be apocryphal. In any case, around the early 1900s, the name Tin Pan Alley came to refer to not only this cacophonous New York City thoroughfare that contained many of the top music publishers of the day but also any music business center anywhere as well as the style of the music produced by the original Tin Pan Alley tunesmiths.

By this time the Tin Pan Alley music publishers were a bona fide industry that knew how to effectively market popular songs. They knew the intricacies and idiosyncrasies of the popular music market and were experts at exploiting tunes. They understood the importance of promotion—that is, that songs had to be vigorously promoted in order to sell them—and their practice of promoting tunes was called song plugging.

The ambitious publishers of Tin Pan Alley used every method they could that would result in the sale of sheet music of their songs to the public. Song pluggers would pitch their company's tunes to singers, bandleaders, musicians, theatrical directors, minstrel troupes, and other performing acts in music halls, saloons, beer halls, burlesque houses, vaudeville houses, Broadway theaters, restaurants, cafes, and hotels. Once their songs were on the bill, they would promote their performances, making the rounds at night to the halls and theaters and joints where their songs were sung, hitting perhaps a half dozen to a dozen venues an evening. They utilized all different types of ploys to engage their audiences and hopefully get them to cotton to their new tunes. As their songs were being sung, for example, they would stand up and join in, hoping to inspire other members to do the same. Or they would plant ringers in the venues to sing along when new songs were introduced to get others to join in and help popularize the new tunes. These pretenders were often lads of about thirteen or fourteen years of age, known as "boy sopranos," who with their cherubic voices would join in on the refrains to make the catchy melodies stand out more in musical shows (they could earn, perhaps, $5 a week for their services). They would employ "water boys," who strolled down the aisles of theaters serving cups of water to audience members (not really their main function) and would join in singing the refrains of showstoppers, or the exceptional songs of shows, or sing along with particular singers they were hired to accompany (their main function). They would ride around the streets of New York City on flatbed trucks and sing new songs through megaphones to the accompaniment of a piano player on board the slow-moving vehicle. They would play original songs in nickelodeons before and after the presentation of silent movies and get audiences to sing along with them as the lyrics were shone on a screen beneath pictures of models acting out the song lyrics. They would go to retailers where there was a piano such as five-and-dimes and department stores and demonstrate new songs there by playing and singing their tunes to customers. Their goal was to get the music to stick in people's heads so they would purchase the sheet music of their company's songs. They often failed to launch a song, but they often succeeded also. Many songs sold more than a million copies of sheet music—some well over 10 million copies—earning small fortunes for their publishers and writers from a single tune (in the early 1900s sheet music generally sold at about twenty-five cents per copy—previously it was about forty cents per copy—with the writer earning about a nickel per copy; the price even dropped lower, to about a dime, just before World War I, with the tunesmith getting just a penny in royalty, but over time the cost of sheet music rose, as did the writer royalty). But it wasn't just from sheet music that songwriters earned income from their songs. Piano rolls were also a source as well as phonograph records when the copyright law was revised in 1909 to give copyright owners the exclusive right of mechanical reproduction (meaning record companies had to license and pay for the use of songs in recordings).

With the water boys and boy sopranos getting an early exposure to show business, some would go on to careers as song pluggers for music publishers or piano players in nickelodeons or even as vaudeville entertainers. For instance, there was Willie Howard (born Wilhelm Levkowitz), who got his start by answering an ad for boy sopranos placed by composer Harry Von Tilzer to sing refrains of his songs in shows. Fourteen-year-old Willie would run from school each day to make the midafternoon show at Proctor's 125th Street Theatre, where for $3 a week he would stand behind a screen and sing the sentimental ballads of Von Tilzer. Like other boy sopranos, his career as a water boy lasted until his voice dropped when puberty set in. In Willie Howard's case, he was in Washington performing in the show *The Little Duchess* when one day his singing voice suddenly dipped to sound like frog-like bellows, and Florence Ziegfeld, the producer, promptly put him on a train home. But Willie's sudden demise as a water boy didn't stop his show biz pursuits, as he went on to great fame as a comedian. Other well-known water boys and boy sopranos included Joe Santly, who went on to become a stage actor, composer, and music publisher (he was in a vaudeville act called Santly and Norton, wrote songs such as "Before We Say Goodnight" and "Hawaiian Butterfly," and worked as a professional manager for Jerome H. Remick as well as started a publishing company with his brothers, Lester and Henry); Joseph Edgar Howard, who directed, produced, and wrote scores for musicals and also penned numerous hits songs such as "I Wonder Who's Kissing Her Now," "Hello, My Baby," and "When You First Kiss the Last Girl You Love"; and Gus Edwards, who wrote scores for Broadway shows, as well as penned numerous hit songs including "By the Light of the Silvery Moon," "Sunbonnet Sue," and "School Days" (he is also credited with having discovered such entertainment luminaries as Eddie Cantor, Eleanor Powell, Ray Bolger, Elsie Janis, George Jessel, and the Lane Sisters; a motion picture biography of his life was made in 1939 called *The Star Maker* starring Bing Crosby).

The route to a published or hit song in these days was relatively simple: the songwriter signed an agreement with a music publisher transferring rights to his or her song for an agreed-upon royalty. The publisher would then have a staff arranger create a piano sheet-music copy for it that could be sold in retail stores. The publisher's song pluggers would go out and promote the song as people needed to hear (and like) it before they would purchase the sheet music. But the competition to get singers to perform songs could be fierce and in this early era of the music business the seeds were planted for later forms of sketchy inducements to get artists to record songs. In trying to get singers to introduce their new songs to the public, song pluggers could be so relentless that they might pursue singers wherever they could find them—at work, on the street, at restaurants, even at home, and give them things like cash, clothes, jewelry, or perfume, or even pay their rent. This practice of offering money or considerations to people to get them to perform (or later broadcast on radio) songs (or records) became known as payola.

In the Tin Pan Alley era (and before), songs were often written to conform to the commonly used AABA structure. A structure is the pattern of a song in terms of its refrains (or choruses) and bridges, each section consisting of a particular number of measures. Commonly, letters are used to designate the sections, with A for the first section, B for the next section, and so forth. The popular AABA structure has four eight-bar sections, or thirty-two measures in total. The A section is the main melody (the catchy part) and is called the refrain or chorus; the B section is the bridge, and is the same length as each A section. The AABA song structure has proven very effective with the public and has been likened to a musical version of home-home-vacation-home, meaning home is what you love most (where you are most comfortable), and then you go on vacation that takes you away and it's nice, but then you're anxious to get back to your favorite place to be (the A section). The AABA pattern was to remain a standard song structure through the rock and roll era. Such American songbook standards as "Winter Wonderland" and "When You Wish Upon a Star" have an AABA structure.

In Tin Pan Alley the songwriters often sequestered themselves in music publisher cubicles and crafted the catchiest songs they could. They would write out their tunes on lead sheets, or music manuscripts, and then a staff arranger would write a piano (or sheet music) copy or whole band arrangement, which could then be offered for sale. In these days, many middle-class homes had piano parlors where families would gather around the instrument and sing popular songs as another member read the sheet music and played the piano.

At the same time, the Tin Pan Alley publishers were like "song stores" where entertainers made the rounds to find new potentially popular songs. These would largely include vaudeville acts, who might tour music halls around the country. In the publishing company offices were small rooms with pianos where a pianist would demonstrate the company's new tunes. They were skilled musicians who could play in any key the singer wished. If a singer took a song, it could be in the act's repertoire for a good period of time, and its wide exposure could make the song a hit. Many famous composers of the era got their start demonstrating other writers' songs before they started crafting their own tunes that became hits.

From the time Tin Pan Alley took root around 1880 through 1910, its songs were largely sentimental and by later standards may be judged sappy, schmaltzy, lovey-dovey, and corny, not to mention maudlin, as some seemed intent on plucking the strings of hearts and eliciting tears from the listener. With their innocent and decorous content, the conventional tunes of early Tin Pan Alley reflected the prim morality and quixotic ideals of the times; others reflected the current events. America was rising onto the world stage as a superpower as millions of immigrants were flooding into it and Tin Pan Alley filled the appetite for the public patriotic spirit by supplying a plethora of rousing marches. There were also exciting new inventions like the first heavier-than-air machine ever to be flown successfully in 1903 and Tin Pan Alley responded with a bevy of airplane songs. There was even a hit song using the make of a car in the title—"In My Merry Oldsmobile" (Vincent Bryan and Gus Edwards) in 1905. But love themes ruled, and even though America was separated from England by the Atlantic, it was still very much the Victorian era in America as reflected by its mushy tunes.

The pursuit of young women by adoring men was a ubiquitous theme of the time (and of course is a timeless theme of pop songs). In 1892's "Daisy Bell (A Bicycle Built for Two)" (Harry Dacre), a poor love-struck young man pleads with Daisy to consent to tie the knot with him: "It won't be a stylish marriage/I can't afford a carriage/But you'll look sweet/On the seat/Of a bicycle built for two." A more whimsical approach to getting the girl was in 1903's "Bedelia" (William Jerome and Jean Schwartz), in which the singer riffs on the opening phrase "Bedelia/I want to steal ye." Even the car song, "In My Merry Oldsmobile," was more about swooning than driving: "Come away with me Lucille/In my merry Oldsmobile/Down the road of life we'll fly/Automo-bubbling you and I/To the church we'll swiftly steal/Then our wedding bells will peal/You can go as far as you like/With me in my merry Oldsmobile."

Just the simple matter of asking out a girl on a date was fodder for a pop tune and it spawned not only a hit but also one of the great standards of all time and the unofficial anthem of baseball. In 1908's "Take Me out to the Ball Game" (Jack Norworth and Albert Von Tilzer), "baseball mad" Katie Casey was asked a question one day by her sweetheart: "On a Saturday her young beau/Called to see if she'd like to go/To see a show but Miss Kate said/'No, I'll tell you what you can do'"; then Katie launches into the immortal refrain of the song title.

Various other themes caught the public fancy. There were Irish-themed love songs like "Sweet Rosie O'Grady" (Maude Nugent Jerome) in 1896 and "My Wild Irish Rose" (Chauncey Olcott) in 1899; toy-themed songs such as "March of the Toys" (Victor Herbert) and "Toyland" (Victor Herbert and Glen MacDonough), both in 1903; patriotic songs such as the march "National Emblem" (E. E. Bagley) in 1906 and the U.S. Navy song "Anchors Aweigh" (George D. Lottman, A. H. Miles, Domenico Savino, and Charles A. Zimmerman) in 1907; and songs that expressed love using expressions of the sun and moon such as "Wait Till the Sun Shines Nellie" (Andrew B. Sterling and Harry Von Tilzer) in 1905, "Moonbeams" (Henry Blossom and Victor Herbert) in 1906, "Shine on Harvest Moon" (Nora Bayes and Jack Norworth) in 1908, and "By the Light of the Silvery Moon" (Gus Edwards and Edward Madden) in 1909. In fact, it was the verses of this last romantic ditty that became synonymous with Tin Pan Alley's sappy but immortal reputation for putting out songs with the cliché "moon-June-spoon" lyrics: "By the light of the silvery moon/I want to spoon/To my honey I'll croon love's tune/Honeymoon/Keep shining in June/Your silvery beams will bring love dreams/We'll be cuddling soon."

The pitfalls of a union of a young woman glowing in her golden youth and a man whose luster is waning but whose pockets are filled with gold were poetically captured in the 1900 hit song "A Bird in a

Gilded Cage." But this wasn't the first artistic ode to this May-December theme. The British painter William Quiller Orchardson addressed it in his 1883 painting *Le Marriage de convenance*, which depicted a young lady, her head bent forward and resting in her left palm as she stares sullenly at the floor, sitting at one end of a long table across from her elderly husband in a regal room. In the song Arthur J. Lamb's famous verse set to a haunting lachrymose melody by Harry Von Tilzer went:

> She's only a bird in a gilded cage,
> A beautiful sight to see,
> You may think she's happy and free from care,
> She's not, though she seems to be,
> 'Tis sad when you think of her wasted life,
> For youth cannot mate with age,
> And her beauty was sold for an old man's gold,
> She's a bird in a gilded cage.

Some composers of the time were so famous that they may be said to be their own genre. Perhaps the most famous of these celebrated songwriters was George M. Cohan, a prolific musical comedy composer who scored several huge hits in early Tin Pan Alley—"Give My Regards to Broadway" and "Yankee Doodle Boy," both in 1904; "Mary's a Grand Old Name" in 1905; "You're a Grand Old Flag" in 1906; and "Harrigan" in 1907—as well as later ones too, including the famous World War I song "Over There." An energetic screen biography of Cohan with many of his famous songs called *Yankee Doodle Dandy* was released in 1942. It starred James Cagney, who won an Academy Award for Best Actor for his portrayal of Cohan. A trailer for the movie said about the tunesmith, "He took the heart-beat of a nation and set it to music" (Cohan died just weeks before the movie's release but was shown a screening of it by the producers); and a Broadway musical based on Cohan's life called *George M!* debuted in 1968.

Other hits of the early Tin Pan Alley era went on to become standards in the perennial pop music songbook. Few tunes have celebrated the joys of city living as 1894's "Sidewalks of New York" (Harry Dacre) with its famous opening refrain "East Side, West Side, all around the town." "Bill Bailey Won't You Please Come Home" became a favorite of Dixieland and jazz bands with its rollicking refrain in which the narrator pleads for the return of her man: "Won't you come home, Bill Bailey, won't you come home?/I moan the whole night long/I'll do the cooking honey, I'll pay the rent,/I know I done you wrong."

Some songs become so successful that they become synonymous with, and virtual anthems of, their subject. That happened in 1906 with Will D. Cobb and Gus Edward's "School Days," a nostalgic look back at the "readin' and 'ritin' and 'rithmetic/Taught to the tune of the hickory stick."

Numerous songs that were hits in these days transcended the usual popular song success and became so iconic that they became standards, classics known to successive future generations. Examples include "Alexander's Ragtime Band" (Irving Berlin), "Danny Boy" (Fred E. Weatherly), "You Made Me Love You, I Didn't Want to Do It" (James V. Monaco and Joseph McCarthy), "St. Louis Blues" (W. C. Handy), "By the Beautiful Sea" (Harry Carroll and Harold Atteridge), and "Rock-a-Bye Your Baby with a Dixie Melody" (Joe Young, Jean Schwartz, and Sam M. Lewis). But the hits weren't all the standard fare of love songs. Tin Pan Alley lyricists combined their sense of humor with their mastery of words and came up with successful ditties with such diverting titles as "If You Don't Want My Peaches, You'd Better Stop Shaking My Tree" (Irving Berlin), "Oh! How She Could Yacki, Hacki, Wicki Wacki Woo" (Charles McCarron, Stanley Murphy, and Albert von Tilzer), "Since Maggie Dooley Learned the Hooley Hooley" (Edgar Leslie, Bert Kalmar and George Meyer), "When Yankee Doodle Learns to Parlez Vous Francais" (Ed Nelson and William Hart), "Everything Is Peaches Down in Georgia" (Grant Clark, Milton Ager, and George Meyer), and "Would You Rather Be a Colonel with an Eagle on Your Shoulder or a Private with a Chicken on Your Knee?" (Sidney Mitchell and Archie Gottler).

Ironically, the most successful song of the Tin Pan Alley era was not written by a Tin Pan Alley composer or published by a Tin Pan Alley publisher. It wasn't even written as a popular song or for commercial purposes, but as an educational song. Yet it went on to become the most recognized tune in the world, not only soon after its time but also through the decades all the way up to today. The song was originally a kindergarten song that was titled "Good Morning to All" and published by the Chicago firm Clayton F. Summy Co. in an anthology of children's songs called *Song Stories for Kindergarten*, and that had an introduction by an educator named Anna E. Bryan. Its authorship is credited to two sisters, Mildred J. Hill and Patty S. Hill. Sometime after "Good Morning to All" was published, new words were set to its melody and in the first decade of the twentieth century, the tune was universally recognized as "Happy Birthday to You." The song owes its success to its simplicity (with a one-octave range, the average person can sing it), melody (it's catchy), brevity (family and friends can sing the short song accompanying the relatively short celebration of blowing out the candles on the cake), and utility (birthdays are celebrated everywhere all the time). Musically, the song's appeal lies in its tension-and-release mechanism. There are four rounds of "happy birthday" in the song. The end notes of the first two rounds whose words are "to you" leave an unresolved feeling (even more in the second round when the note with "to" is a step higher than it was in the first round). The relief finally starts coming in the third round when the tune reaches its apogee with the octave jump to the note with the syllable "birth" after which the notes start to descend but still end on an unresolved note (whose word is the name or last syllable of the name of the birthday celebrant), and the whole enterprise of building musical tension and leaping toward a grand conclusion is aesthetically resolved in the fourth and final round when the song comes to a satisfying end. Probably no single work of any composer, from Mozart to Beethoven to Gershwin to Lennon & McCartney, has become so universally known and performed as the Hill sisters' lyrically mutated, short (one eight-bar verse), buoyant tune (now in the public domain), which is used to celebrate birthdays around the clock around the world.

Songwriting is a craft that can require painstaking effort, but prior to Tin Pan Alley, songwriters weren't particularly savvy in their business relationships with music publishers, nor were some of them particularly concerned about how much money they could make off their work. Some, like the nineteenth-century songwriters Stephen Foster ("Oh, Susanna," "Beautiful Dreamer," "The Camptown Races") and Septimus Winner ("Listen to the Mockingbird," "Ten Little Indians" "Oh Where, Oh Where Has My Little Dog Gone?") sold millions of copies of sheet music although they may not have become rich from their efforts— Foster died broke—but many tunesmiths wrote out of pure love or inspiration or for the betterment of society and didn't care that they made little or no money at all. That all changed when music publishing became a centralized industry and the primary aim was for its product—popular songs—to make money. At the same time, changing technology gave the industry new ways to deliver music to the public, which could mean additional sources of income for its writers and publishers but in order for that to happen the copyright law needed to be revised.

The origin of the U.S. copyright law may be traced back to England's Statute of Anne, which was formally titled "An Act for the Encouragement of Learning, by Vesting the Copies of Printed Books in the Authors or Purchasers of Such Copies, during the Times therein Mentioned," enacted in 1709 and entering into force in 1710. It was the world's first copyright law and when England established its colonies on the east coast of America it applied its legal system of the Statute of Anne and English common law to the colonies. An author or copyright owner thus had the right to print, publish, copy, and vend his or her work, or to authorize others to do so.

After America won independence from England the thirteen former colonies, now states, established their own governments, many adopting provisions of their colonial charters. Beginning with Connecticut in January 1783, the states began ratifying local copyright statutes and by April 1786 all the thirteen original states had copyright statutes with the exception of Delaware. The statutes were enacted under the Articles of Confederation, the new country's first constitution, and they were patterned after the Statute of Anne. The state copyright statutes were not uniform, with the exception of a couple of provisions: protection was accorded only to American citizens or residents and registration of the work by the author or copyright owner was required as a condition of copyright protection.

The Articles of Confederation resulted in a weak federal government and held the new states together so loosely that some had their own currency and militias and consequently the thirteen states functioned as if they were almost thirteen separate countries. The nation was on the verge of falling apart until the U.S. Constitution was signed on September 17, 1787, in Philadelphia. In drawing up the law of the land, the Continental Congress continued to recognize the value of intellectual properties and empowered Congress in Article 1, Section 8 "to promote the progress of science and useful arts, by securing for limited to authors and inventors the exclusive right to their respective writing and discoveries." Almost three years later, on May 31, 1790,

Congress enacted the first federal copyright statute in the United States; there was now a single system of copyright law for all the states in the country. The law provided copyright protection for books, maps, and charts for a term of fourteen years, with the privilege of renewal for an additional fourteen years. The author or owner of a work made copyright registration at the U.S. district court where he or she resided. Only published works were accorded statutory protection; for an unpublished work authors generally relied on state common law.

The first general revision of the U.S. copyright law was enacted on February 3, 1831, and it provided copyright protection for musical compositions and also extended the first term of copyright from fourteen years to twenty-eight years, while leaving the renewal term at fourteen years. This revision took place at around the time minstrel shows were starting to develop and become popular in the United States, and songs were an important part of this new style of entertainment.

The U.S. copyright law underwent a second general revision that was enacted on July 8, 1870, and this was significant, for it centralized copyright deposit and registration at the Library of Congress (in 1897 a Copyright Office was established at the Library of Congress as a separate department); pursuant to this revision registration at U.S. district courts was no longer in effect.

The first international copyright protection for U.S. works came as a result of the International Copyright Act of 1891, sometimes referred to as the Chace Act, or "International Copyright Act." The need for international protection was illuminated some years earlier when the British theatrical impresario Richard D'Oyly Carte and composing team of Gilbert and Sullivan came to the United States to oversee business interests of the team's comic opera *The Pirates of Penzance*. The show opened in New York City on December 31, 1879, at the Fifth Avenue Theatre located at 28th Street and Broadway, and the first unauthorized production of the show occurred in September of the next year when a Boston theater group performed it at the Booth Theatre at 23rd Street and Sixth Avenue. The Chace Act provided that the works of nonresident foreign authors could receive copyright protection in the United States as of March 3, 1891, on the condition that their countries extended copyright protection to the works of U.S. authors, although as the venerable publisher Isadore Witmark pointed out, the difference in copyright laws between countries, with some countries laws' having complicated formalities, could create logistical challenges. But with the Chace Act it might be said that the American music business first became legitimately internationalized. Its Tin Pan Alley publishers traveled to England to exploit their songs and found a receptive market there; English artists performed and recorded their tunes, popularizing not only themselves but also American songs. At the same time, the Chace Act ostensibly ended the practice in America of U.S. firms publishing popular English songs such as the heartbreaking breakup-story song with a happy ending "Mary and John" and the music hall Cockney song "My Old Dutch" without paying any royalties.

By the early 1900s the phonograph player had become a popular staple in American homes—it was often either this machine or a piano that was the centerpiece of the middle-class living room. The popularity of the phonograph player was a result of the public's love of music and desire to own recordings of the music they enjoyed. The copyright law didn't address the reproduction of music in phonograph recordings since the last general revision of the law was in 1870, before the invention and development of the phonograph. But that would soon change.

The third general revision of the copyright law was enacted on March 4, 1909 (effective on July 1, 1909), and it addressed the reproduction of music works in phonograph recordings, as well as made several other changes that were important for songwriters and owners of musical compositions: it extended the renewal term of copyright from fourteen years to twenty-eight years, bringing the total term of copyright to an original term of twenty-eight years and a renewal term of twenty-eight years (twenty-eight plus twenty-eight); it provided for copyright registration of certain classes of unpublished works, including musical compositions; it brought into general law the 1897 performance right amendment providing an exclusive right to copyright owners for public performances of their musical works—there was little compliance with this mandate that required performers of copyrighted musical compositions to license (and pay for) public performances of songs until the formation of the first American performing rights organization in 1914; and it provided a compulsory license for the making and distribution of phonograph recordings. This last addition provided that once a nondramatic music work was recorded and distributed with the permission of the copyright owner, then anyone could record and distribute mechanical reproductions of that work as long as the person complied with the terms of the compulsory license. In essence, the compulsory license provision enabled a system for making cover records and prevented discrimination by the song owner. In this way the song owner, or music publisher, could not choose who could or could not record and distribute his musical work, and it accorded with the Constitution's mission of empowering Congress "to promote the progress of . . . [the] useful arts." The original royalty for sale of a mechanical reproduction (recording) of a music work under the 1909 law was two cents per mechanical reproduction of a song. Thus, for every recording of a song that was sold, the label would remit two cents to the music publisher, who would split it (usually 50/50) with the songwriter. The two-cent mechanical royalty rate would continue until the fourth general revision of the U.S. copyright law went into full effect on January 1, 1978, after which it increased incrementally over time.

The mechanical right would provide writers and publishers of songs with one of their most important sources of song income. Over the years, sheet music sales would decrease and record sales would increase, and the mechanical right enabled songwriters and music publishers to participate in the revenue from sales of recordings. It would always be a flat penny royalty rate, unlike artists and producers, who would earn a percentage of the retail or wholesale price of their singles or albums, but in the long run it could be quite lucrative, as while an artist and producer get a percentage royalty rate for their particular recordings, the music publisher and songwriter get their mechanical royalties for every recording of their song released, so if a song is covered by multiple artists, the music publisher and songwriter will collect mechanical royalties for all these artists' record sales of their song (plus there could be other types of royalties).

The songwriter and music publisher's invaluable statutory mechanical right came as a result of a Supreme Court decision in the case of *White-Smith Music Publishing Company v. Apollo Company*. The case involved two songs, "Kentucky Babe" and "Little Cotton Dolly," that had been published in sheet music and were subsequently sold in the form of perforated rolls (player piano rolls) by Apollo Company, a manufacturer of player pianos that are used with perforated sheets. The composer of the two songs, Adam Geibel, sued Apollo for copyright infringement for reproducing his songs, copyrighted around March 17, 1897, but Apollo maintained that their perforated sheets, or piano rolls, were not copies of the work, which was what the copyright owner had the right to reproduce his work in. A circuit court of the United States for the Southern District of New York ruled in favor of Apollo, and the decision was upheld by the circuit court of appeals of the second circuit, and by the Supreme Court of the United States with the principle that a player piano roll was not a "copy" of the musical composition but a mechanical reproduction. However, Congress, in its Copyright Act of 1909, included a provision that whenever the owner of a copyright has used, permitted, or knowingly acquiesced the use of the party's copyrighted song in a mechanical reproduction of the work, then any other person may make similar use of the song upon payment to the copyright owner of a royalty of two cents for each unit manufactured and the rendering of payments at times provided by the law.

With a mechanical right now part of the U.S. copyright law, song publishers could now legally license and collect revenues for the reproduction of popular songs in piano rolls. Indeed, there was a thriving industry in the first quarter of the twentieth century for player pianos and piano rolls. The antecedent of the player piano actually goes back much further in time and shows that mechanical reproduction of music has been a long-time pursuit of people. In August 1927, Charles F. Stoddard, the director of the research laboratory of the American Piano Company, gave an address titled "The Evolution of the Music Roll" in which he said,

> I have a photograph of an old print dated 1657, thirty-seven years after the Pilgrims landed at Plymouth Rock, which shows a beautiful pipe organ operated by such a roll. The entire mechanism was driven by an overshot water wheel. In Latin is a complete description of this organ which tells exactly how the music was laid out. I shall read a translation of the Latin:
>
> Transfer the Pythagorean melody to the aforesaid phonotactic cylinder. Since the melody consists of 54 times, or measures, the whole circumference of the cylinder should be divided into 54 equal parts; then each part should be subdivided into three parts since each note of this melody equals one-third of a measure, In the figure the heavy lines drawn longitudinally on the cylinder mark the first division into 54 parts, the dotted line shows the subdivisions into three parts. Then transfer to the cylinder the melody and fix the

teeth which correspond to the notes in the proper places. (Roehl, 1961)

Around the time of Stoddard's speech, there was a plethora of automatic music machines that could reproduce popular tunes, many of these machines now forgotten. There were, for example, coin-operated electrical pianos (which functioned like jukeboxes and could be installed in venues such as hotel lobbies, cigar stores, ice cream stores, candy stores, and billiard parlors), orchestrions (player pianos that could reproduce sounds such as a piano, violin, flute, piccolo, snare drum, bass drum, tympani, triangle, and cymbal and be used in theaters and amusement venues), and reproducing pipe organs, It is unclear if the manufacturers of these devices took out mechanical licenses to reproduce songs, but there were toy mechanical gimmicks also. Here is the text for an ad for the "Rolmonica":

> Rolmonica is the only mouth organ that plays music rolls. All you have to do is turn the crank and blow. Built into a hinged bakelite frame, the Rolmonica measures 4 by 5/8 inches. Two cranks, one for winding and the other for re-winding, the rolls which can be changed easily. Blowing or drawing breath draws the same note. Length of perforation regulates tempo. (Roehl, 1961)

The cost of the Rolmonica was $1.00 and included four rolls. Additional rolls sold for forty-seven cents and included these songs in separate rolls, as shown in these four examples: (1) "Swanee River," "Endearing Young Charms," "Wild Irish Rose," "Humoresque"; (2) "Carry Me Back to Old Virginny," "Kiss Me Again," "Annie Laurie," "Mighty Lak' a Rose," "When You and I Were Young Maggie"; (3) "Turn on the Heat," "Little Kiss Each Morning," "Chant of the Jungle," "La Paloma," "Perfect Day"; (4) "Stein Song," "Me and the Girl Next Door," "There's Danger in Your Eyes," "I Love You Believe Me," "Tiptoe thru the Tulips" (Koenigsberg, 1987).

Another device that played popular tunes with perforated rolls was the Play-a-Sax, which sold for $2.89 with its rolls selling "3 for 39 cents." An advertisement for it read:

> You can Play-a-Sax the minute you get it. . . . Just put on the music roll, turn the crank and blow. Plays 16-note perforated music rolls

with accompanying chords. All metal with gold finish. Length 12 inches. One music roll included, "Way Down Upon the Swanee River." (Roehl, 1961)

The ad also featured four music rolls containing popular songs of the time offered for sale: (1) "I Get the Blues When It Rains," "Sweethearts on Parade," "Sidewalks of New York"; (2) "Mean to Me," "Tiptoe thru the Tulips," "Am I Blue?"; (3) "Singing in the Rain," "Lover Come Back to Me," "Wabash Blues"; (4) "Piccolo Pete," "If I Had a Talking Picture of You," "Let Me Call You Sweetheart" (Roehl, 1961). Some of these songs were in copyright such as "Am I Blue?" and "Tiptoe Thru the Tulips With Me," both written in 1929, so presumably the manufacturer of the rolls paid royalties to these songs' publishers, but "Swanee River" (Stephen Foster's 1851 song, also called "Old Folks at Home") was in the public domain at this time, so no license was needed to reproduce the song in a roll.

Thanks to Congress, in the early part of the twentieth century, and the music publishers who lobbied its members for the inclusion of a compulsory license for the mechanical reproduction of songs, songwriters and music publishers would have a valuable source of income from their works as the public's buying habits changed from sheet music to records. The mechanical royalty would be an important and perennial source of income for music publishers and professional songwriters.

On Saturday evening, December 10, 1910, the curtain rose at the Metropolitan Opera in New York City for the premier of Giacomo Puccini's new opera, *La facciulla del West* (*The Girl of the Golden West*). Puccini was the renowned Italian composer of such operas as *La Bohème* and *Madama Butterfly* and was in town for the opening performance of his new work, which the thirty-year-old opera company commissioned. The opera starred the renowned Italian tenor Enrico Caruso, as well as soprano Emmy Destinn and baritone Pasquale Amato, and was conducted by the distinguished maestro Arturo Toscanini. So great was the demand for tickets that scalpers were selling them at prices starting at $75. The last morning rehearsal at the Metropolitan Opera had been completely packed with an audience that included many of the opera company's regular singers who were not in the production as well as many well-known stage performers who were in the city, the most prominent newspaper critics and journalists of New York, and regular box-office subscribers. After the first act of the morning rehearsal the principals came on stage repeatedly, finally with Puccini himself, who was greeted with frenzied screams of "Bravo!"

It was during his visit to New York City that Puccini had a meeting, according to one account, which if true, resulted in one of the most significant developments in the American music business. Puccini met with George Maxwell, the American representative of G. Ricordi, his Italian publisher. He asked Maxwell how much he might earn from public performances of his compositions at venues such as nightclubs and restaurants. Maxwell told him that although U.S. copyright law provided copyright owners with an exclusive right for nondramatic performances of musical compositions, there was little compliance with it, and that performances of his works would probably not result in any revenue. Puccini was agitated by this situation—he responded that public performances of musical compositions in Europe resulted in royalties—and not long after Maxwell and composer Raymond Hubbell proposed to copyright attorney Nathan Burkan the idea of creating an American performing rights organization to ensure compliance with the performing right of the copyright law.

The legal right of composers and authors of musical compositions to license and earn royalties for public performances of their works first went into force in 1851, when the performing rights organization, the Société des Auteurs, Compositeurs et Editeurs de Musique (SACEM), formed in France. The purpose of this organization was to license the performing rights of musical compositions on behalf of copyright owners to music users. At this time there was no legal recognition in the United States of a performing right, but an act of January 6, 1897, provided a nondramatic performing right for copyrighted musical compositions. In effect, this meant that anyone who performed a musical composition in public without permission would be subject to the penalties of copyright infringement. This new exclusive right promised to be an important source of income for songwriters and music publishers, for it meant that whenever their songs were played in public for profit they would earn a performance royalty.

As it turned out, there was little compliance with this new public performance right in the beginning. Songwriters and music publishers made money off popular songs by the sale of sheet music. Songs were generally brought to public attention by singers, musicians, and bandleaders who performed them in various types of venues. They were responsible for some songs selling millions of copies of sheet music. With the 1897 performing right amendment, anyone who wanted to legally perform a copyrighted song in public for profit now had to obtain the permission of the owner of the song. Permission meant the paying of a performance license fee, so in effect, this meant that venues or performers had to pay to play songs, which they interpreted as being unfair since they now had to pay to popularize the songs they played, which enriched the writers and publishers of those songs, while they themselves may have been struggling financially to earn a livelihood from playing music. The musicians and the venues where they performed threatened to boycott performing any songs for which they were required to pay a performance license fee, but the publishers, fearful that a boycott would severely diminish sheet music sales of their songs, told the musicians and venue operators that they wouldn't require a license for the performance of their songs and to continue playing their tunes gratis.

Spurred by Puccini, some prominent American music publishers and songwriters hoped to do something about the lack of compliance with the statutory performing right of copyright owners of musical works. A meeting was set up for composers and songwriters to meet at Lüchow's restaurant on 14th Street near Union Square in New York City in October 1913. However, due to inclement weather or confusion about the purpose of the meeting, only nine of the thirty-six invited men showed up. Renowned composer Victor Herbert was still enthusiastic about starting a performing rights organization, and the group planned to meet again.

That seminal meeting took place at the Hotel Claridge in Times Square in Manhattan on the evening of February 13, 1914, and over one hundred songwriters and publishers from the music world were in attendance. This resulted in the creation of the American Society of Composers, Authors and Publishers (ASCAP), the first performing rights organization in America, and it was patterned after the French society, SACEM. Many of the most prominent American songwriters and music publishers of the day became its first members.

Representing songwriters and music publishers for the licensing of the nondramatic performing right of their compositions, ASCAP promoted its purpose. The first ASCAP license was issued on October 1, 1914, to Rector's Restaurant at 1600 Broadway in the theater district, and it authorized the eatery's in-house orchestra to play ASCAP songs. Soon eighty-five hotels signed licensing agreements. Their license fees averaged $8.23 per month, which barely covered the operating expenses of the new music licensing society, so no performance royalties could be paid to its members. There were many other establishments in New York City that played music but that did not take out a music performance license, so it was known that a court ruling was needed.

The John Philip Sousa march "From Maine to Oregon" had been performed without authorization in the dining room of the Vanderbilt Hotel on Park Avenue and 34th Street, and the publisher brought the operator of the hotel to court for an unlicensed performance. The ruling favored the plaintiff, but the verdict was appealed, and the circuit court reversed the decision on the basis that patrons of the dining hall had come to eat rather than hear music.

ASCAP and its members were surely disappointed but ready to try again. The next composer to sue was Victor Herbert, who was dining at Shanley's Restaurant in Times Square and appalled at a high bill he received at the same time some of his compositions were being played for which he earned nothing. So he brought suit against Shanley's for the unauthorized performance of his waltz "Sweethearts" on April 1, 1915. At the U.S. District Court for the Southern District of New York, Judge Learned Hand ruled against Herbert, and the decision was upheld by the circuit court of appeals. With defeat after defeat now the question of whether songwriters and music publishers would earn revenue from public performances of their music was in doubt. However, *Herbert v. Shanley Co.* made its way to the Supreme Court, and on January 22, 1917, the Court unanimously upheld the right of copyright owners to license their works for public performance, even if no admission is charged. In his decision Associate Justice Oliver Wendell Holmes Jr. wrote,

> If the rights under the copyright are infringed by a performance where money is taken at the door, they are imperfectly protected. Performances not different in kind from those of the defendants could be given that might compete with and even destroy the success of the monopoly that the law intends the plaintiff to have. It is enough to say that there is no need to construe the statute narrowly.

The defendant's performances are not eleemosynary. They are part of a total for which the public pays and the fact that the price of the whole is attributable to a particular item which those present are expected to order is not important. It is true that the music is not the sole object, but neither is the food which probably could be got cheaper elsewhere. The object is a respect of surroundings that to people having limited powers of conversation or disliking the rival noise give a luxurious pleasure not to be had from eating a silent meal. If music did not pay, it would be given up. If it pays, it pays out of the public's pocket. Whether it pays or not, the purpose of employing it is profit, and that is enough.

This landmark decision affirmed ASCAP's existence and the right of songwriters and music publishers to derive revenue from the public performances of their music was firmly established. It wouldn't be until 1921 that ASCAP's licensing income exceeded its overhead and legal costs, but with its hard fight all the way up to the Supreme Court the victory was won for songwriters and music publishers. Over the years, performance rights revenues for broadcasts and other public performances of songs would turn out to be one of the most important, if not *the* most important, source of popular song income. But also, importantly, performing rights organizations (PROs) provide an efficient system by which song rights holders can license their music to establishments that play music and society can efficiently have access to copyrighted music. The PROs provide a practical way for the clearance of rights for song licensing. Music is performed practically everywhere—on radio, television, and streaming services; at concert halls, stores, shopping malls, bars, hotels, dance studios, arenas, stadiums, colleges, and numerous other venues. Around the world there are hundreds of thousands of music users who want to perform copyrighted music, which includes millions of songs. Since permission is needed by the users to perform copyrighted music—some users such as streaming services perform millions of compositions annually—it would be virtually impossible for them to contact each of the owners of the songs separately and negotiate performance licenses. At the same time, it would be economically unfeasible for music copyright owners to negotiate separate licenses with each of its music users and then to monitor performances of their works by these music users. Thus, as central clearinghouses the performing rights organizations simplify the clearance of rights and ease the burden of direct licensing. As bulk licensors of copyrighted music, they enable copyrighted music to be performed in public expeditiously and efficiently and serve a valuable function for society.

Today, there are performing rights organizations in most countries around the world as copyright laws of most countries recognize the performing right of a musical composition. This gives the owners of musical compositions the exclusive right (subject to certain limitations as stated in countries' copyright laws) to license their musical works for public performance. These foreign societies operate similarly to the American organizations: they charge license fees to music users and, after deducting their operating expenses, distribute the collected fees as performance royalties to the writers and publishers of the publicly performed works.

Musical compositions are commonly performed in countries outside of their writers' and publishers' home countries. Because performing rights organizations have reciprocal agreements with PROs in other countries, the writers and publishers of publicly performed compositions outside their home countries can have their works licensed in foreign countries and get credited for performances of their works there and get paid for such performances through their domestic PRO. Indeed, with the system of PRO reciprocal agreements, the international licensing of copyrighted music is handled efficiently, enabling music that originates in one country to be played globally and legally and for creators and copyright owners to be paid for the performances of their music virtually anywhere.

The first million-selling record came in the early 1900s as Tin Pan Alley was basically shaping the popular music industry of America. Its writers and publishers were coming up with songs that the public took to with great fervor, with sheet music selling briskly. Now, with phonograph players growing in popularity, the recording industry would become a more important player in the music industry. The introduction of the Victrola in 1906, a new style of record player in which the speakers, previously external and an eyesore and dust-collector, were built inside the unit, would be a more attractive entertainment unit for the home, resulting in more players—and more records—being sold.

But the first million-seller disc was not of a popular song, but is reportedly of the aria "Vesti la Guibba" from Ruggero Leoncavallo's opera *Pagliacci*, recorded and released in 1902 by the famous Italian tenor Enrico Caruso. Nevertheless, with the phonograph record, sheet music had a welcomed competitor (with both the public, and with songwriters and publishers, starting in 1909, when the copyright law was revised to include a mechanical right), in how popular songs were sold to the public, with labels such as the American Graphophone Company and Monarch distributing records to the public.

As the music companies of New York City were bringing sheet music and records of Tin Pan Alley tunes to the American public, a new form of music was taking shape in the south of the country. After the Civil War, many African Americans made their way to New Orleans, which was considered an open-minded city. Music was vibrant in New Orleans, and here African Americans, some the children of former slaves, sung black folk tunes and spirituals, blues, and religious hymns. Many also took up instruments, even though they were unable to read music. But they played by instinct and ear, being able to not just recreate popular tunes from their minds but also improvise on them as notes poured out of their instruments while staying in the chords of songs so they could play together as an ensemble. Individual musicians could improvise as tunes were being played, or all the musicians in the group could play extemporaneously at the same time, too. This music would come to be called jazz, and it would become one of the most popular idioms of popular music.

This new indigenous form of music was born in the Storyville sector of New Orleans, where prostitution was legal by city ordinance. One of its pioneers was a cornet player named Charles "Buddy" Bolden, who fellow musicians raved as being a virtuoso on his instrument. Jazz was expressed in different ways, one of which was called ragtime.

Ragtime, a form of syncopated music (that is, with the upbeat accented) played primarily on the piano, was gaining popularity around the mid-1890s, but really took off in 1899 with the publication of Scott Joplin's "Maple Leaf Rag." Other composers such as James Scott, Tom Turpin, and Joseph Lamb helped popularize ragtime with their compositions, and several female composers did also, including Adaline Shepherd ("Pickles and Peppers"), Charlotte Blake ("The Gravel Rag"), Julia

Lee Niebergall ("Horse Shoe Rag"), and May Aufderheide ("The Thriller Rag").

Tin Pan Alley was always quick to pick up on music trends and bring them to mainstream audiences in popular-song form. It did this with the new music coming out of New Orleans in popular tunes as Hughie Cannon's 1904 "Bill Bailey Won't You Please Come Home," Irving Berlin's 1911 "Alexander's Ragtime Band," and W. C. Handy's 1914 "St. Louis Blues."

As Tin Pan Alley was making its mark on the American public, pioneers in the phonograph player were also making their advances. In the 1880s Edison and Alexander Graham Bell were making improvements on Edison's relatively new invention as well as other men such as Chichester Bell (no relation of Alexander) and Emile Berliner, who developed the flat disc in 1887. At the start of the last decade of the nineteenth century, many people couldn't afford to buy a record player, but they still liked the idea of listening to recorded music, whose repertoire was growing. The phonograph wasn't marketed aggressively to the public because it hadn't been adopted fully as an entertainment device but rather as a machine for dictation. In that regard, it wasn't immediately embraced by the general public, but as improvements were made, it would become a popular medium for playing music.

Popular songs seemed to follow the sentiments of the Victorian era as Tin Pan Alley's tunes through the end of the Victorian era were often sappy and endearing. The rigid morals of that era slowly evaporated after the death of England's Queen Victoria in 1901, although Tin Pan Alley continued to hold onto them as reflected with songs such as "By the Light of the Silvery Moon" in 1909, "Let Me Call You Sweetheart" in 1910, and "I Want a Girl (Just Like the Girl That Married Dear Old Dad)" in 1911. But social, cultural, political, and other changes were taking place that would change the country, and as always, be reflected in the tunes of Tin Pan Alley, the musical mirror of popular culture.

In 1898 the United States fought Spain in the Spanish-American War and annexed Hawaii, Puerto Rico, and Guam. In the first decade of the twentieth century, President William McKinley was assassinated and America was rising on the world stage as a superpower. From 1900 to 1910 Americans were introduced to bubble gum, hamburgers, pizza, comic strips, Jello, bibles in hotel rooms, teddy bears, paper cups, the Victrola, bloomers, piano parlors in homes, and the permanent wave hairstyle. Americans were starting to dance the fox trot in 1914. These and other cultural happenings were the backdrop for the popular hits of the decade, and a changing morality that would presage new and exciting forms of popular music to come soon. But political tensions had been fomenting in Europe for years now and, following the assassination of Austrian Archduke Franz Ferdinand in Sarajevo, came to a head on July 28, 1914, when World War I broke out. The world was changing, and Tin Pin Alley would be there to buoy its spirit in song.

3

BOOZE, AIRWAVES, AND CELLULOID
SPARK THE BIZ

As World War I raged on with the Allied and Central powers fiercely engaging in combat with trench warfare, fighter aircraft, armored tanks, mortar cannons, howitzers, railway guns, flamethrowers, and chemical warfare—the conflict would result in a staggering 16 million combatant and civilian deaths—the music business was doing its part to bolster the spirits of both soldiers and public alike. From 1914, when the war began, to its couldn't-come-soon-enough end in 1918, the music business each year paraded an ensemble of patriotic fare for marching, drinking, reminiscing, cheering, and commiserating with such tunes as "Keep the Home-Fires Burning, Till the Boys Come Home" and "When You're a Long, Long Way from Home" in 1914; "Pack up Your Troubles in Your Old Kit-Bag" and "When the Boys Come Home" in 1915; "Roses of Picardy" in 1916; "Over There," "Good-Bye Broadway, Hello France," and "When Yankee Doodle Learns to Parlez Vous Francais" in 1917; and "Oh! How I Hate to Get up in the Morning," "K-K-K-Katy," and "Would You Rather Be a Colonel with an Eagle on Your Shoulder, or a Private with a Chicken on Your Knee?" in 1918.

The grim conflict didn't stop the Alley from dishing out its usual concoction of catchy upbeat ditties, however, as it did with such future standards as "By the Sea," "The Aba Daba Honeymoon," "I Love a Piano," "For Me and My Gal," "After You've Gone," and "Rock-a-Bye Your Baby with a Dixie Melody," and it also kept feet dancing and toes bouncing with its fox trots, jazz, and ragtime. In the last year of the decade, and in the wake of the "The Great War," Tin Pan Alley even showed its sense of humor with such big hits as "Oh How I Laugh When I Think How I Cried about You," "My Home Town Is a One-Horse Town, But It's Big Enough for Me," "I Wish I Could Shimmy Like My Sister Kate," and "All the Shakers Are Shoulder Shakers, Down in Quaker Town." And also in that last year of the decade, 1919, the first bona fide superstar singer of the popular music business, Al Jolson, swept the country with his "Swanee," a one-step (and conscious follow-up to the one-step hit of the preceding year, "Hindustan"), written by George Gershwin and Irving Caesar; the pair discussed their ideas for the song in a restaurant and went back to Gershwin's home, where they completed it in twenty minutes (Gershwin's father, in a poker game in another room, heard the song being sung and left the table to accompany the young duo by playing an improvised kazoo).

So now the war was over and people reveled to the beat of the popular tune and likewise to a swig of liquor as music was performed in bars, saloons, beer halls, dance halls, and restaurants. For adults, music and alcohol seemed as natural a coupling as toast and jelly or salt and pepper, but a temperance movement in the United States arose years earlier that culminated in 1920 with the ratification of the Eighteenth Amendment, which imposed a national legal ban on the making, transporting, and selling of alcoholic beverages. During the time of this ban, commonly known as Prohibition, booze would no longer be served where there was music (at least legally), and music would have to find another arena in which it could be plied to the public.

That other arena came soon enough. Prohibition drove the serving of liquor underground in bars or rooms called speakeasies, and people flocked to these establishments, as carousing was part of their lives. There were thousands of speakeasies in cities like Chicago and New York, and many were controlled by gangsters who supplied them with illicit liquor, or moonshine. It was such a competitive scene, in fact, that speakeasy proprietors endeavored to find the best musical talent they could to perform in their venues, but that talent would need to musically complement the spirited nature of these places, and that talent performed jazz, hot jazz. Musicians such as Louis Armstrong, Fats Waller, Bix Beiderbecke, and Duke Ellington were among the featured attractions in these establishments, which were often multiracial, and they became nationally famous. Flappers, young women who wore short skirts, wore their hair in bobs, smoked, drank, and danced the shimmy, Charleston, tango, and Lindy Hop, frequented speakeasies, all in the wake of the Nineteenth Amendment adopted on August 18, 1920, granting women the right to vote. Popular songs were also performed in speakeasies, so with these illegal establishments Tin Pan Alley had another area in which to promote its tunes.

The speakeasy scene would fall when the stock market crashed at the end of the 1920s, but it was a decade in which music was a vital part of the culture. Since music was craved by the public, the Alley would be there to satiate its appetite, whether the venues in which its songs were performed were legal or not. Like in previous times, music and booze fed off each other in the Roaring Twenties, showing theirs is a symbiotic relationship and that where there's booze, there is likely to be music.

In 1920, when underground drinking establishments were launched in the wake of Prohibition, it was at the same time a watershed time aboveground, for it marked the advent of commercial radio broadcasting in the United States. Commercial radio broadcasting had been gearing up for years—in 1893 Nikola Tesla conducted experiments in wireless communication, and he was followed by other scientists such as Guglielmo Marconi and Reginald Fessenden, whose experiments would lead to improving radio. The U.S. government's first control of the new wireless communication medium came with the Wireless Ship Act of 1910, which required that vessels with at least sixty persons on board sailing two hundred miles from the U.S. coast must contain wireless radio equipment that could communicate over a distance of one hundred miles, followed by the Radio Act of 1912, which required that all ships keep continuous radio watch and stay in contact with nearby vessels, and that all amateur radio operators in the United States be licensed by the federal government.

From the early days of radio, it was easy to see that it would be an important entertainment medium and could have a profound effect on the promotion of music. In November 1916, David Sarnoff, a traffic manager at the American Marconi wireless telegraph company (and future head of Radio Corporation of America, or RCA), wrote in a memo to his supervisor, "I have in mind a plan of development which would make radio a household utility in the same sense as the piano or the phonograph. The idea is to bring music into the house by wireless." Sarnoff actually wasn't the first industry professional to envision the benefit of radio to music. Lee de Forest, an inventor and pioneer in broadcasting, preceded him in this prognostication, having already aired over his Bronx, New York, experimental station, 2XG, news and entertainment programs including songs.

Although by 1920 radio communication was known to the public, the idea now that sounds in all their distinct textures, layers, and tones could travel invisibly through the air and be heard from a receiver in the home a distance away just as if they were heard in-person at their source of origin indubitably struck some as another miracle of science. That marvel became a reality when the station KDKA of the Westinghouse Electric and Manufacturing Company in East Pittsburgh made the first commercial radio broadcast on November 2, 1920. (The announcer asked that anyone hearing its broadcast of the presidential election results to contact the station, as "we are anxious to know how far the broadcast is reaching and how it is being received.") Stations quickly proliferated as the public seemed to enjoy radio's programming.

With radio now emerging as a popular entertainment medium, the music industry would find it to be a great promotional vehicle for its songs and records, as the old vaudeville theaters, burlesque halls, beer halls, and other venues where songs were sung had largely disappeared. Indeed, culture and technology are always changing, and radio more or less ratified a cardinal rule of the music industry, that it needs to monetize popular new technologies, if possible, for its product.

In 1921 there were just five radio stations broadcasting in the United States, but the number jumped to 30 the next year, 571 in 1925, and 618 in 1930. Music was part of the mix of early radio programming, along with romance shows, comedies, news programs, baseball games, soap operas, serial shows, quiz shows, and other types of shows. Music would emerge as radio's most popular format, and from its beginning through the 1940s, there were numerous shows that featured popular music and would be the DNA for future styles of radio programming.

There was, for instance, the show called "Your Hit Parade" that debuted in 1935 and ran for eighteen years that played the top songs of the week. While its personnel of announcers, conductors, singers, and musicians changed over the years, the show's initial premise (different permutations of the show occurred over the years) may be indicated by the opening remarks of announcer Andre Baruch for the Wednesday,

May 27, 1936, broadcast of the show airing on the National Broadcasting Company network:

> Lucky Strike presents "Your Hit Parade," the 15 most popular songs in America this week played by Al Goodman and the Lucky Strike Orchestra. Each week Lucky Strike checks the sheet music and phonograph records you buy, the tunes you request, the principal orchestra leaders and the melodies that are your favorites over the air. These factors show what songs you like best each week and how they rank in your favor. Then we bring you the Top 15 as "Your Hit Parade." It's fascinating to watch this ever-changing list of popular melodies.

In an effort to promote the show and lure listeners, the announcer invited listeners to predict the top three songs for the following week by writing their titles on a postcard and mailing the card to the offices of the American Tobacco Company, 111 Fifth Avenue, New York, before the following Sunday night by midnight (only one entry per person was allowed and those who submitted more than one entry would be disqualified). Winners were to receive a free regular carton of 200 Luck Stripe cigarettes. It didn't cost anything to enter and nothing had to be bought. Emphasizing throughout the program that the popularity of songs was measured "coast to coast," the first song played on this particular show was "Goody Goody" (a later hit for the doo wop group Frankie Lymon and the Teenagers) and the top song of that particular week was ("with the contradictory title," the announcer noted) "Lost."

Another popular radio program featuring music was Chesterfield Supper Club, which ran in the 1940s and was hosted by singer Perry Como (singers Jo Stafford and Peggy Lee later came on board). This program featured popular songs and might have a guest play an instrumental performance of a classical piece, as actress Diana Lynn played on piano Grieg's *Piano Concerto in A Minor*. The announcer opened the show by saying "Welcome to the Supper Club. Your table is ready," then informed the audience who was the entertainment that night.

"Kay Kyser's Kollege of Musical Knowledge," which first went on the air in 1938 and was broadcast for eleven years, quizzed contestants on their ability to name song titles based on an orchestra playing snippets of popular songs. Host Kay Kyser would intersperse the show with joking between him and his staff, who addressed him as "Professor," and introduce contestants by telling where they were from. The radio show was performed before a studio audience. Contestants competed against one another with the winner decided by the show's judges.

In "Beat the Band," a radio show from the 1940s that was described on the air as "a musical game," listeners were invited to "beat the band if you can" by sending in questions; the show's sponsor, General Mills, paid $10 for every question used and $20 for questions that "beat the band." The show featured singers and Ted Weems's orchestra and was hosted for much of its time on the air by humorist Garry Moore. An example of the show's style may be given with this snippet from a show hosted by Garry Moore. A question was submitted that read "Casper Milquetoast went to call on his best girl and found her in the arms of a man who looked like a cross between King Kong and Goliath. The title of a tune popular about thirty-five years ago tells you what he did." A band member answered, "Goodnight Sweetheart," but that was wrong. The correct song title was "He Walked Right in, Turned around, and He Walked Right out Again," from 1906, which Moore said "sold a million copies." Moore chided the band member for not being able to answer the question, and the band member said he wasn't around thirty-five years ago, so how was he supposed to know the answer to the question, to which Moore responded, "You heard about Columbus discovering America, didn't you? And you weren't here either." The band member who missed was told to throw fifty cents into the bass drum. After he got the next question wrong, Moore told him to move his chair closer to the bass drum. Then the band played a new popular song.

While radio promoted the sale of records and sheet music, which of course was to the financial benefit of labels and artists, and music publishers and songwriters, it was also recognized that stations were profitable business enterprises making money off the playing of music, and that with stations broadcasting music, they were using the performance right of song owners for profit. This was appreciated by music publishers and songwriters from the beginning of radio, who saw the new communications medium as a great potential new source of income, especially since the staple of songwriter and music publisher income—sheet music sales—would likely be diminishing with this new source of free entertainment (this proved to be true) and also with the concern that record sales might decrease since radio was a free source of entertainment (this did not prove to be true, just as it was inaccurately later conjectured that the free medium of television would have a devastating effect on the motion picture industry).

The issue of licensing public performances of music for profit had been settled after a hard battle (*Herbert v. Shanley Co.*) that went all the way up to the Supreme Court, so it was thought that the request for radio stations to license and pay for the broadcast of music would be uncontested and accepted. But it turned out that radio stations did not want to pay for performance licenses for broadcasting music, offering various rationales: songs were not being publicly performed but were rather spun only before the announcer (they weren't called deejays then) and engineer, and even if they were transmitted by wire, that would not constitute a public performance, as music carried on wire is not a public performance. It was a contentious issue, but the right of music copyright owners to license their works for broadcast over radio stations was affirmed in the case of *Witmark & Sons v. Bamberger & Co.* in 1925. This was another important victory for songwriters and music publishers, who were now assured that they would be paid when their songs were played on the air.

When radio first started, ASCAP was sympathetic to it being a new entertainment medium that needed to build itself into a profitable enterprise. It waived or reduced its licensing fees so stations could use its income to become economically viable. But after some time passed and radio got on its legs, it came time for the songwriter and music publisher licensing society of performing rights to charge radio stations for their use of music. At first, ASCAP requested a percentage of broadcaster revenues. Deeming the requested license fees unfair, radio was loathe to pay the fees requested by ASCAP—which allegedly had a monopoly on licensing popular songs—but the parties eventually settled for the performing rights society to get a license fee and a share of revenues. With what was to come, it may be said that the battle was over but not the war.

By the late 1930s approximately eight hundred radio stations were licensed to broadcast music, and the majority of records purchased by American consumers was released by three record companies. The broadcasters paid annual license fees to ASCAP that amounted to about $6 million, but this revenue was distributed to just over one thousand songwriters and less than 150 music publishers. There were four radio networks at the time and ASCAP distributed its radio license fee revenues on the basis of live performances on the radio networks during evening hours only. Songwriters and music publishers did not receive any performance income when recordings of their musical compositions were broadcast or when their songs were performed live on independent radio stations. There were thousands of songwriters and music publishers who were unable to share in the performing rights licensing revenue collected by ASCAP.

It was felt by some that an alternative source of licensing was needed, and that happened in September 1939 when a group of broadcasting executives met during the annual convention of the National Association of Broadcasters and established Broadcast Music Inc. (BMI). BMI considered itself an alternative to ASCAP—writers of any genre were welcome and no one needed any kind of track record to qualify for affiliation. The broadcasters pledged half the license fees they paid to ASCAP in 1937 to fund this new venture. On October 15, 1940, it was reported at a stockholders' meeting that BMI had built a repertoire of over 25,000 music copyrights, which would become a main source of programming for broadcasters for almost a year.

In March 1940 ASCAP decided to change its licensing structure by reducing the fees paid by individual radio broadcasters and charging the broadcasting networks, which previously were exempt from paying license fees, a hefty percentage of their revenues. The PRO defended its position by asserting that thanks to ASCAP-licensed compositions—it licensed the works of the most popular tunesmiths of the day such as Irving Berlin, George Gershwin, Victor Herbert, Jerome Kern, Cole Porter, John Philip Sousa, and Richard Rodgers—the broadcasters' income had grown and that the weight of the license escalation fell on the networks since they were most able to afford it. When ASCAP's agreement with broadcasters expired at the end of the year, most broadcasters did not enter into a new licensing agreement with the PRO. This meant radio stations couldn't air the songs of the big Tin Pan Alley tunesmiths that were popular with the public. Instead they played BMI-licensed works and public domain tunes such as those by the nineteenth-century writer Stephen Foster. An agreement was finally reached in May 1941, however, and the tunes of America's first PRO once again found their way into the nation's homes on their radios. But BMI took a strong interest in attracting the writers and publishers of songs that had been largely ignored by ASCAP, such as country and western music.

Over the years the federal government has enacted various statutes to regulate interstate business practices. In 1890 it enacted the Sherman Antitrust Act to stop prices from being raised artificially and to keep the marketplace competitive. With ASCAP having been the performing rights licensor of the overwhelming majority of popular music, it risked a federal antitrust action. Indeed, with the possibility that an inquiry into the criminal accusations lodged against it regarding competitive matters could end badly, the performing rights organization agreed to a consent decree with the federal government. The 1941 Consent Decree, which was subsequently updated, would have heavy repercussions for the licensing of music not only in the immediately ensuing decades but also all the way to the digital age, and restricted how ASCAP could conduct its business.

Liquor may have been driven underground with Prohibition and some popular music with it, but not all music was relegated to the subterranean world of moonshine joints. The 1920s was also notable for events in the concert and music theater worlds. A young composer named George Gershwin was asked by the bandleader Paul Whiteman near the end of 1923 to write a symphonic jazz composition that Whiteman's orchestra could play in a serious music setting; jazz was a relatively new musical genre and its reputation was not entirely savory and Whiteman wanted to show it as a dignified form of music. Gershwin was a rising star in the music world with a busy composing schedule— he wrote stylish popular tunes that were performed by well-known vocalists and a few years earlier wrote a national pop song hit called "Swanee" with lyricist Irving Caesar—but he consented.

With the idea for a rhapsody coming to him on a train trip to Boston, Gershwin got around to writing his composition for the upcoming concert in early January 1924. A few weeks later he completed a piece for two pianos, which was given to the Whiteman orchestra's pianist and arranger Ferde Grofé to orchestrate, and the composition was called *Rhapsody in Blue*.

Whiteman's concert was held at Aeolian Hall in New York City on February 12, 1924. With the premier of Gershwin's jazz-symphonic composition, it became a celebrated event, one of the notable concerts of twentieth-century history. There were a variety of selections per-

formed at the concert—including jazz pieces and jazz-pop songs such as
"The Livery Stable Blues," "Limehouse Blues," "Ice Cream and Art,"
"Alexander's Ragtime Band," "A Pretty Girl Is Like a Melody," and "To
a Wild Rose"—but it was *Rhapsody in Blue,* which Gershwin himself
played on the piano with the orchestra accompanying him, that stood
out from the other selections and that launched the concert to fame.
Gershwin's remarkable piece, which begins with a trilling and embou-
chure-bending clarinet glissando that breaks into a thoroughly exciting
and dramatic composition with a magnificent piano part, showed jazz
could be a genre for people of all music tastes. Indeed, it was, in a larger
spectrum, jazz, framed in a grand, illuminated, vibrant symphonic picture, meant to exalt the popular, relatively new musical genre for the
general public. The premier of *Rhapsody* also cemented the composer's
reputation at the pinnacle of popular music and jazz.

Near the end of 1927, Jerome Kern and Oscar Hammerstein II's
Showboat premiered on Broadway and the introduction of this musical
play was considered a watershed event in musical theater. The New
York theater world had musical comedies and plays into which songs
were interpolated but didn't necessarily advance the plot of their shows.
Sometimes songs were written or inserted as vehicles for particular
headliners who could bring in audiences. But shows were lacking with
genuine credible stories and characters who audiences could take seri-
ously and relate to in emotional ways. Kern wanted to adapt Edna
Ferber's novel called *Show Boat* for the musical stage and present a
musical show in ways it hadn't been done before. He recruited lyricist
Oscar Hammerstein II to write the books and lyrics for the musical,
which incorporated themes such as racial tension and heartbreak, and
which became a theater-world sensation. In 1927 several songs from
the show became popular song hits, including "Bill," "Can't Help Lovin'
Dat Man," "Make Believe," "Ol' Man River," and "Why Do I Love
You." The impact of this show was profound. It would lead to other
serious musicals like Rodgers and Hammerstein's *Oklahoma, Carousel,
The King and I*, and *The Sound of Music*; spur hit records and endless
covers; generate numerous standards in the popular music songbook;
and spark labels to release cast albums of musical shows, which ever
since have been a perennial audience favorite, not to mention an important source of income for labels, music publishers, composers and lyricists, singers, musicians, and retailers. Indeed, songs from Broadway

shows, whether through recordings, live performances, broadcasts, streams, or other areas, could generate significant revenue for the music business.

By the late 1920s the music business had undergone some profound changes. Tin Pan Alley, the locus of the popular song business in America and the lodestar for popular music centers in other places, was gone, at least in a geographical sense. Its publishing houses had once occupied a turf along 28th Street, but as the theater district moved some blocks north into the 1940s, so had the publishers abandoned their buildings, with many making the short migration north along with the theaters, or finding other streets and buildings into which they could build their publishing nests. The whole business of introducing and popularizing songs in vaudeville and burlesque halls and restaurants and saloons had ceased or was in its last days as these venues and the forms of entertainment they offered were dying as popular songs now found their popularity swelling in other venues: musical theater, radio, and the new entertainment medium of talkies, or sound motion pictures.

Great, catchy songs could propel a Broadway musical to box-office success, and songs in shows didn't necessarily have to advance the plot prior to *Showboat*. By getting airplay on network radio by the mid-1920s, more people could be exposed to songs in a shorter time than by any previous method. But radio, with its fast turnover of records, meant that the life of a song was shorter. Previously, it could take a song perhaps a year to make its way across the country as traveling singers and song pluggers performed it in venues in various cities, and sheet music could sell briskly in that time period. Now, with airplay, audiences from coast to coast could hear a new song at virtually the same time. Network broadcasts of a new song could immediately catapult it to hit status.

The introduction of sound into motion pictures gave new opportunities to music publishers to exploit their copyrights; while print had long been the medium for owners and creators of songs to make money, now technology offered new ways to get music out to the public and publishers and writers saw how a single song could have multiple sources of income. Following sheet music, which for many years was the main source of income for writers and publishers of songs (albeit sheet music sales lessened as playing piano in the home became less popular), there were records (from which they could earn mechanical royalties and which promoted the sale of sheet music), then radio airplay (from which they earned performance royalties and which also promoted the sale of records and sheet music), and now here were motion pictures (from which they could earn synchronization fees and which promoted the sale of sheet music and records). The first major sound motion picture, *The Jazz Singer*, featured not just dialogue but songs, including the future Tin Pan Alley standards "Toot, Toot, Tootsie! (Goo' Bye)," "Waiting for the Robert E. Lee," "Blue Skies," and "My Mammy"—and showed that film was a new entertainment medium in which songs could be introduced to the public. The debut of sound motion pictures in 1927—the year in which Charles Lindbergh made his historic solo flight across the Atlantic Ocean, from Garden City, New York, to Paris—marked the beginning of the end of silent movies.

With sound motion pictures, songwriters and music publishers had a new way to bring tunes to the attention of the public and derive revenue. Some successful Tin Pan Alley writers went west to California to work for the major studios that released most of the films. The Academy Awards, which recognized outstanding achievements in film, were first presented in 1929 to honor movies from the previous two years. The first "Best Song" award went to composer Con Conrad and lyricist Herb Magdison for their song "The Continental" from the 1934 RKO Radio song-and-dance musical *The Gay Divorcee* starring Fred Astaire and Ginger Rogers. Many Tin Pan Alley writers won Academy Awards, such as Harry Warren and Al Dubin for "Lullaby of Broadway" from the 1935 Warner Bros. movie *Gold Diggers of 1935*, Jerome Kern and Dorothy Fields for "The Way You Look Tonight" from the RKO film *Swing Time*, and Jerome Kern and Oscar Hammerstein II for "The Last Time I Saw Paris" from the 1941 Metro-Goldwyn-Mayer movie *Lady Be Good*. Motion pictures helped many popular songs become iconic, perennial standards known around the world such as the "Best Song" Academy Award–winners "Over the Rainbow" from *The Wizard of Oz*, "When You Wish Upon a Star" from *Pinocchio*, and "White Christmas" from *Holiday Inn*.

With film studios like Paramount seeing how popular songs in movies could bring people to theaters, they put songs in movies and started purchasing music publishing companies to acquire the copyrights to songs for which they couldn't get the synchronization rights. To help movie producers locate the owners of musical compositions for licensing or purchase, the trade organization Music Publishers' Protective Association (MPPA; whose name changed to the National Music Publishers Association in 1966) assisted them. The MPPA was established in 1917 by twenty-four music publishers to protect rights of music publishers with regard to royalties. When sound was beginning to be incorporated into motion pictures, the MPPA started to license synchronization rights for music publishers, whether they were members of the association or not.

In 1936, under the direction of its chairman, John G. Paine, the organization's licensing services were extended to include electrical transcriptions, which were an important programming tool in radio's early days and through the 1940s. Electrical transcriptions are acetate, or disc recordings, of radio shows cut as the shows were being performed. In radio's early years, most programming was live and stations employed actual instrumentalists and vocalists to perform live on the air. But with the different time zones in the United States, a program broadcast live nationally had the problem of being heard at different times in the various zones. The stations addressed this problem by broadcasting in their East Coast studios live programs and at the same time recording them on discs, usually 16-inch acetates playable at 33 1/3 rpm (as opposed to the 78 rpm records offered for public sale then). These electrical transcriptions could then be shipped to stations in other time zones for broadcast when they wished, or the programs could be sent over a telephone line to stations, which would record them as they were being played. Another option for remote stations was to have the studio that had the original transcription of the show play it at the time the remote station wished to broadcast it, a process called "time shifting" that allowed shows to air in the central United States or on the West Coast on the same day as it originally aired. Electrical transcriptions typically contained thirty-minute programs with fifteen minutes on each side, and were cut with a 3/1000-inch-wide microgroove. Electrical transcriptions were the chief means to store and rebroadcast radio programs (and also to store programs for archival purposes), but were phased out when magnetic recording became available.

Of concern to music publishers and songwriters with sound motion pictures was not only income from the synchronization of musical works to film but also performance royalties. The licensing of performing rights for movies goes all the way back to the silent era of films. At that time, when silent movies were shown in theaters, there might be a piano player or small ensemble or orchestra playing as the movie was exhibited. ASCAP, which had formed in 1914, attempted to license the theaters where silent movies were exhibited, but the theater operators refused to pay the license fees. ASCAP filed a number of suits and in 1923 the silent movie theaters took out a blanket license for the performance of musical works played in the theaters while the silent movies ran. The fee paid by a theater operator to ASCAP annually was based on how many seats there were in the theater.

When sound was introduced to movies, it was at first played by phonograph recordings that played in conjunction with the speech and action on the screen, and then later onto the soundtrack of the film. The right to synchronize music to film is held by the copyright owner, or music publisher. The main writers and publishers at the time were members of ASCAP. When film producers requested a license to synchronize their music to their films, the publishers would license the synchronization right but withhold the performance right, which they licensed separately to theater operators. Since many film producers had purchased music publishing companies, they would share in the performance license fees allocated to the music publishers.

The theater operators objected to having to pay for the performance of music in the movies they exhibited. Two claims were filed at the U.S. District Court for the Southern District of New York in 1942 but no litigation action was taken on them through 1946. The case, *Alden-Rochelle, Inc., et al. v. American Society of Composers, Authors and Publishers, et al.* was tried in March 1948. Court cases had held that copyright owners joining their copyrights and acting in conjunction was a violation of anti-trust laws, even if owning a copyright confers a monopoly in that work for the owner of copyright. The practice of ASCAP publishers granting to motion picture producers the right to reproduce songs in films but reserving the performing right to those songs, which in turn they licensed to theater operators, limited exhibition of the film to only those theaters that had an ASCAP license. This arrangement was mirrored in the agreement between movie producers and theater operators, which provided that in order to exhibit the producers' films, the theaters had to have an ASCAP performance license. The producers' film monopoly and ASCAP's music monopoly were deemed to restrain trade and be a violation of anti-trust laws. As a result, the practice became that producers license from music publishers the synchronization and performance rights to musical compositions, and theaters do not need a performance license for the exhibition of films with music (although they do need a license for the performance of copyrighted music before or after the films they exhibit).

Legal issues notwithstanding, the big screen has always been one of the best promoters of the popular song.

The 1920s brought with it many hit records, and despite the lack of music promotion from Prohibition's closing of bars, radio, along with music publishers and record labels, thrived—at least up until the end of the decade when the stock market crashed. In 1927 the annual music business revenues reached a tidy $27 million. In 1933, four years after the stock market crashed, music business revenues plummeted to $5.5 million. While the country was still embedded in the Great Depression, the Twenty-first Amendment was passed, repealing Prohibition. This brought to an end the banning of alcohol in public venues and sparked the opening of bars and saloons across the nation.

The end of World War I brought on a recession that affected the music business. As if this economic decline didn't have a negative enough impact on the record business, radio emerged in the early 1920s, and it was a free entertainment medium that now competed with records, which were a commercial product offered for sale. But the record industry was salvaged by various factors such as the rise of jazz and its star musicians such as Jelly Roll Morton, Sidney Bechet, and King Oliver; the popular songs of the Roaring Twenties; the popularity of singing stars such as Al Jolson, Bessie Smith, and Fanny Brice; and the introduction of electrical circuitry in the recording process, which considerably improved sound reproduction and essentially marked the end of acoustic recording. In 1927 the Automatic Music Company of Grand Rapids, Michigan, began manufacturing coin-operated record players that could play several records, which came to be called jukeboxes. With such factors as these making the record industry look promising, a young business giant, Radio Corporation of America, took control of Victor in 1929.

But the industry tumbled when the stock market crashed on October 29, 1929, which, along with other causes, resulted in the Great Depression. It was a devastating economic turndown that changed daily life for most Americans—a quarter of the American workforce was out of jobs, many people became homeless, soup kitchens opened to feed the poor, and suicide rates spiked. Tin Pan Alley tunesmiths, who never missed a beat in reflecting in song the spirit of society, were sure to capture the gloom and melancholy of the Great Depression. Among those who chronicled the difficulties of the Depression era in song were Richard Rodgers and Lorenz Hart in 1931 with "Ten Cents a Dance," a song about a female "taxi dancer" in a music hall who laments having to dance for a dime with unsavory men and endure blasting music that hurts her ears; Jay Gorney and E. Y. Harburg with their 1932 "Brother, Can You Spare a Dime?" about a man who had once built a railroad and a tower and was building a dream but now had lost his job and was pleading for small change; and Al Dubin and Harry Warren in 1933 with "Boulevard of Broken Dreams" about a stroll along "the street of sorrow" where soulless people whose schemes have been shattered wake up "with tears that tell of broken dreams." But the tunesmiths of Tin Pan Alley, perennial optimists at heart with their signatory upbeat fare, for the most part rather cared to consecrate in song during these somber years positive themes such as falling in love and happiness. Indeed, the Depression years were filled with hopeful, buoyant songs such as the following (all of which became standards): "Happy Days Are Here Again" and "Singin' in the Rain" in 1929, "On the Sunny Side of the Street" and "Get Happy" in 1930, and "I've Got the World On a String" in 1932.

Still, with America's economy in dire straits during the Depression years, people struggled every which way, including just to buy food. Buying records and sheet music was a luxury few could afford, and the 1929 stock market crash was the record industry's darkest hour. Could people afford to buy records again? With music available as free entertainment on radio, *would* people want to buy records again? The record industry's annual gross of $75 million in 1929 fell to $46 million in 1930 and to $18 million in 1931. In an attempt to combat the decline, RCA introduced a long-playing record in 1931. It was a 12-inch disc that played for about eight minutes on each side at 33 1/3 revolutions per minute rather than the standard 78 rpm. It failed, for few turntables in circulation could operate at 33 1/3 rpms and the records wore out after a few playings.

With the growing popularity of motion pictures, coupled with radio, the future for records seemed bleak. Top officers at radio-oriented RCA believed that radio's live entertainment could not be challenged by "canned" records. In 1933, when total retail record sales dipped to $5.5 million, many believed records were near their end as home entertainment.

But just when the bottom seemed to be reached, help was on its way, in no small way aided by the jukebox. In 1933 the repeal of Prohibition caused thousands of nightclubs and bars to open across the country, almost all equipped with coin-operated record players. By 1934, 25,000 jukeboxes were operating in the United States. Five years later, 250,000 machines accounted for sales of 19,000,000 records. Many performers developed cult followings via these small-change music players: Louis Armstrong, the Dorsey Brothers, Bing Crosby, the Mills Brothers, and Guy Lombardo. Thousands of dance bands across America were playing popular tunes in dance halls and other venues. Among the well-known musicians who led big bands in the Swing Era were Benny Goodman, Duke Ellington, the Dorsey Brothers (Jimmy and Tommy), Artie Shaw, Isham Jones, Glenn Miller, Fred Waring, Ted Weems, Harry James, and Count Basie; many singers who performed with the big bands went on to great fame, including Frank Sinatra, Perry Como, Mildred Bailey, Helen Forrest, and Peggy Lee.

Industry record sales rose to $26 million by 1938, and RCA sold a small record player (designed to be jacked into radio sets) for $19.50— almost a giveaway. The industry was once again thriving, and the Columbia Broadcasting System purchased the Columbia Phonograph Co. In 1942 two songwriters, Buddy DeSylva and Johnny Mercer, in collaboration with a record store owner, Glenn E. Wallichs, formed a new label, Capitol Records.

What not long before seemed like a doomed future for the record industry was now blooming again. Out of the depths of the Great Depression, the music industry was on its way to prosperity, thanks to booze, which was now legal and plentiful and bringing people into bars and saloons where jukeboxes blared records of popular recording artists, and thanks to the airwaves, which brought popular music to the masses all across America, and thanks also to the silver screen, which brought movies to the public, who could escape from their ordinary lives and be thrust into musicals, romances, adventures, dramas, animated features, westerns, fantasies, and other genres of cinema in which popular songs enhanced their enjoyment of these larger-than-life stories and which made their way into radio and clubs and elsewhere. Booze, radio, and movies saved the music business but helped sink Tin Pan Alley as people flocked to bars and found other sources of entertainment. Gone now were the days of vaudeville theaters and music halls, of song pluggers and water boys and singing waiters, and of the home piano parlor. Those all had reached their peak around the turn of the century. Sheet music sales were dwindling now—the industry was changing to one in which its most important product was not sheet music but records. Some of the big music publishers were being gobbled up by the big motion picture studios—the Warner Bros. music companies by the mid-1930s owned such a sizable share of American popular songs that it offered separate performance licenses to music users. The world was changing, to be sure, and the music business was too, and as it happened Tin Pan Alley, whose end was near, would pass to the record industry the baton of bringing music to the public.

4

THE ROAD TO ROCK AND ROLL

Confetti rained down on the seas of revelers swarming the streets below. Women gaily kissed strange sailors who happened to be lingering nearby. Flags were zealously waved by exhilarated participants under bright blue skies. Church bells pealed, horns were honked as cheers of victory, and cars were hoisted up into the air by jubilant sailors. People danced, sang, screamed with joy in round-the-clock nonstop celebrations. In cities around the world crowds in the thousands and millions filled public squares in a state of euphoria. The war was over!

The war years, 1939 through 1945, were a turbulent time for the nations of the earth. A torrent of cataclysmic fighting wreaked havoc on humanity on a scale unlike ever seen before. By World War II's devastating end, some sixty to eighty million people had perished. Never before in human history had people annihilated each other with such ferocity as they had during the terrible years of the war's duration. Carpet bombings of cities, atomic bombs, concentration camps, and mobile warfare with armored tanks were just some of the means by which human life was laid to waste.

After World War II ended on September 2, 1945, people were looking for diversion, escape, and amusement, and they found these gratifications in movies, the new medium of television, and, as always, music. But there was a major change in the music that made its way to people as vintage popular songs, jazz, and swing music by this time were regarded as old and worn, and people were ready for something different.

And that undeveloped form was slowly materializing in the margins of the music business. Brewing in the mists of the music-making scene was a confection of sounds that heralded the arrival of a new musical genre.

African American bands were common from the time of New Orleans ragtime in the Gay 1890s through the swing era of the 1930s and 1940s. The instrumentation in these bands grew over time: ragtime bands typically consisted of a cornet, trombone, clarinet, guitar, and bass; Dixieland bands in the early 1900s were characterized by a piano, trumpet, guitar, banjo, clarinet, trombone, and drums; the so-called red-hot bands also of the early 1900s were usually composed of a piano, cornet, trombone, clarinet, double bass, and drums; and Duke Ellington's premier band of the swing era featured an instrumentation of piano, clarinets, trumpets, trombones, saxophones, bass, and guitar. The music played by these African American bands could be sizzling hot and wildly energetic, sounding like a sweeping musical force with different instruments soaring in different directions yet all playing together as a synchronized whole.

While some of these bands continued on in the post–World War II years, a new generation of African American musicians ushered in a new kind of music—rhythm and blues. Early R&B was characterized by a rhythm section keeping a steady beat driven by a thumping bass with soulful vocals, and a jamming piano and a riffing raspy sax coming in for their solos. Musicians in these combos also played electric guitar (which jazz musicians began using in the 1930s and blues musicians in the early 1940s) and electric organ. "Rocket 88," an R&B single recorded in March 1951 by Jackie Brenston and His Delta Cats with a foot-tapping boogie woogie beat and upper-register piano riffs and howling sax solos, is considered by some to be the first rock and roll record, although some critics dispute that. Other records have also been considered the first rock and roll recording, such as the African American doo-wop group the Crows' "Gee," a 1953 release that hit the R&B and pop charts in 1954, or Goree Carter and His Hepcats' April 1949 recording of "Rock Awhile," or Jerry Leiber and Mike Stoller's "Kansas City," written in 1952 and recorded by Little Willie Littlefield, or Lloyd Price's "Lawdy Miss Clawdy," which was an R&B hit for him in 1952. Chuck Berry, Etta James, Little Richard, and Wild Bill Moore were some of the other early R&B pioneers whose music could be considered rock and roll. R&B music, which for the most part was targeted to black audiences, was commonly marketed by independent labels such as Atlantic, Chess, Apollo, Savoy, King, Specialty, and Imperial, although large labels such as Decca and RCA Victor also released records of R&B artists.

As R&B was emerging as a commercial force with black audiences, at its dawn the mainstream record charts were filled with mostly white crooners and orchestras such as Bing Crosby, Dinah Shore, Frank Sinatra, Frankie Lane, Vaughn Monroe and His Orchestra, and Peggy Lee. But the mainstream charts weren't devoid of African American artists. The Ink Spots, Nat King Cole, and Count Basie and His Orchestra, among others, all had hit records, although those records were more mainstream-sounding rather than the new sound coming out of R&B.

Writers who were members of ASCAP, home of the old guard of standard-making Tin Pan Alley tunesmiths such as Herbert, Gershwin, Kern, and Berlin, continued to churn out infectious chart-making Tin Pan Alley fare (including songs from Hollywood and Broadway) from 1946 through 1949, so the music brought to the public during these years wasn't all that different than from preceding years. Some of the most popular songs of that time include "All I Want for Christmas (Is My Two Front Teeth)," "La Vie en Rose," "Zip-a-Dee Doo-Dah," "Once in Love with Amy," "Mona Lisa," "Some Enchanted Evening," and "Rudolph, the Red-Nosed Reindeer."

During the late 1940s post-war years, BMI writers, some of whom had been shut out at ASCAP, were penning country and western songs that were becoming more mainstream, more pop-sounding. *Country and western* was now the term for the genre of the erstwhile-disparaged "hillbilly" category and its direction now presaged a turn from its pure roots to one of mainstream assimilation. Hank Williams's 1951 "Hey Good Lookin'" was a cross between country and rockabilly. With songs like "There's a New Moon over My Shoulder" and "You Two-Timed Me One Time Too Often," Tex Ritter leaped off the country charts and crossed over onto the mainstream charts. The country and western genre was also boosted by Chet Atkins, Homer and Jethro, and Hank Snow and with producers such as Owen Bradley and Bob Ferguson, who were making records that changed the old country sound. Western swing, an upbeat, danceable form of country and western music that was about twenty years old at this time, and which had its roots in other

genres such as cowboy and Dixieland, and whose stars included Bob
Wills and the Texas Playboys and the Light Crust Doughboys, was also
a forebear of rockabilly and country rock.

Country and western, jazz, and vintage pop were all part of the mix
from which rock and roll emerged, but it was R&B that was the main
ingredient. There was a whole slew of songs going back to at least the
1920s that had the feel, the sense, and the sound of what would come to
be called rock and roll, and these rock precursors were written and
performed by mostly black artists, the majority of whom remain little
known in the annals of popular music history. The music ranged from
bluesy songs with complementary vocals and guitars strumming out
slow rhythms to up-tempo tunes with jamming pianos on which the
keys were rapidly tickled on the upper registers. As the songs pro-
gressed toward the late 1940s and into the early 1950s, they resembled
more and more closely the future music genre dubbed rock and roll.
Stretching back from the 1920s and earlier, a plethora of recordings
(markedly different from typical Tin Pan Alley fare) carried the DNA
for rock and roll, such as Tampa Red and Georgia Tom's "You Can't
Get That Stuff No More," Sister Rosetta Tharpe's "Up above My
Head," Arthur Crudup's "I'm Gonna Dig Myself a Hole," Muddy Wa-
ters's "Muddy Jumps One," The Treniers' "Rockin' Is Our Bizness,"
Ray Brown's "Boogie at Midnight," The Clovers' "Fool, Fool, Fool,"
Elmore James's "Dust My Broom," and Ruth Brown's "Mama, He
Treats Your Daughter Mean."

Culture constantly moves, and it's often navigated by young people
who invent new ways or manners of speech and comportment, fashion,
and thinking, and this culture often reflects or is reflected by the music
young people put out. And that youth music in which its bards express
their feelings about love and sex and anxiety and sundry other emotions
is not stagnant, as they find new ways to musically articulate the basic
themes of life, which is to say new ways to write songs; as a result, new
genres or subgenres or fusions or hybrids of pop music come about for
the next generation. Once the initial seeds germinate, if they catch on
and diffuse, they can create a nova of expressions in the form of popular
music.

By around the mid-point of the twentieth century, the young people
of the day yearned for a music of their own. The popular music of the
1920s, 1930s, and 1940s was jaded and square, and these youths wanted

a new kind of music they could relate to—not the jitterbug or swing or Lindy or Charleston. Not the stale or dated pop tunes of their parents' generation. And the new, exciting form of music they wanted was almost there. That almost-there genre was called rhythm and blues, and with its bluesy vocals, sexy raspy saxophone, and boogie piano, it drew them in—young whites and blacks alike. It made them want to move, to dance, to snap their fingers and move their legs. But it was music made by African Americans, and African American music at the time was officially for African Americans, and for adult white society—parents, deejays, record company operators—it wasn't white enough yet.

This yearning by young people was encapsulated in a front-page article in the April 24, 1954, issue of *Billboard* titled "Teenagers Demand Music with a Beat, Spur Rhythm and Blues." The article, by Bob Rolontz and Joel Friedman, states,

> Rhythm and blues, once limited in sales appeal to the relatively small Negro market, has blossomed into one of the fastest growing areas of the entire music business. Rhythm and blues record sales last year reached an all-time high of $15,000,000. . . . More than 700 disc jockeys across the country devoted their air time exclusively to rhythm and blues recordings. Many disc jockeys who once restricted their programming only to popular records are following the change in listener tastes by including rhythm and blues selections with their popular offerings. . . .
>
> Teenagers have spearheaded the current swing to R&B, and are largely responsible for keeping its sales mounting. The teenage tide has swept down the old barriers which kept this music restricted to a segment of the population.

White teens so much enjoyed R&B that white artists found they could sell lots of records by recording, or covering, R&B songs. Many R&B singles crossed over onto the national singles pop chart, but white artists and their labels found they could have greater success with cover versions of R&B tunes than the R&B artists had with their own songs. In turn, black artists felt they were being exploited by the white record industry and white artists, who could have greater success with their music than the black artists with having a built-in audience for them with white consumers by closely recording R&B tunes. In early 1955 R&B singer LaVern Baker's recording of "Tweedle Dee" was released and landed in the top five of the *Billboard* R&B chart and also in the top fifteen in the pop singles chart; in February 1955 white singer Georgia Gibbs's cover of the song on the Mercury label landed in the top ten of the national pop singles chart. Baker subsequently wrote to Charles Coles Diggs Jr., Michigan's first African American Congressman, requesting that the U.S. copyright law be revised to prohibit "note for note" copying of black artists' records by white artists. Although there are different stories of what came out of this, probably no copyright legislation resulted from it. But while it may have resulted in greater sensitivity to black artists' concerns about their music being exploited by whites, there were some African American artists who appreciated the economic returns they received for white artists covering their songs. Pat Boone covered Fats Domino's "Ain't That a Shame," and his record made the top position on the *Billboard* pop singles chart (Domino's version topped the magazine's R&B chart). At a concert some time later, Domino called Boone to the stage and showed off his ring resembling a piano and before launching into "Ain't That a Shame" announced "Pat Boone bought me this ring with this song."

Mirroring the racial divisions in the United States, popular music was also divisive. There was black music—the blues, ragtime, jazz, black swing, and R&B; and there was white music—Tin Pan Alley tunes, white jazz, white swing, country and western. Of course, there were overlaps in each area—white artists who did ragtime, black artists who did popular music, whites who performed the blues, blacks who played country—but each had its segregations, and their music was largely thought of as having separate constituencies of black or white audiences, respectively. And for each there was a long history of whites covering black tunes, and blacks covering white songs. As the mid-1950s approached, this was coming together, a merger of both music and audiences, but still there were walls between the two. It wouldn't be until legal and social factors impeded that the walls would be torn down, although not completely.

In that sense, rock and roll, as an official new pop music genre, was just waiting for the right song by arguably the right white artist to bring it to the mainstream, meaning white teenagers, as society at the time segregated white music from black music and would call whatever music black musicians came up with "rhythm and blues." It wouldn't exactly be R&B; it would, as it evolved, synthesize other genres and styles, too, such as blues, country, western swing, jazz, ragtime, honky-tonk, spirituals, folk, and traditional pop; the boogie piano of R&B would be mostly replaced by the twangy or wailing electric guitar, and it would have lyrics that addressed primal teenage anxieties, desires, likes, dislikes, and concerns. And importantly, it would be the performance style and arrangement of the song, transforming it into a white record. Everything was in place, but rock and roll needed a Big Bang to reach the masses.

The right song for the right white artist to give birth to rock and roll came along with "(We're Gonna) Rock around the Clock" with Bill Haley and His Comets as the artist, although Haley's group wasn't the first to record and release the song. But Haley's version radiated the necessary magic that brought the song to life, although its initial release as a B-side in 1954 was less than spectacular; it wasn't until fifteen months later when it was on the soundtrack of a new youth rebel movie, *The Blackboard Jungle*, that this high-energy, mega-wattage, feel-good, make-you-want-to-dance, catchy, white-sounding record with rhythmic lyrics sparked a rock and roll wildfire, and on July 9, 1955, "(We're Gonna) Rock around the Clock" on the Decca label soared to the number 1 spot on the *Billboard* Top 100 (in 1958 the magazine's singles chart was changed to the Hot 100), becoming the first rock and roll recording to reach the national mainstream singles chart summit.

With the planting of the rock and roll flag at the top of the pop mountain, the rock and roll universe formed into existence, but it needed a supernova superstar artist to bring it to the masses, to certify its existence, to make it a bona fide pop genre, and to make it the international, no-language-barrier anthem of a new generation of youths. That would come shortly with a twenty-one-year-old from Memphis, Tennessee, having the energy and charismatic wattage of an aurora borealis, or rather, as he would later be dubbed, "The King of Rock and Roll."

In expressing the yearnings and emotions of the new young generation, and with its blaring guitars, raspy sax solos, and stylized vocal deliveries, rock and roll was considered rebellious youth music, but it wasn't by any means the first rebellious youth music; rebellious youth music goes all the way back hundreds of years ago, in fact. During the colonial days of America, for instance, the New England clergyman Cotton Mather, in his diary entry of September 27, 1713, wrote about the humorous and sentimental tunes people would sing: "I am informed, that the Minds and Manners of many People about the Countrey are much corrupted by foolish Songs and Ballads, which the Hawkers and Pedlars carry into all part of the Countrey" (Mather, 1912). The cultural inclinations of the fifty-year-old Mather would indeed be mirrored by future generations of older people, who found popular songs dissolute and unsavory. Jazz, a hot, driving music that began spiraling into mass popularity beginning in the early 1900s, was considered rebellious to those with Victorian sensibilities at the time. Moreover, pre–rock and roll music of various genres wasn't all so prim and proper, as one might expect of the times. Even hillbilly music could be downright suggestive, as can be heard in such recordings as Betty Lou and the Hartman's Heartbreakers' 1930s' "Let Me Play with It," "Feels Good," and "Give It to Me, Daddy."

Exciting new musical genres aside, it just doesn't happen that new styles of art gain mass popularity without some form of circulation. Circulation can range from word of mouth to business practices to technology. In the case of rock and roll, it was the confluence of all three that lead to the spreading of its popularity.

Serendipitously, there were technological changes just around the time of the advent of rock and roll that expedited its circulation and commercial success. In 1948 Columbia came out with the 33 1/3 rpm vinyl disc that was lighter than the 78 rpm disc and could hold much more music. The next year, RCA came out with the seven-inch 45 rpm single. Both new formats, which made record playing and collecting easier, would catch on with consumers and aid in the sale of records. The 45 rpm single would be the conduit through which record labels would release their new best commercial pop songs (the occasional B-side hit notwithstanding) and would be the medium through which records were promoted to radio stations with a Top 40 format. The relatively new medium of television also helped, with shows that would feature teen-oriented music and dancing.

Changes that abetted the popularity of rock and roll also came in the way records were distributed. After World War II, a new wholesaler called the "one stop" started operating. At first, the one stop functioned as a specialized sub-distributor to service jukebox operators who normally stocked their jukeboxes with numerous records. Jukebox operators might have had dozens of coin-operated machines to stock with records, and to obtain these records from multiple labels was time-consuming, inconvenient, and costly. The one-stop served to be a convenient single source from which they could obtain product issued from any record label. Having one source, a single entity from which they could transact all their record purchases, was a welcome alternative for these operators, and the practice of using one stops spread to independent record stores so they too could have the convenience of making all their different label purchases from a single source. Having originally serviced jukebox operators, one stops started out primarily selling 45 rpm singles but later added on vinyl albums and tapes. It might cost a small retailer slightly more to buy from a one stop as opposed to a local label distributor, but one stops were also welcomed by small retailers who could not get credit from local distributors.

In the 1950s another type of wholesaler of phonograph records would become important in the distribution chain and in bringing product to consumers. This wholesaler was called the "rack jobber," and it served to operate the record departments in mass-merchandise and other non-music outlets such as department stores, variety stores, discount stores, supermarkets, and drugstores. Records could be a draw in non-music retail operations, but their operators were not professionally knowledgeable enough about the music industry to know what records to stock, where and how to get them, how to organize the display of product, how to handle returns and exchanges of unsold records, how to maintain an accounting system for stock, how to train the sales staff, and how to implement merchandising programs that could aid in the selling of this specialty item. Rack jobbers had the expertise to run these outlets' music departments profitably, and it was their investment that paid for the inventory of product in the music departments they ran. The rack jobber assumed the risks that actual retailers incurred, with the outlet paying rent, salaries, and certain other expenses, and the rack jobber remitting to the outlet or its proprietor a percentage of sales revenue. So successful was the rack jobber in the 1950s and the following few decades that they grew in number and accounted for a significant portion of the record industry's retail sales.

As part of their merchandising efforts, rack jobbers might print sheets or pamphlets of the latest hits or related songs for customers of the music departments of the stores they serviced. For example, for Korvettes, a department store chain that was in business from 1948 through 1980, Alpha Distributing Corp. would compile 45 rpm "Top Hits" lists that broke down into different categories. Its January 1976 "Top Hits" lists, for example, 45s—#1 through 50 with titles and artists of the current hit singles; then Up and Coming Hits #51 through 55; Heavy Disco Sounds #56 through 60; and Hits of the Past #61 through 75. The sheet instructed consumers to "request by number" the records they wanted. So if a consumer requested record numbers 1, 51, 56, and 61 (the first records listed in each of the aforementioned groups), for example, he or she would receive Barry Manilow's "I Write the Songs," Elton John's "Grow Some Funk of Your Own," Jeff Evans's "I'll Be Seeing You," and Tony Orlando and Dawn's "Tie a Yellow Ribbon Round the Old Oak Tree/My Sweet Gypsy Rose," respectively.

Another multi-location department store in New York at the time was A&S. For the week of September 9, 1972, a pamphlet printed by Double B Records & Tape Corp. lists the top fifty hits, with titles and artists' name followed by More Hits numbers 51 through 80. A customer who purchased the top five hits of that week would get Looking Glass's "Brandy," the Carpenters' "Goodbye to Love," Gilbert 'O'Sullivan's "Alone Again (Naturally)," Three Dog Night's "Black and White," and Argent's "Hold Your Head Up." Also in the pamphlet was a reproduction of *Billboard*'s Top LP's and Tapes.

Once consigned to specialty record stores, records were now available in general mass-merchandising outlets thanks to these new record wholesalers that came into existence after World War II. Jules Malamud, the executive director of the National Association of Record Merchandisers (later renamed the Music Business Association), said in a 1961 keynote speech at the organization's annual convention that with consumer interest in recorded music growing, their needs weren't being met by record stores, which conducted themselves like "exclusive specialty shops," and that these specialty stores "were caught napping by the aggressive record merchandisers" who are "a legitimate avenue of record distribution fulfilling a function which no other part of the record industry can handle, and without which a great amount of dollar volume in phonograph records would be lost" (*Billboard*, March 6, 1971, p. N–8). Three years later, George Marek, the vice president and general manager of RCA Victor Records, who was the keynote speaker at NARM's annual convention, said: "Several important trends emerge from the last decade. The first and obvious one is the evolution of record merchandising which has made records available in America's high traffic shopping outlets and has put music among the bananas and eggs and lipstick and shaving cream" (*Billboard*, March 23, 1968, Narm Special, Narm 5). Indeed, thanks in part to the specialty record wholesaler, records were becoming a popular household item. Over time, as stereo enhanced the listening experience and the growing popularity of pop music with consumers spurred their desire to purchase pop albums in great quantities, one stops not only found themselves moving beyond supplying singles to jukebox operators and selling albums to small retailers, but some combined with rack jobbers.

By the late 1950s the music business's dynamics had been altered profoundly. The advent of the 33 1/3 rpm album and the 45 rpm single, stereo fidelity, the new youthful genre of rock and roll, one stops, rack jobbers, and Top 40 radio all happened within about a decade starting in the late 1940s. Whereas music publishers had once been powerful by being the song supplier, record companies were now the new powerhouse, as consumers wanted to purchase records more than sheet music. The public was generally more interested in listening to the new music than playing it. And there was another change, one to the detriment of the songwriter who wasn't an artist. Rock and roll brought with it artists who wrote their own music, so there was less reliance on music publishers to supply outside songs for artists.

To produce a new kind of music is one thing, but to bring it to the masses, it needs promotion, and in the case of rock and roll, its first chief messenger to the teenagers of the day was an unlikely candidate for the position. The end of World War II brought a new generation of teenagers to the cultural scene. The jitterbugging youths of the 1930s swing era were now adults, many of them veterans of World War II, with families of their own. This new generation of teens came of age through the doom-and-gloom years of the Second World War, and many found relief in music. America still had its political and sociological problems with African Americans being discriminated against and northerners regarding southerners as bigots and hicks, but music with its universal appeal had a way of breaking down barriers, of becoming a common bond for young disparate folks. And so niche music genres coalesced with old-fashioned white music to become rock and roll, the anthem of the new youth, the voice of a new generation, destined to uproot the enduring music of the old fogies that had been carrying on too long and had had its day. Electric guitars and organs and wild-haired young singers singing not that square stuff but hip stuff, stuff you could do cool dances to, throbbing music to which you could bop your head, snap your fingers, or purr along to with its "oohs" and "aahs" and "babies," fun songs that perked you up and made you feel oh so cool—yeah, that was the music a new generation would rock to.

Cool came. And the message heralding its arrival came paradoxically not from a youthful peer but a thirty-year-old, tie-and-jacket clad, fast-talking former deejay of classical music who was unlike the square hosts of erstwhile radio fare such as *The Major Bowes Amateur Hour*, *Stop the Music*, *Rudy Vallee Show*, *Chesterfield Supper Club*, *Beat the Band*, or *Kollege of Musical Knowledge*. The courier's name was Alan Freed, but true to form, this emissary of the new youth music, this emcee of rock and roll (who claimed he coined the term), would adopt a hipster moniker with which he would be known on the air: Moondog.

5

SCREAMING FOR ELVIS AND THE BEATLES

The post-war years of the 1950s were a mixed bag of high-wire political tensions and a welcomed respite from the global calamity of the Second World War. The decade roiled with the Korean War, McCarthyism, and the Cold War, but there was also economic prosperity, growth of the suburbs, and expanding families whose children came to be known as baby boomers. By the end of the decade almost 90 percent of Americans had televisions (an astronomical increase over the number who had TVs in the mid-1940s when the medium of commercial television was just beginning), phonograph players were ubiquitous in American homes, and popular culture was alive with the hula hoop, Davy Crockett coonskin hats, Barbie dolls, poodle skirts, and the beatnik. The future baby boomers were engrossed in such kids' TV fare as *The Howdy Doody Show*; *Kukla, Fran and Ollie*; and *The Mickey Mouse Club* and family sitcoms such as *Leave It to Beaver*, *Father Knows Best*, and *The Donna Reed Show*. As American decades of the twentieth century went, it was relatively tranquil, but with a potpourri of cool but lesser-known genres of popular music sizzling under the mainstream radar, it was a ripe time for a new youthful style of pop music to explode onto the scene and enrapture teenagers around the world.

Over in Cleveland a disc jockey was shepherding in this new youth music. In 1951, Leo Mintz, the proprietor of Record Rendezvous at 300 Prospect Avenue, told this deejay, Alan Freed, that lots of teenagers, not just African Americans but white teens, too, were coming into his shop to buy 78 R&B discs, and asked if he could play this music on the air. After obtaining the consent of his station's executives, Freed agreed, and having adopted the on-air appellation Moondog, put on a show called "The Moondog Rock and Roll House Party." It caught on so well that on March 21, 1952, Freed sponsored the Moondog Coronation Ball at the Cleveland Arena at 3717 Euclid Avenue. The venue had a capacity of about ten thousand, and after it was filled, another ten thousand or so youths, many of whom had purchased tickets to the event, became unruly outside and forced themselves through the doors to let themselves in. As a result, the police shut down the coronation ball shortly before 11 PM. Freed was criticized by everybody from the media to civic leaders and went back on the air to apologize and tell what he called the truth of what happened. He also asked his listeners to call in their support of him to his station, WJW, and said if not enough support was given, he would go off the air. His listeners swamped the station with support and bonded his stay at WJW, but all the adverse attention helped give burgeoning rock and roll a reputation as rebellious youth music. (Rock and roll would earn an even more negative reputation in relation to Freed when at a concert he sponsored in May 1958 the police repeatedly stopped the show, as attendees were dancing in the aisles, and Freed announced, "It looks like the police in Boston don't want you kids to have fun," with the subsequent result being a melee breaking out that continued on the streets; there were reported stabbings and robberies, and Freed was accused of inciting a riot, but the charges were later dropped for a lack of evidence.) Freed's reputation grew as young people flocked to his program, and soon the nation's biggest radio market came calling. In 1954 Moondog found himself deejaying at station WINS in New York City.

By this time rock and roll was still in its embryonic stage, and it was African American music that was mostly attracting teens, including white teens. It was difficult for African American artists to break into the mainstream, although a few did, such as Nat King Cole ("Answer Me, My Love"), Sarah Vaughan ("Make Yourself Comfortable"), and Sammy Davis Jr. ("Hey There"), perhaps because their hits lacked the elements of energetic rhythms and soulful vocalizations that characterized rhythm and blues and were more or less pop tunes. For the most part, the record charts in 1954 and 1955 were dominated by white artists such as Eddie Fisher, Tony Bennett, the Four Aces, Jo Stafford, Frank Sinatra, the Ames Brothers, Kay Starr, Perry Como, Doris Day, the Crew-Cuts, the McGuire Sisters, the Chordettes, Andy Griffith, Teresa Brewer, Georgia Gibbs, Hugo Winterhalter, Tennessee Ernie Ford, and Les Baxter. The charts reporting the best-selling and most-played records on radio of the day were like a loaf of white bread sprinkled with a few poppy seeds.

At this time not only was the bestselling records chart predominantly white, but it was also old white; the upper echelons were filled with songs of Tin Pan Alley sensibility. But rock and roll and R&B records occasionally infiltrated the list. There was, for instance, "Shake, Rattle and Roll" and "Dim, Dim the Lights (I Want Some Atmosphere)" by Bill Haley and His Comets, both on the mainstream singles charts in December 1954; and "Earth Angel (You Will Be Mine)" by the Penguins in January 1955. But even Bill Haley and His Comets' "(We're Gonna) Rock around the Clock," which perched at the top of the singles chart, didn't bring on an onslaught of rock and roll records to the singles chart summit; it was bumped off about two months later on September 3 by Mitch Miller with his Orchestra and Chorus's march-like recording of "The Yellow Rose of Texas."

In these days the A&R (artists and repertoire) people at the labels wielded great power. They pretty much determined what songs their label's artists would record and set up the recording sessions, and perhaps selected the producer and arranger and musicians. They would meet with songwriters and music publishers to find songs for artists to record, as at the time many of the signed artists did not write. A songwriter's career could be made by having his or her song chosen for recording by an A&R man (as most of those in those days were male). To a good extent, their tastes shaped public taste. A&R directors (sometimes called "music directors") at the major labels had a very strong impact on the records that became hits at the time, although they famously passed on some artists who went on to become stars at other labels, such as Elvis Presley, who signed with RCA Victor. Some, such as Hugo Winterhalter (at MGM, Columbia, RCA Victor, and Kapp) and Mitch Miller (Mercury and Columbia), recorded and released records under their own name with their own ensemble (Hugo Winterhalter and His Orchestra, Mitch Miller and the Gang).

The top records on the charts were mostly issued by major labels (or their subsidiaries) or well-established independent labels. Among these were Columbia, RCA, Capitol, Decca, Coral (owned by Decca), Epic (owned by Columbia), MGM, Brunswick, Dot, Mercury, and Cadence. Their rosters were filled with mostly white artists, although some African American artists were signed to major labels such as Eartha Kitt on RCA and Nat "King" Cole on Capitol.

At the time some people derogatorily referred to African American records as "race records." Even after the U.S. Supreme Court decision on May 17, 1954, in *Brown v. Board of Education* in which racial segregation in public schools was declared unconstitutional, this disparaging label was still used, and some white radio deejays even refused to play black records. In mid-1950s America popular music was, to an extent, segregated.

Dancing around the fringes of the mainstream record market by the mid-1950s were small black labels or white-owned labels that put out R&B or country records such as Chess, Peacock, Holiday, End, Essex, Rama, Specialty, Jamie, and Arcade Records. Hard-working, aggressive, and passionate about the music they released, the owners of these small labels or their upper management would promote their releases in various special ways such as going out on their own and directly convincing DJs to play their records, or hand-selling their records to independent retailers. Out of these small independent labels came many hit artists and songs such as Willie Mae "Big Mama" Thornton's "Hound Dog" on Peacock; Bo Diddley's "I'm a Man" on Checker (a subsidiary of Chess); and Howlin' Wolf's "How Many More Years?" and Chuck Berry's "Maybellene" on Chess.

Another small label that was to spawn a legendary artist was Sun Records, owned by a former disc jockey with a penchant for rhythm and blues, Sam Phillips. Elvis Presley's discovery and rise to fame is a classical American success story. He was born on January 8, 1935, in a two-room hut in Tupelo, Mississippi; his twin brother, Jesse Garon Presley, was stillborn a half hour after him. At his family's church, Elvis was exposed to gospel music. His fifth-grade teacher at East Tupelo Consolidated School entered him in the Tupelo State Fair talent contest, and he came in fourth place. In 1948 his family moved to Memphis, where he attended Humes High School, and after graduation he worked for a tool company and then drove a truck. During a break from his truck-driving one summer day in 1953, Elvis went to a recording studio, the Memphis Recording Service, and paid $4 to record a couple of songs on an acetate disc as a gift for his mother, Gladys. He returned to the studio in January 1954 to record some more songs, and met its owner, Sam Phillips. Phillips, also the proprietor of Sun Records, was looking for a white male singer to record some songs in a soulful style and invited the nineteen-year-old to sing. At the session in early July 1954, Elvis recorded "That's All Right"; it became a regional hit, and the young singer started appearing on local television shows. Elvis worked hard to promote his records, performing at parks, schools, shopping malls, on the Shreveport-based country music radio show "Louisiana Hayride," and in touring country-and-western music shows, and had five regional hits in the south. With his youthful good looks and hip performance style, when Elvis sang there was hysteria in the crowds. Teenage girls screamed, cried, and clenched their fists with ardor for the new singing idol. A shake of his legs or a fancy dance movement by the rocker was enough to set the crowds off into frenzy. Fans reached out to touch him if they were near the stage, and cops had to hold them back. With Elvis's career taking off, Sam Phillips knew a major record label was needed to catapult him to national stardom, and in November 1955 RCA bought his contract from Sun Records for the then-high price of $35,000 plus an additional $5,000 for Elvis as a bonus.

Under the direction of his new label, Elvis, in January 1956, went into a Nashville recording studio to record some new songs. It was in this year that he became a national sensation with several records reaching number 1 on the Top 100: "Heartbreak Hotel," "I Want You, I Need You, I Love You," "Don't Be Cruel/Hound Dog" (spending eleven weeks at the top position), and "Love Me Tender." In January 1956 Presley signed an agreement with William Morris for the talent agency, perhaps the most powerful agency in show business, to represent him for performing engagements. That year, Presley made several national television appearances: the CBS-TV music variety program *Stage Show*, the shows of Jimmy and Tommy Dorsey, Milton Berle, and Steve Allen, and two of his three famous appearances on *The Ed Sullivan Show*, with the third appearance in January 1957. Presley was initially turned down by Sullivan, but then after his appearances on the other shows, Sullivan changed his mind and paid the young singer $50,000 for the three bookings (in his first appearance he was famously filmed from above the waist so his gyrating hips would not be seen).

By mid-1956 Elvis was being managed by Colonel Tom Parker. Parker was his third manager, after Scotty Moore, who played guitar in his Sun recording sessions, and Bob Neal, a Nashville promoter who Sam Phillips hired to publicize Elvis's concerts when he was under contract to Sun. Songwriter Mae Axton, who worked for Neal and co-wrote Elvis's first national hit, "Heartbreak Hotel," introduced Parker to Presley.

In the competitive world of popular music where achieving stardom often defies calculated planning, numerous factors can be attributed to what made Elvis Presley the original superstar of rock and roll. On the physical side he was young and tall (six feet) with an athletic physique; he had thick, shiny, coal-black hair and cool, seductive looks, indeed the rare bulls-eye right look of a true superstar. With his high cheekbones, pompadour, piercing black eyes, and hint of being a bad boy, he was handsome in a way unlike his counterpart pop superstars of the 1920s, 1930, and 1940s, Al Jolson, Bing Crosby, and Frank Sinatra, respectively. He exuded testosterone-sizzling off-the-meter sexiness and was highly photogenic. As far as talent, he had a captivating singing voice; he recorded great make-you-want-to-dance, -sing, or -cry rock and roll songs; he had the swagger of a rock star before there was even a rock star (you could say he invented, or at least cultivated, it); he had the dazzling dance moves of a rock star (derived doubtlessly from African American R&B artists); he had his own inimitable style of performing in the way he shook his legs, swiveled his pelvis, curled his upper lip, moved his neck and shoulders; he dressed in a way that appealed to young people; he came across in a charming, country-boy way. It all added up to magic, magnetism, and charisma, and he became the prototype of a rock and roll star. As early pictures of Elvis exemplified, he set in stone the image of the rock and roller as the long-haired youth with sideburns strumming the guitar and bopping enthusiastically to the beat.

Other factors that contributed to Presley's success include the arrangement and production of his recordings; the timings of his releases; the background musicians and singers on his recordings; the appealing Americana story of his impoverished family background and how a poor, country boy rose to fame; his (to some people, at least) whimsical, unusual, or country-sounding first name; his early touring and self-promotion; his signature style and looks that could easily be imitated; his timing to come on the pop music scene when rock and roll was just beginning and the public was yearning for an artist to become its break-out star and symbol. With his appeal, music, and charm, he filled an emotional need for fans of pop music. He had that special allure, that magic something that cannot be put in words, that inimitable awesome allure that makes a superstar.

But even the most talented and charismatic entertainers need assiduous marketing and promotion to make them stars, and Elvis received such support from his label, manager, concert promoters, and others involved in his career. As Presley's manager, Colonel Parker oversaw all aspects of his career, which, his infamous exorbitant (50 percent) commission aside, make a textbook case of how to promote and maximize revenue of a potential rock star. In that sense, it might be said that rock and roll (with Presley as its star pupil) wrote the rules of talent and record promotion all the way up to the Internet age.

It was obvious that Presley had star potential and Parker aimed to exploit his client in all areas of entertainment, including motion pictures. Presley's William Morris agent arranged a screen test with Paramount producer Hal Wallis (the producer of *Casablanca*, which won an Academy Award for Best Picture), who then signed him to make pictures. A couple weeks before Elvis's "Love Me Tender" became the number 1 recording on November 3, 1956, he began what would be a robust movie career by filming a Civil War drama with the same title that was released in mid-November 1956 and became a smash hit. The first of some thirty-one or so feature films he would star in, he would continue making movies until 1969, sometimes making two or three films a year. Although many of his films were critically panned, Elvis's star quality often shined in the characters he played on the big screen, adding a new dimension to how others viewed his talent—*Jailhouse Rock*, *Kid Galahad*, and *Viva Las Vegas* were some audience favorites—and his films were for the most part profit-makers and helped him pick up fans outside of his music base.

During the summer of 1956 Elvis and his manager entered into an agreement with H. G. Saperstein and Associates for the company to handle the singer's merchandising. Saperstein, in turn, would line up licensees to make products with Elvis's name, picture, or likeness, and as a result, "Elvis" products flourished and generated revenues in the millions of dollars. According to a September 29, 1956, article in *Billboard* by Joel Friedman:

> A merchandising campaign expected to eclipse sales of $20,000,000 worth of goods before the end of the year, and which it is hoped will pale by comparison such staunch competitors as Mickey Mouse, Hopalong Cassidy, and Davy Crockett, is currently gathering steam behind the music industry's most controversial and at present most successful figure, Elvis Presley. . . . 18 licensees are currently producing a variety of approximately 30 products, all in the Elvis Presley motif and all bearing his name or likeness. Presley's guitar has almost become somewhat of a trademark. Merchandise includes such items as hats, T-shirts, blue jeans, handkerchiefs, bobby-sox, canvas sneakers, shirts, blouses, belts, purses, billfolds, wallets, charm bracelets, necklaces, magazines, gloves, mittens, a statue, book-ends, a guitar, lipstick, cologne, stuffed "hound-dogs," stuffed dancing dolls, stationery, greeting cards, sweaters and most recently, a glow-in-the-dark picture of Elvis, whose image lasts for two hours after the lights have been turned off, is also available.

There were numerous other products in the Presley merchandising solar system. There were head scarfs with colored images of Elvis printed on them and titles of his records. There were flasher badges on which an image of Presley's face and the imprint "Sincerely Elvis Presley" changed back and forth to another image of him playing guitar and singing, all in color. There was the "Elvis Presley Autographed Special" portable phonograph player, which RCA heavily promoted. Louis J. Collins, RCA's Radio and Victrola division sales manager, said "Network radio and co-op space ads will carry the lion's share of the job, with dealers being supplied with newspaper mats and a special spot radio transcription, recorded by Elvis himself. Dealers will also get special selling cards, including streamers, counter cards, posters and handbills" (*Billboard*, November 3, 1956, p. 22). Some of the phonograph players came with sets of Elvis's records.

There were Elvis Presley trading cards, glossy photos, movie photos, souvenirs, fan clubs with regular newsletters (Presley's image was carefully projected through his numerous photos, and in modern-day parlance, it would be said that he branded himself with his photos). Radio stations did all sorts of promotion events. For instance, in the fall of

1956 the Chicago station WAIT sponsored an Elvis Presley letter-writing contest, and according to *Billboard* received "a total of 1,099,127 pieces of mail in two weeks" (*Billboard*, November 3, 1956, p. 20). The winners of the contest were given airplane tickets to fly to New York and meet the "king" himself.

In March 1958 Presley entered the U.S. army and the following September shipped out with his division to West Germany, where he arrived on October 1. He would be away for two years, but his personal manager, label, and publishing manager knew that even the world's most famous music entertainer would need to stay in the spotlight in order to sustain his career. Besides keeping the merchandising going, they planned for RCA to release new Elvis recordings. In February 1958 Presley's "Don't" reached the number 1 spot. RCA's marketing muscle kept on grinding with radio promotion, and several other of the singer's records made the top 20 of the *Billboard* national singles chart: "Wear My Ring around Your Neck," "Hard-Headed Woman," "I Got Stung," "One Night," "I Need Your Love Tonight," "Big Hunk of Love," and "My Wish Came True." He was away for two years, but even the most popular music entertainer in the world, which he was, could be forgotten by his fans by being out of the limelight. On March 3, 1960, after he was discharged, Presley's plane landed at McGuire Air Force Base in New Jersey, where a large group of screaming fans were waiting anxiously to greet him. The rock and roll idol was back home in America; with RCA continuing its promotional efforts, Presley's "Stuck on You" reached number 1 in April 1960, and his "It's Now or Never," a revamp of the Italian standard "O Sole Mio," in August 1960, also hit the national singles chart summit position (a trip to the top of the pop singles mountain that he frequently made, following "Heartbreak Hotel" in April 1956, "I Want You, I Need You, I Love You," "Don't Be Cruel/Hound Dog," "Love Me Tender," "Too Much," "All Shook Up," "(Let Me Be Your) Teddy Bear," "Jailhouse Rock/Treat Me Nice," "Don't/I Beg of You," "Hard Headed Woman," "A Big Hunk O' Love," and "Stuck on You" [Bronson, 1985]).

To bring Elvis back into the spotlight and remind the public he was back from West Germany, Presley appeared on *The Frank Sinatra Timex Special: Welcome Home Elvis* on May 12, 1960, which was broadcast over the ABC-TV network. It was a sharp marketing move for one star who was aging and for another star who had been away for two years, although merchandising sales efforts kept Presley in the public eye. Sinatra and Presley were the biggest pop music superstars of the 1940s and 1950s, respectively, so a show sprinkled with humor and the two singing together was just the natural thing to do. After Elvis sang a song with loud female shrieks heard coming from the audience, Sinatra and comedian Joey Bishop joined the young singer on stage. The three then bantered together in a kind of classic comedy routine designed to get laughs and warm the audience:

Sinatra: Elvis, I tell you something, that was great, and I'm glad to see the Army hasn't changed you. Wasn't it great? [Looks at Bishop.]

Bishop: I never heard a woman screaming at a male singer. [Sinatra shoots him a dirty glance, then in a mock gesture of defiance puts his hands on his hips.]

Sinatra: Don't you remember me, Charley?

Bishop: Mr. Presley, would you think it presumptuous of Frank if he joined you in a duet?

Presley: I would consider it quite an honor. [He looks at Sinatra.] I would like to do one of your songs.

Sinatra: All right.

Presley: I mean, you know, with you.

Sinatra: Fine, you know, I always wondered, as a matter of fact, while you were singing Elvis, I thought to myself, I wondered what would have happened if I recorded "Love Me Tender" instead of you. I wonder if it would have made any difference. [He looks at Bishop.]

Bishop: I think it would have about 2 million records *less*.

The audience chuckled, the orchestra began playing, the two tuxedo-clad superstars began rhythmically flexing their shoulders to the beat, and Sinatra quipped, "We work in the same way, only in different areas." Then Sinatra began singing "Love Me Tender" followed by

Presley singing "Witchcraft" and back and forth, and at the end, arms clasped around each other's shoulders, the two superstar singers harmonized together. "Man, that's pretty," Sinatra smiled. Female screams poured out of the audience every time Presley started singing.

Col. Parker managed Elvis's music business affairs and set the deals for him, which his client pretty much followed as told. Parker arranged for Presley to have some music publishing companies in partnership with a larger music publisher, Hill and Range. Parker set down the rule that for songs Presley recorded, he would get a piece of the publishing, usually about a third or half interest (this would generally not apply to previously published songs), and Elvis would also often get co-writing credit on original songs he recorded, even if he did not participate in the writing. Fortunately, this practice of acquiring publishing rights to songs owned by others and of obtaining writing credits to songs that the artist did not participate in writing dissipated with future music stars over time (although some may argue not completely).

In the mid-1950s rock and roll took off and became the new pop music of youths. Elvis Presley, with his banner year in 1956, catalyzed its popularity more than any other artist, but numerous other developments contributed to the new pop music genre becoming the anthem of teenagers. There was the Top 40 radio format in which not only were the bestselling records played on the air (not a new concept), but also it was a style of programming generally on AM stations designed to appeal to youthful audiences with their hip DJ patter and promotional activities such as album or concert ticket giveaways (the format is commonly credited to broadcasting pioneer Todd Storz of Omaha). Another contributing factor was television shows that featured rock and roll artists. Ed Sullivan, Steve Allen, and Milton Berle were among the hosts of shows that brought on musical acts, but there was another show that was exclusively devoted to rock and roll artists and that brought rock and roll into the homes of Americans. It was called *American Bandstand* and following a swinging opening theme song, it featured teenagers in the studio dancing to hit songs lip synched by their artists; hosted by Dick Clark it was broadcast live each weekday afternoon, and by the end of the decade it had a reported audience of 20 million.

Transistor radios were popular and cheap at the time, and tweens and teens had them and would tune into Top 40 radio stations, getting drawn in by rock and roll and pop including novelty records designed to appeal to youths such as "The Purple People Eater" and "The Witch Doctor." In the latter part of the decade labels started releasing records in stereo, which enhanced the listening experience, even though it took a while for people to replace their mono players with equipment that could play stereo.

As the new music of the youth generation, rock and roll songs embellished characteristics that were established by its predecessors. It had, for instance, made-up words and expressions that had a special catchy appeal about them, some of which became cultural buzz words and phrases. These linguistic fabrications could be found in such songs as "Who Put the Bomp (In the Bomp Ba Bomp Ba Bomp)," "Sh-Boom," "Be-Bop-a-Lula," and "Tutti Frutti." It had plasticity, where words or syllables could be stretched, molded, twisted, or shaped, or syllables could be added on either in front of or at the ends of words, all in a playful way (like "Ba ba ba ba-Barbara Ann" in the song "Barbara Ann" or "tooken" for *taken* to rhyme with *lookin'* in Hank Williams's "Hey, Good Lookin'").

Breaking the rules of grammar may not have originated with rock and roll (lyrics seem to lend themselves to grammatical faux pas), but improper grammar seemed to take off in rock and roll lyrics with the rampant use of double negatives, run-on sentences, and sentence fragments. Informality and slang are also part and parcel of the pop vernacular, so there is prodigious use of words that are traditionally not considered proper English but are how people talk such as *ain't* (for "am not"), *wanna* (for "want to"), *lotta* (for "lot of"), *gimme* (for "give me"), *cos* (for "because"), *'em* (for "them"), and *don't-cha* (for "don't you"). There is a catchiness to words or syllables that successively repeat (such as the word *lolly* in "Lollipop," *duke* in "The Duke of Earl," and countless songs with "oh oh oh oh" or the like), and so word and syllable repetition is another characteristic. Linguistic fare such as *baby*, *babe*, *ooh*, and *ooh baby* became a natural constituent of rock and roll jargon. Such words tend to be perceived as making the songs cool, as opposed to the syrupy and sentimental expressions of Tin Pan Alley lyrics, which favored words like *darling* and *sweetheart* (although these words can be found in many rock and roll songs).

Many of these linguistic characteristics can be found in pre–rock and roll songs, such as made-up catchphrases as found in songs such as

"Inka Dinka Doo" and "Bibbidi Bobbidi-Boo" or adding syllables to words to make rhymes such as the word "good-bye-ing" to rhyme with *dying* in "Let It Snow! Let It Snow! Let It Snow!" Lyrics are sometimes fashioned to fit the melody or beat or to make a particular point, and so pop song lyrics by their nature are malleable and inventive in all sorts of ways, all in the spirit of making the songs fun or expressive. As musical works, pop songs are more expressions of the heart than the brain, although they may pack a deep intellectual punch that leaves the listener pondering its meaning; indeed, one of the joyous if not fun aspects of pop songs is that listeners may read into their meanings in any way they wish, and people typically find all sorts of interpretations for the same words. Some people even ponder if the writer is sending a cryptic message or code such as in John Lennon and Paul McCartney's "Lucy in the Sky with Diamonds," which was commonly interpreted as referencing the drug LSD, with the first letters of the main words of the title.

Rock and roll, and later pop songs, often had similar themes or the same words in their titles and could be categorized (as well as compared and contrasted) in this way. Consider, for example, the following groupings of songs from the 1950s through 1970s: letters or mail ("Please Mr. Postman," "Love Letters in the Sand"), angels ("You Are My Special Angel," "Johnny Angel"), sixteenth birthday ("Happy Birthday Sweet Sixteen," "Sixteen Candles," "Sweet Little Sixteen"), dreaming ("Dreamin'," "Dream a Little Dream of Me"), clowns ("Cathy's Clown," "Tears of a Clown"), chapels ("Crying in the Chapel," "In the Chapel in the Moonlight," "Chapel of Love"), fools ("Poor Little Fool," "Fools Rush In," "A Fool Such as I"), hotels ("Heartbreak Hotel," "Hotel California"), ribbons ("Scarlet Ribbons," "Tie a Yellow Ribbon 'Round the Ole Oak Tree"), eyes ("Pretty Blue Eyes," "Smoke Gets in Your Eyes"), sea ("Sea of Love," "Beyond the Blue Sea"), girls ("Seven Little Girls Sitting in the Back Seat," "Girl Watching"), morning ("Angel of the Morning," "Morning Has Broken"), places ("Way Down Yonder in New Orleans," "Venus," "Kansas City"), wild ("Wild One," "Wild Thing"), a person's name ("Maybellene," "Diana," "Runaround Sue," "Charlie Brown," "Johnny B. Goode," "Tom Dooly," "Donna the Prima Donna"), rhyming titles ("Tallahassee Lassie," "Tutti Frutti," "Wooly Bully"), the name of an instrument ("Alvin's Harmonica," "The Happy Organ"), stars ("Little Star," "Starry, Starry Night," "Catch a Falling Star"), and doctors ("Witch Doctor," "Doctor My Love," "Doctor's Orders"). All this shows that a single word can evoke many kinds of responses and consequently launch a multitude of disparate lyrical themes, which is one reason why pop songs can have so many forms of expression.

Rock and roll exploded into the national consciousness around the mid-1950s, but it wasn't the only music that was embraced by the public at the time. On the trade magazine singles charts (there were singles charts published in the music industry's three main magazines at the time, *Billboard*, *Cash Box*, and *Music Vendor*, later renamed *Record World*) were records of other genres, although the lines between genres are often blurred and there is even some subjectivity in selecting what genre a record is primarily in, as it can have characteristics of one or more other genres. The mainstream singles chart, which for many years was viewed as the ranking of the bestselling and most-listened-to pop songs (in recent years streaming activity was added as a criteria), included crossovers from other genres such as jazz, R&B, and country, and its top singles can even be dominated by a non-pop (in its strict musical sense) genre as hip hop dominated the top spots of the mainstream singles chart around 2018. Indeed, as the diversity of popular music and public taste has evolved, that has been reflected in the mainstream singles chart, which reflects the convergence of different genres. The mainstream "pop" chart is no longer truly pop in the pure sense of "pop" with its white-bread hooks and verses. It is whatever the public embraces, and that can be a combination of different genres at the same time monopolized by a particular genre or two such as hip hop or dance music. Occasionally, one single artist or genre may even come to dominate the top five or ten positions, indicating a surge in popularity for that particular artist or genre at the moment, but such chart monopolizations are usually temporary, and other genres or artists of different styles may come to dominate those top chart positions in the future.

At any time, the current shape of commercial pop music can be discerned by the artists and songs on the mainstream singles charts. A perusal of the 1950s charts shows that perhaps no other popular music era, up to that time, at least, had such a heterogeneous potpourri of pop-style mainstream hit music. In the decades before there was a pretty homogenous mixture of standard Tin Pan Alley pop songs (including instrumentals) with some jazz hits (particularly during the

1930s Big Band era) and the occasional country or Latin or other-genre hit. Black artists certainly had hits, but they were not really considered rhythm and blues or other subsequent genres.

The 1950s had a more varied hit music tapestry. There were traditional crooners such as Bing Crosby and Grace Kelly, who had a hit with "True Love," Frank Sinatra with "All the Way/Chicago," Eddie Fisher with "Dungaree Doll," and Tony Bennett with "In the Middle of an Island/I Am."

R&B, a relatively new genre, was represented by such artists and songs as Fats Domino with "Blue Monday," "Blueberry Hill," and "I'm Walkin'"; Chuck Berry with "School Days," "Rock and Roll Music," and "Johnny B. Goode"; Little Richard with "Jenny, Jenny"; Sam Cooke with "You Send Me"; the Coasters with "Yakety Yak"; Lloyd Price with "Stagger Lee" and "Personality"; Jackie Wilson with "Lonely Teardrops"; the Coasters with "Charlie Brown"; and Sammy Turner with "Lavender Blue."

There were the new rock and rollers who were trying to tear down the curtain of vintage pop, and they included Buddy Knox and the Rhythm Orchids with "Party Doll," Danny and the Juniors with "At the Hop," Paul Anka with "Diana," Buddy Holly and the Crickets with "Peggy Sue," Bobby Helms with "My Special Angel" and "Jingle Bell Rock," Frankie Avalon with "Venus," Ritchie Valens with "Donna," Dion and the Belmonts with "A Teenager in Love," and Freddie Cannon with "Tallahassee Lassie" and "Way Down Yonder in New Orleans."

There were what might be called pop rock-and-rollers (with the emphasis on *pop*), and their ranks included Pat Boone with "Love Letters in the Sand," Tab Hunter with "Young Love," the Tune Weavers with "Happy, Happy Birthday Baby," Bobby Darin with "Splish Splash" and "Mack the Knife," The Crests with "Sixteen Candles," and Neil Sedaka with "Oh! Carol."

There were hip country acts that tried to marry country with rock and roll, and their roster included The Everly Brothers with "Bye Bye Love" and "Bird Dog," Jerry Lee Lewis with "Whole Lot of Shakin' Goin' On" and "Great Balls of Fire," Jimmie Rodgers with "Honeycomb," Johnny Horton with "The Battle of New Orleans," and Stonewall Jackson with "Waterloo."

Calypso and Caribbean-flavored artists also had chart hits such as Harry Belafonte with his "Banana Boat (Day-O)" and Terry Gilkyson and the Easy Riders with "Marianne." There were young pop balladeers such as Johnny Mathis with "It's Not for Me to Say" and "Misty," Andy Williams with "Butterfly" and "I Like Your Kind of Love," Debbie Reynolds with "Tammy," and Perry Como with "Catch a Falling Star/ Magic Moments." Novelty acts also hitched onto the singles charts, such as David Seville with "Witch Doctor," Sheb Wooley with "The Purple People Eater," and The Chipmunks with "The Chipmunk Song," which were especially popular with kids, and occasionally, a kids' pop tune could enjoy immense popularity, as happened with "The Ballad of Davy Crockett," which around March 1955 enjoyed chart hits by three artists—Bill Hayes, Fess Parker, and Tennessee Ernie Ford.

In this time of rock and roll bursting onto the pop scene, instrumental artists also charted, such as Perez Prado with "Cherry Pink and Apple Blossom White," Dave "Baby" Cortez with "The Happy Organ," and the Tommy Dorsey Orchestra with "Tea for Two Cha Cha." And there were the new doo wop acts who fused R&B, pop, and rock and roll in vocal-centric performances featuring male leads and attractive harmonies who scored on the charts also (antecedents of the doo wop style could be found in the smooth harmonies of such African American vocal groups of the 1930s and 1940s as the Ink Spots and Mills Brothers). The doo wop chart-makers included Frankie Lymon and the Teenagers with "Why Do Fools Fall In Love," The Platters with "Twilight Time" and "Smoke Gets in Your Eyes," The Five Satins with "In the Still of the Night," The Flamingos with "I Only Have Eyes for You," Little Anthony and the Imperials with "Tears on My Pillow," The Skyliners with "Since I Don't Have You," and The Mello-Kings with "Tonite Tonite."

Recordings of Broadway and Hollywood songs also made the charts, but hit songs from musicals and movies were nothing new, as tunes from shows such as *Show Boat* and *Good News* (both Broadway musicals that premiered in 1927) and from movies such as *The Wizard of Oz* (1939) and *Pinocchio* (1940) made the Hit Parade of prior years. All in all, however, with rock and roll, R&B, and doo wop emerging into the mainstream, vintage pop battling to maintain its long-time presence, and myriad hybrids and fusions of pop music hitting the charts, it was arguably unprecedented as a pastiche of hit popular music.

The pop music of the latter half of the 1950s was mostly rock and roll and doo wop and traditional pop with the emphasis on rock and roll, but by the end of the decade, there appeared to be some rumblings in the rock and roll universe. The U.S. government started looking into the illegal practice of DJs and TV show hosts being paid to play records on the air, and there were those who declared that rock and roll, the beloved music of teens, was over. Indeed, rock and roll had its detractors from its beginnings. There were those who called it the devil's music, and some would say it led to promiscuity among young people. Some groups of people even held bonfires in which they burned rock and roll records. In what may be viewed as a pop gesture of defiance, in 1958, Danny and the Juniors, the ABC-Paramount Records group that scored a top 10 hit in December 1957 with "At the Hop," released an anthemic rock and roll survival song called "Rock and Roll Is Here to Stay" asserting just that.

By the end of the 1950s, the death knell had not yet sounded for rock and roll; rock and roll records still made up about half of the singles chart-makers. But the thing about popular music is that it is dynamic—it constantly changes forms and evolves, rarely remaining static for very long. As the times change, songwriters and singers sweep in with new forms of expression, replacing older ones and keeping the music scene fresh. New talent seeks to grab the public's attention, and even a single artist can upend the music scene, as happened around the mid-1950s with that kid with the pompadour from Tennessee. Just a handful of years earlier rock and roll launched modern pop music like a powerful rocket; eventually this first stage of modern pop would jettison as other new forms would evolve, but surely no one could have imagined the impact and new sound that would come shortly from across the Atlantic Ocean.

As the year 1960 rolled in, the number 1 song on the pop singles chart was a country and western number, Marty Robbins's "El Paso." But this wasn't a harbinger of what was to come in the decade, as although country and western would become more pop-sounding and have its genre modified to just a single word, "country," the decade of top pop music would be moving in other directions. In 1960 numerous rock and roll songs charted, such as Mark Dinning's "Teen Angel," Paul Anka's "Puppy Love," the Hollywood Argyles' "Alley Oop," the Drifters' "Save the Last Dance for Me," and Chubby Checker's smash-hit dancing sensation "The Twist." But the top records of the year included those by numerous middle-of-the-road artists such as Connie Francis, Steve Lawrence, Andy Williams, Connie Stevens, and the piano duet Ferrante and Teicher. Apparently, older consumers were listening to and buying popular music, so there was still an audience for Tin Pan Alley–type songs.

As the early 1960s moved along, however, pop music continued in a very "pop" (and non–Tin Pan Alley) direction. While there were fewer middle-of-the-road artists landing on the pop singles chart, there were many of the same hit rock and roll artists from the late 1950s charting, plus, it might be said, more of the same in terms of the songs. "Spanish Harlem," "Runaway," "Mother-in-Law," "Those Oldies but Goodies (Remind Me of You)," "Tossin' and Turnin'," "The Duke of Earl," "The Wanderer," "The Lion Sleeps Tonight," "Sealed with a Kiss," "Johnny Angel," "Breaking Up Is Hard to Do," "Big Girls Don't Cry," "Hey Paula," "I Will Follow Him," "It's My Party," "Those Lazy-Hazy-Crazy Days of Summer," "Surfin' U.SA."—these were all catchy chart-makers, but these and other hit tunes were not carving out any creative new path for pop music. Among the chart-making artists then were the Beach Boys, Neil Sedaka, the Contours, the Four Seasons, Bobby Vinton, Gene Pitney, Brian Hyland, Freddie Cannon, Shelley Fabares, Jay and the Americans, Johnny Tillotson, Roy Orbison, the Tokens, Dion, and African American artists such as Sam Cooke, Gene McDaniels, the Marvelettes, and the Marcels. There were new dances—the Peppermint Twist, the Watusi, the Mashed Potato. Foreign language songs even became pop hits—"Sukiyaki" was a *Billboard* Hot 100 number 1 hit in Japanese for Kyu Sakamoto in June 1963, and "Dominique" was also a *Billboard* number 1 hit in French for the Singing Nun (Jeanne-Paule Marie Deckers) a few months later in 1963. Rock and roll and doo wop even became parodied in songs with fun-sounding phrases such as "rama lama ding dong" (from "Who Put the Bomp," recorded by Barry Mann) and "bomp ba-ba bomp a danga dang dang a dinga dong ding" (from "Blue Moon" recorded by The Marcels). The chart-making artists of the time put out diverting and feel-good sing-along pop tunes, and it was all clean, innocent fun. But then just as political events started taking a turn, so, too, did the musical landscape.

Near the end of 1963 there was talk on some Top 40 AM radio stations about a new group from England that was tearing up a storm there. Rumors spread among young people about this group—they had mop top haircuts, wore collarless suits, and spoke with that engaging English accent. But if you hadn't heard or seen them, you didn't know what to expect. Oh, and they had a funny name: The Beatles. The Beatles? What kind of name is that for a rock and roll group? But excitement built, and with great anticipation, teenage music fans anxiously awaited the arrival of this mysterious new group. On February 7, 1964, some four thousand screaming fans at Heathrow Airport in London bid the Beatles—John Lennon, Paul McCartney, George Harrison, and Ringo Starr—goodbye as they departed for America. Some radio stations were playing their music already, but for the most part, the American public did not know what to expect. Two days later, on February 9, the Beatles performed on *The Ed Sullivan Show* to a frenzied studio audience and with a staggering 73 million people watching on television. Top 40 radio such as WABC in New York City, perhaps the quintessential pop radio station in the country, enthusiastically embraced the Fab Four. They were championed there perhaps most prominently by DJ Cousin Brucie, as well as by another New York City DJ, Murray the K over at WINS, who would later dub himself The Fifth Beatle. In no time the Beatles pushed aside the American pop artists and dominated the top of the singles charts. In March 1964, just two months after they debuted on the American charts with "I Want to Hold Your Hand" (at position number 45 in January), the Beatles occupied the top three positions on the pop singles chart with "I Want to Hold Your Hand," "She Loves You," and "Please Please Me." By the end of the year they had numerous other top five singles: "Twist and Shout," "Can't Buy Me Love," "Love Me Do," "Do You Want to Know a Secret?" and "A Hard Day's Night," as well as four other songs in the top twenty—"P.S. I Love You," "And I Love Her," "I Feel Fine," and "She's a Woman." Their sound was new and fresh, youthful and vibrant, but not exactly the rock and roll or American pop of the 1950s and early 1960s. In 1964, Beatlemania hit America.

On August 15, 1965, the Beatles played before 56,000 screaming fans at Sea Stadium, in Queens, New York City. The stadium was filled to capacity, and the concert, which was filmed, set a record for U.S. concert attendance at the time. The crowd went wild and it was pure pandemonium there with the fan noise so loud the music could barely be heard. Cops had to carry out young women who fainted. It wasn't just Beatlemania; it was rock and roll fan frenzy at its apotheosis.

The phenomenon that was the Beatles wasn't just due to their timeless music, however. There were keen marketing forces behind them, just as there were behind Elvis Presley, who became the archetype for pop music star promotion. Like Presley's manager, Colonel Parker, the Beatles' manager, Brian Epstein, navigated the group's marketing.

Twenty-seven-year-old Epstein was running his family owned North End Music Store in Liverpool, when at lunchtime on November 9, 1961, he and an assistant went to the nearby Cavern Club to check out a group he had heard about from young customers in his record shop. He eventually took over the management of the Beatles and continued until his death in 1967.

With few exceptions, there weren't many previous rock and roll groups in the early years of the genre in which all the members stood in front of audiences playing instruments and singing hit songs they wrote. Sure, there was Bill Haley and His Comets and Buddy Holly & the Crickets, and the Beach Boys to name a few, but a majority of the pop chart-makers were individual singers (backed by studio musicians in making records) such as Chubby Checker, Ray Charles, Gene Pitney, Ben E. King, Neil Sedaka, Connie Francis, Carla Thomas, Brenda Lee, Johnny Horton, Sam Cooke, Andy Williams, Lou Christie, Little Peggy March, Bobby Rydell, Ricky Nelson, and Brook Benton, or groups whose members just sang and didn't play instruments or write their hit material such as the Shirelles, the Platters, the Marvelettes, the Four Seasons, and the Orlons. The Beatles played instruments—groups like the Crickets and the Beach Boys may have personified the makeup of a rock and roll band, but the Beatles with their lead guitar, bass guitar, rhythm guitar, and drums codified that image. They wrote songs—they all did, even if the group's chief writers, Lennon and McCartney, wrote most of their songs. They had the right looks—Paul famously was the "cute one"—and the perfect personalities to complement their music—in interviews they came across as charming, funny, witty, and not intimidating. They wore mod suits and trail-blazed new fashion standards, being widely copied with their haircuts and attire.

By the time the so-called Fab Four crossed the pond, they were experienced rock and rollers at giving live shows, having honed their performance skills at various clubs in Hamburg such as Indra, Kaiser-keller, and the Top Ten club, and at the Cavern Club in Liverpool in the early 1960s. The group, with its core being Lennon, McCartney, and Harrison, went through various drummers before settling on Ringo Starr.

The Beatles' early songs were buoyant effusions of love, with their themes compactly encapsulated in their titles. In 1963 their tunes included "I Want to Hold Your Hand," "All My Loving," "She Loves You," and "I Saw Her Standing There." The next year they had hits with such songs as "Can't Buy Me Love," "I Should Have Known Better," "A Hard Day's Night," "I Feel Fine," "Tell Me Why," "If I Fell," and "Eight Days a Week," followed in 1965 by such tunes as "In My Life," "Yesterday," "Michelle," "You're Going to Lose That Girl," "Drive My Car," "Nowhere Man," "You Won't See Me," and "Help!" While their songs weren't exactly unique in the crowded and competitive pop field—were they all that set them apart from such other pop fare as "Will You Love Me Tomorrow?" "Crying," "The Wanderer," "Duke of Earl," "Breaking Up Is Hard to Do," "Walk Right In," "It's My Party," and "Blowin' in the Wind"?—they were exuberant expressions of love that, with the group's fresh sound and charisma (not to mention the hype that surrounded the Beatles) and the group's reputation of writing their own songs (with a few exceptions), they captured the public's fancy. But the Beatles changed with the times, or, it might be said, helped change the times, by progressing from innocuous love tunes to songs with more daring themes, with "Day Tripper" (perhaps about drugs) in 1965 being one of their early songs in this vein. Their *Sgt. Pepper's Lonely Hearts Club Band* and *Magical Mystery Tour* albums, both recorded and released in 1967, took them into new territory, at least the way some people interpreted their songs, with allusions to sex and drugs.

Although Lennon and McCartney were masterful pop songwriters, they and the other Beatles weren't afraid to express their admiration for other songs or genres, and the Beatles made cover records of R&B songs (the Isley Brothers' "Twist and Shout" and Chuck Berry's "Roll over Beethoven"), Tin Pan Alley pop ("Ain't She Sweet"), show music ("Till There Was You" from *The Music Man*), and old folk tunes ("My Bonnie"), all, of course, in rock and roll or pop arrangements, and having a new sound, their own sound, their inimitable Beatles brand of rock and roll. This is an example of why the term *rock and roll* came to be applied as a generic term to successor forms of popular music, so long as the artist incorporated the rock and roll sounds and styles of electric guitars, keyboards, and drums.

The Beatles' success and longevity owes much to the fact that they could be wonderfully prolific and continually come up with great new hits and grow creatively through time. In 1964 the Beatles had already established themselves as hit-makers, but the pop music landscape was fiercely competitive, with bands always having to prove themselves with new hits to sustain their popularity, and the Beatles, it might be said, rose to the occasion. Indeed, "rose to the occasion" does not even begin to state strongly enough their imperial ascendancy. They glowingly surpassed expectations by producing new records that seemed to eclipse each other in artistry and quality, inventiveness and cleverness, imagination and genius. Their subsequent songs, albums, and sounds went off in new directions, incorporated new sounds, interpolated songs within songs, and were all so well received that they even helped shape the cultural landscape. Their U.S. albums, *Meet The Beatles!*, *The Second Beatles Album*, *A Hard Day's Night*, *Beatles '65*, *Help!*, *Rubber Soul*, *Revolver*, *Sgt. Pepper's Lonely Hearts Club Band*, *Magical Mystery Tour*, *The Beatles (White Album)*, *Yellow Submarine*, *Abbey Road*, *Hey Jude*, and *Let It Be* were so packed with hit singles that both their singles and albums regularly made the top spots on the charts, and even their album cuts enjoyed immense popularity. The Beatles' album art complemented their artistic growth with new directions also and even a bit of mystery, as exemplified by the cover artwork for *Sgt. Pepper's Lonely Hearts Club Band*. Like Elvis, the Beatles made movies (though not anything near the volume of Presley) and had a merchandising bonanza behind them with an array of products.

The Beatles seemed to have launched a new music scene in America. They were followed on the charts in 1964 by numerous other English groups—the so-called British invasion—including the Rolling Stones, Animals, Herman's Hermits, Dave Clark Five, Peter and Gordon, Gerry and the Pacemakers, Billie J. Kramer and the Dakotas, the Zombies, the Searchers, and the Kinks. By the time the Beatles arrived in America, Elvis's heyday was past, but the Beatles ignited a music scene that was to have an immense worldwide cultural impact.

6

A GOLDEN AGE OF POP HITS

Friday, November 22, 1963, started out as an ordinary day in America. People commuted to work, kids traipsed off to school, those weary from the work week undoubtedly looked forward to the weekend ahead. On people's minds also was Thanksgiving, which was just five days away. There would be family meals with turkey, cranberry sauce, and mashed potatoes and, for many, no work or school. With the weekend respite and holiday ahead, Americans could blithely look forward to a bit of serenity—but not for long. As the morning got underway, no one could have imagined that in just a short time a horrifying event would stun the world and history would forever be changed.

At 11:39 a.m. C.S.T. Air Force One, touched down at Love Field in Dallas, Texas, carrying John F. Kennedy, the president of the United States, his wife Jacqueline, and others. The plane took off from Fort Worth, where at 8:45 a.m. C.S.T. the president gave a speech at a Chamber of Commerce breakfast inside the Texas Hotel where he talked about how America tries to advance freedom around the world and how Texans have helped maintain the security of the United States. "So I am glad to come to this state," he said, "which has played such a significant role in so many efforts of this country." Soon after landing at Love Field the president, Mrs. Kennedy and others boarded a motor-cade to go to downtown Dallas. It was a forty-five-minute ride away.

It was a bright peaceful day in Dallas, temperature in the mid-sixties, as the 1961 Lincoln Continental cruised down Main Street carrying the president of the United States, John F. Kennedy and his wife Jacque-

line in the back seat, Texas governor John B. Connelly and his wife
Nellie in the seat in front of the Kennedys, and two Secret Service
agents in the front, one the driver. Following the open "bubbletop"
limousine were cars of Secret Service agents and reporters, and in one
of the vehicles was Vice President Lyndon Johnson and his wife Lady
Bird.

Proceeding on Main Street in Dallas, the presidential motorcade
made a right turn onto Houston Street. The president was headed for
the Trade Mart, where he was scheduled to give an address at the
Citizens Council annual meeting. Moving slowly, the motorcade then
turned left onto Elm, and then toward a triple underpass. The route
was lined with many Texans. People were smiling and cheering and
trying to get a glimpse of JFK. Unbeknownst to those on the street,
however, there was a sniper aiming a rifle with a telescopic sight from
an upper floor of the Texas School Book Depository at 411 Elm Street.
The calm of the day was suddenly interrupted. At 12:30 p.m. cracks of
fire could be heard. The president had been hit in the neck by a bullet.
A second bullet struck Governor Connelly. And yet another bullet entered the back of Kennedy's head on his right side. The president
slumped over onto his wife, and the limousine raced to Parkland Me-
morial Hospital, where John F. Kennedy was pronounced dead at 1:00
p.m.

Between McCarthyism in the early 1950s, when there was a cam-
paign to root out Americans who were members of the Communist
Party and dislodge them from their workplaces, to the Cuban Missile
Crisis in October 1962, in which Russia agreed to remove guided mis-
siles from Cuba pursuant to the U.S. quarantining Cuba and assuring it
wouldn't invade the island nation, America had been relatively peaceful. But the Kennedy assassination struck at America's heart, and its
shockwaves reverberated in many ways that helped shape the decade
including the cultural zeitgeist.

The 1960s were a time of momentous political and cultural change,
when an unpopular war was sundering a nation, when civil rights were
being fought for resulting in peace marches and riots, when fashion and
arts and social mores and education were rapidly changing, when the
tranquility of the 1950s was metamorphosing to questioning and misgiv-
ings and unrest and actions, when young people were shaping and being shaped by the times. As a result, pop music itself would undergo

dramatic changes, too, both fomenting discontent and being factionalized by it into less mainstream forms that would continue to sprout
other unconventional forms that would enlarge the universe of pop
music like never before.

The decade all started innocently enough. On September 26, 1960,
John F. Kennedy and Richard Nixon engaged in the first of four nationally televised debates in a local television station in Chicago. These were
not the first presidential debates—the political tradition began in 1858
with Abraham Lincoln and Stephen Douglas—but they were the first to
reach a national audience as it was broadcast live on national television.

In the early 1960s, the baby boomers were just tots, kids, tweens,
and teens, but as youngsters they were perhaps more interested in TV
programming that catered to their tastes. They had everything from
Popeye cartoons and Three Stooges shorts to *Lassie*, *Walt Disney
Presents*, *Gunsmoke*, *Bonanza*, *The Twilight Zone*, and *The Ed Sullivan
Show* with *The Flintstones*, *The Jetsons*, *The Beverly Hillbillies*, *The
Munsters*, *The Addams Family*, and *Gilligan's Island* soon to be added
to their television mix. Many of these TV shows had catchy theme
songs—those from such shows as *The Flintstones*, *The Beverly Hillbillies*, and *The Addams Family* were virtually part of the Boomers' up-
bringing—and they could readily imitate the catchphrases of the characters (such as Fred Flintstone's "Yabba dabba doo!") or the theme
songs' gimmicks (such as *The Addams Family*'s snap of the fingers).
Baseball players such as Willie Mays, Sandy Koufax, Hank Aaron, Ro-
berto Clemente, Mickey Mantle, and Roger Maris were cultural icons
for them. Kids took photos with their Kodaks and Polaroids at the time,
but the flashlight that went off with a snap of the finger was temporarily
blinding.

The early 1960s Boomers imbibed in the innocent pleasures of
youth, but that innocence came to an abrupt end on November 22,
1963, when news poured out that President John F. Kennedy was assassinated in Dallas, Texas, and the nation went into shock (it became a
cliché that people would always remember where they were when they
heard the news). As if the assassination weren't enough of a shock, two
days later, on November 24, another thunderbolt was to strike. At 11:20
a.m., as Lee Harvey Oswald, the alleged assassin of President Kennedy,
was being led through a basement corridor of the Dallas County Jail, a
local nightclub owner named Jack Ruby standing in a crowd of report-

ers lurched forward and shot Oswald with a pistol. Unlike the Kennedy assassination, these proceedings were televised live to a national audience.

The cruel reality of the world hit, and the Boomers grew up fast. And as they matured, they would come to be involved with myriad issues that would strike at their hearts. The decade would be fraught with other serious happenings such as the Vietnam War and the anti-war movement, the assassinations of Martin Luther King Jr. and Senator Robert F. Kennedy, the civil rights movement, the women's liberation movement, and the gay rights movement. Drug use became common. Boys grew their hair long. The late 1960s was the age of counter-culture with hippies and slogans like "flower power." "Free love" became a mantra of the generation. The times were alive with a cultural revolution. The 1960s was the Baby Boomer's decade of coming-of-age, and music—pop songs—was their soundtrack.

The transition from the 1950s to the 1960s was marked not just by cultural and political changes but by popular music transformations also. Out of rock and roll blossomed a new form of popular music that may be regarded as just "pop" or "pure pop" or "contemporary pop." It generally didn't have the common I, IV, V chord sequence of rock and roll tunes. It didn't have the jamming piano and sax riffs of rock and roll. It was hip and youthful but more, well, "poppy." It would have been outdated, if not corny by this time, for 1960s pop songs to glorify in its titles and lyrics the word *rock* like in the 1950s hits "(We're Gonna) Rock around the Clock," "Rockin' Robin," or "Jailhouse Rock." Instead, it used new trendy lingo like "Groovin'," "A Goovy Kind of Love," or "Groovy Situation" (although of course there were some exceptions to this).

The Beatles and the British invasion artists ushered in a new sound, and in their wake American pop artists continued making youthful music that was fun and catchy but with a more updated or more sophisticated sound, although some people would call their songs as well as the British invasion groups' songs "rock and roll." Perhaps that is because groups like the Beatles, the Rolling Stones, the Dave Clark Five, the Hollies, the Who, the Beach Boys, Tommy James and the Shondells, Paul Revere and the Raiders, Three Dog Night, and Creedence Clearwater Revival continued the generic configuration of rock and roll groups of being a small ensemble of young men playing electric guitars, keyboards, and drums. But many of the rock and roll songs of the 1950s probably wouldn't have worked in the 1960s, and many of the pop songs of the 1960s probably wouldn't have worked in the 1950s, which is all fine as popular music should not be stagnant but dynamic, changing with the times. Every generation should update pop music to fit in with its time, culture, and idiosyncrasies. They may be writing about the same experiences and emotions—looking for love, fawning over females, and unrequited love are timeless themes—but new generations need to express their sentiments in their culture's vernacular and sound.

A close examination of the pop songs of the 1960s would reveal that the lyrics didn't always make sense and sometimes words were even made up (what does *surry* mean in Laura Nyro's "Stoned Soul Picnic"?), or their meaning was ambiguous or unclear, although part of their fun was that they could be deciphered in many different ways. But these pop songs worked as records (and thus songs) because of the delivery, arrangement, attitude, and drive that came across. As a new, or at least updated, form of popular music, "pop songs" of the 1960s were especially catchy, as often happens when new forms of music emerge. Just like the classical compositions that came out of the First Viennese School of Music from Mozart, Haydn, and Beethoven have been especially revered over the centuries if not regarded as seminal and quintessential examples of classical music, so too, may the pop songs of the 1960s be regarded as seminal and quintessential examples of the modern-day pop song.

In the mid-1960s the music scene was gradually changing. There was the usual mass of pop song confections—indeed, this was a pop song age of extremely catchy tunes, and the mere thought of a title of a top twenty tune could instantly ignite in the head of a music fan of that time the song's infectious hook. But other styles of pop songs were entering the mainstream, too. The Vietnam War, which wrought fierce anti-war sentiment in America, brought folk music transmuted into protest songs into vogue with artists such as Bob Dylan; Joan Baez; Peter, Paul and Mary; Pete Seeger; Phil Ochs; Richie Havens; and Arlo Guthrie. In September 1965 Barry McGuire's "Eve of Destruction" landed at number 3 on the Hot 100, and in March 1966 Sgt. Barry Sadler's "The Ballad of the Green Berets" became the number 1 pop record in America; "In the Year 2525" by Zager and Evans peaked at

number 2 in August 1969, and Edwin Starr's caterwauling "War" hit
number 1 in September 1970. These hits showed protest could be pop
sensations, too. Pop of the 1960s, for all its themes of romance and
having fun, could be contemplative and sad too, as was seen in "Abraham, Martin and John," Dion's mellow lamentation of three iconic
Americans who tragically met their end by the pulling of a trigger.

Other English bands such as The Who and Cream hit the American
pop singles charts before the decade was out. Acid rock, hard rock, soft
rock, and psychedelic rock were all new sounds coming out, with heavy
metal, glitter rock, progressive rock, and punk rock on the horizon. But
while songs of these rock sub-genres occasionally leaped onto the mainstream singles chart, for the most part that chart was dominated by
songs of prototypical pop groups, R&B crossovers (especially of Motown artists, although it might be argued they were R&B-pop groups),
and country-crossover artists.

Like the tunesmiths of the Prohibition era and the Great Depression
prolifically wrote the standard pop fare of love and heartbreak songs, so
did their 1960s counterparts. The 1960s mainstream pop songs covered
an array of universal sentiments, expressed in the burgeoning youthful
sound of pop. Sprouting out of rock and roll, these tunes, from the
1960s to the early 1970s (until about the time disco started becoming
mainstream) might now be deemed "classic modern pop." They are
characterized by ultra-catchy hooks and melodies with basically clean
and meaningful lyrics. In their day, these songs dominated the Top 100
singles charts. Their hit records had distinguishable personalities, owing
to the artists' individual styles and the recordings' arrangements, and
productions. These songs are generally quite memorable, many the
kinds of standards that will last through time and be known to future
generations.

There were hundreds of these songs from what might be called the
"golden age of pop." They became hits in recordings by such artists as
the Beatles, the Beach Boys, the Association, the Four Tops, the Rolling Stones, the Supremes, Freddie and the Dreamers, the Young Rascals, the Turtles, the Mamas and the Papas, Bread, the Jackson Five,
the Fifth Dimension, Tommy James and the Shondells, Sly and the
Family Stone, the Doors, the Lovin' Spoonful, and the Dave Clark Five.
Many of these songs had the same basic themes, but they were expressed in different ways, or they covered specific niches of the overall

themes. Indeed, their titles were so telling that one might even conjecture how the lyrics go from the titles alone.

From this arguably golden age of pop there were songs with sexual innuendos such as "The Birds and the Bees," "Hanky Panky," and "Gimme Some Lovin'"; songs about love such as "Happy Together," "Baby, I'm Yours," and "Cherish"; songs about pining for somebody such as "I Saw Her Standing There," "Oh, Pretty Woman," and "Save the Last Dance for Me"; songs about insecurity such as "Will You Still Love Me Tomorrow" and "I Won't Last a Day without You"; songs about defending a lover such as "Don't Say Nothin' Bad (About My Baby)" and "Leader of the Pack"; songs about heartbreak, infidelity, loneliness, and sadness such as "Crying," "Take Good Care of My Baby," "Only the Lonely," and "Rainy Days and Mondays"; songs about illicit love affairs such as "Me and Mrs. Jones"; songs of rebellion or adventure such as "Born to Be Wild" and "Surf City"; songs about the spreading of lies and insincere charmers such as "My Boyfriend's Back," and "Sweet Talking Guy"; songs about surfing such as "Surfin' U.S.A.," "Surfin' Safari," and "Surf City"; songs about cars such as "Hey Little Cobra," "Little GTO," and "Little Deuce Coup"; songs about places such as "On Broadway," "San Francisco," "It Never Rains in Southern California," and "Never Been to Spain"; songs about reminiscing or growing old such as "Those Were the Days," "Yesterday When I Was Young," "Yesterday Once More," and "Your Mother Should Know"; nonsense songs such as "Oh, My My"; songs about working hard such as "Working in the Coal Mine"; tuneful reveries of finding love such as "Where the Boys Are" and "World without Love"; happy songs such as "Sing" and "Joy to the World"; songs of cynicism such as "Kodachrome"; songs about helping others through rough times such as "Lean on Me," "Bridge over Troubled Water," and "You've Got a Friend"; story songs such as "Mr. Bojangles," "Harper Valley PTA," "A Boy Named Sue," "Piano Man," "Tie a Yellow Ribbon 'Round the Old Oak Tree," and "A Whiter Shade of Pale"; songs of family bonds such as "Loves Me Like a Rock"; and songs of unity such as "Love Train." Indeed, many of these songs have become staples of culture, reproduced in movies, TV shows, and commercials, and for modern-day pop music aficionados they comprise the seminal and iconic pop music catalog (see appendix A for a more extensive listing of these songs).

There were also instrumentals of this era such as "Walk, Don't Run," "Pipeline," "No Matter What Shape," "Brian's Song," and "Hawaii Five-O (around the mid-1970s instrumental themes from movies and TV shows such as *Close Encounters of the Third Kind*, *Star Wars*, *S.W.A.T.*, and *Charlie's Angels* became hits, although hit pop instrumentals largely faded in later years).

The 1950s and 1960s were the heyday of the pop novelty song, which may be looked at as the oddball, weird, unique, or surprising tune, and is usually fun in some idiosyncratic, strange, or distorted way. It doesn't usually embrace any of the traditional themes of pop songs such as teenage love, courtship, touching and physical contact, heartbreak, making it through the day, dancing, places, weather, seasons, or cars. Novelty songs of that time were generally characterized by catchy cadences, silly or double-entendre lyrics, amusing words or rhymes or tongue-twisters, and highly infectious melodies and instrumental riffs. The vocal delivery and instrumental performances of the song reflect or mirror the message of the song. Some novelty songs may reflect current fads or even start them. The content is usually light, but novelty songs can be dark. Examples from that era include "The Flying Saucer (Parts 1 and 2)," "The Purple People Eater" (1958), "Witch Doctor (Ooh Eeh Ooh Ah Ah Ting Tang Walla Walla Bing Bang)" (1958), "On Top of Spaghetti" (1963), "A Boy Named Sue" (1969), "Gitarzan" (1969), "Gimme Dat Ding" (1970), "My Ding-A-Ling" (1972), and "The Streak" (1974). Some novelty songs are novelty-dance hybrids, spawning special dance movements such as "The Monster Mash" (1962), "The Mouse" (1965), and "Disco Duck" (1976). Some novelty songs may later find themselves to be politically incorrect such as "Ahab the Arab" (1962) and "Please Mr. Custer" (1960). A novelty song may border on the philosophical-religious like "Spirit in the Sky" (1970). With its chilling lyrics about a mental breakdown and the pitch of the singer's voice increasingly getting higher as if the singer is gradually losing his mind and cracking up and sirens alarmingly playing in the background and the whole thing speeding up and slowing down, the novelty song "They're Coming to Take Me Away, Ha Haaa!" (1966) was banned from broadcast by some radio stations.

A phenomenon of 1960s pop was the fictitious group that scored pop hits on the national singles charts. There were precedents to such apocryphal music ensembles—Ross Bagdasarian's singing Chipmunks had singles hits in the late 1950s with "The Chipmunk Song" (number 1 on the *Billboard* Hot 100) and "Alvin's Harmonica" (in the top five of the Hot 100), but these were intended as novelty records. In the 1960s, the Archies, a studio group of real live musicians, landed in the top spot of the national singles charts with "Sugar, Sugar" and hit the Top 10 in January 1970 with "Jingle Jangle." There were session musicians and singers who became the nameless talent behind such records. The Archies' lead vocals were provided by Ron Dante, who also sang on numerous other hit records. Another phenomenon of 1960s pop was the manufactured music group. The premier example of this would be the Monkees, a pop group assembled for a television series with the group's name. The Monkees, whose members during the show were Davy Jones, Mickey Dolenz, Peter Tork, and Michael Nesmith, had several hit singles including "Last Train to Clarksville," "I'm a Believer," "A Little Bit Me, a Little Bit You," "Pleasant Valley Sunday," and "Valleri" (most of their songs were written by Bobby Hart and Tommy Boyce, who also wrote numerous other pop hits). The concept of manufactured pop group whose members audition for spots would be the basis for boy bands and girl groups of later years.

The 1960s were also a time when spoken-word or musical comedy albums could sell millions of copies. There was, for instance, Vaughn Meader's parody of President John F. Kennedy with his 1962 Grammy Award–winning multi-million-selling album *The First Family* and Allan Sherman's 1962 Grammy-nominated comedy album *My Son, the Folksinger*. Other comedy albums followed, but Sherman also released a single in 1963 that nearly reached the top of the *Billboard* Hot 100. It was called "Hello Muddah, Hello Fadduh," and using a melody from Italian opera composer Amilcare Ponchielli's "Dance of the Hours," it was about a kid at summer camp who in a letter to his parents rolls off a litany of reasons why after one whole day there he wants to come home, until it stops raining and "guys are sailing, playing baseball." Both Meader's *First Family* album and the two aforementioned Sherman records were released before the assassination of President Kennedy, so the times were amenable to such fare, but both music and culture took a turn after the assassination, and it would be hard to imagine these records, or kinds of records, being released in later decades.

Songs about women being enchained by men or breaking free from them go back a long time, as exemplified by "A Bird in a Gilded Cage,"

Harry Von Tilzer and Arthur J. Lamb's 1900 tearjerker reflection of a young woman trapped in a marriage with an older man; in the rock and roll era women's liberation songs flowed freely including the Cookies' 1962 "Chains" (later recorded by the Beatles), Lesley Gore's "You Don't Own Me," which reached the number 2 position in 1964 (just behind the Beatles' "I Want to Hold Your Hand"), and Aretha Franklin's "Respect," which landed at the peak chart position on June 3, 1976. But with the modern women's lib movement beginning in the late 1960s, it was Helen Reddy's "I Am Woman" that became the pop signature song of women's fight for equality, hitting the number 1 spot on December 9, 1972. Gloria Gaynor's disco tune "I Will Survive," in March 1979, also hit the peak position on the American singles chart.

Most of the top chart singles were about the usual concerns of young people, but there were some songs that referenced drug use, or that could be construed that way. The Association's first chart song in July 1966 was "Along Comes Mary" and some interpreted "Mary" as marijuana. Peter, Paul and Mary's recording of "Puff the Magic Dragon," released in 1963, was similarly interpreted as a song about smoking marijuana. The Beatles' "Lucy in the Sky With Diamonds," from the group's 1967 album *Sgt. Pepper's Lonely Hearts Club Band*, was popularly regarded as a reference to LSD (with the clever use of the first letters of its title words: "Lucy," "Sky," and "Diamonds"). The Rolling Stones' "Brown Sugar" (from the album *Sticky Fingers*), which reached the number 6 position in May 1971, was alleged to be about drugs, and more blatantly from the same album was the song "Sister Morphine," which was released two years earlier as a single by British singer Marianne Faithfull in 1969. With Top 40 radio and its heed of controversial lyrics not being so much a factor for album cuts, however, many artists released drug-oriented songs in their albums. Among the first blatant rock drug songs were two from the Velvet Underground's 1967 debut album *The Velvet Underground & Nico*: "Heroin" and "I'm Waiting for the Man," both written by Lou Reed.

Songwriters have always in their way been philosophers, expressing themselves through the poetry of lyrics. They would take themes of human experience, or niches of themes or niches of niches of themes and so forth, and within the economy of a pop song lyric tell a story or impart a message that resonates with listeners. Setting words to music makes them larger than life, or rather aggrandizes them in a memorable and powerful way as pop music effectively does. Indeed, one three-minute pop tune can speak worlds to a person affected by that theme, which is why every line, or even every word, carries significant weight. With rock and roll and its subsequent forms, songwriters have endeavored to appeal to virtually every facet of the human condition, most pronouncedly those of youths and their feelings and emotions and experiences.

With rock and roll leading the charge, records were selling well by the late 1950s, and a trade group decided to bring attention to the recordings that were most purchased by the public. In 1958, the Recording Industry Association of America Inc. (RIAA), the main trade organization for record labels that was founded in 1952 by major labels such as RCA, Decca, Columbia, and Mercury, began a program to certify best-selling recordings under rules it set forth; the program would offer Gold Record Awards, with plaques being given for singles and albums. At the time, for a single to qualify for a Gold Record Award, it had to have shipped 1 million copies. Gold Album awards were not based on units shipped but on dollar sales. For an album to be certified gold, it had to have attained 1 million dollars in sales based on 50 percent of the list price. At that time albums generally sold for under $5, so if the retail list price of an album was $5, 50 percent of the list price would be $2.50, and the album would have had to have sold 400,000 units ($1 million divided by $2.5) to reach the $1 million mark and receive the award for a gold album. Over the years the criteria for certification have changed, with platinum and diamond awards being added to the mix.

RIAA certification is made pursuant to an audit of the label by the trade group. In the early years of the program, not all labels would permit the RIAA to audit their books, and certain hits did not receive Gold Awards (most labels granted the audit over the years, however). In 1958, the first year of the program, four singles and one album received RIAA certification. The Gold Single Awards went to "Catch a Falling Star" recorded by Perry Como on RCA Victor, "Hard Headed Woman" recorded by Elvis Presley on RCA Victor, "He's Got the Whole World in His Hands" recorded by Laurie London on Capitol; and "Patricia" recorded by Perez Prado on RCA Victor. The Gold Album Award went to *Oklahoma*, with Gordon MacRae as the artist on Capitol Records.

There is another organization that recognizes the creative achievements of people in the music industry, including songs and albums. It is the National Academy of Recording Arts and Science (NARAS), which was founded in 1957 in Los Angeles. NARAS, or the Recording Academy, as it is also called, is best known for its annual Grammy Awards, which over the years have grown in categories. Its most prominent awards now are for Album of the Year, Record of the Year, Best New Artist, and Song of the Year. In 2018 NARAS increased the number of candidates in these categories from five to eight, so a wider range of nominees could be included. In 2018 NARAS had approximately twenty-four thousand members, representing creative people in the recording field including artists, musicians, songwriters, composers, producers, arrangers, conductors, photographers, and graphic artists.

Like any new "art," rock and roll needed promotion and distribution to popularize it and bring it to the masses. At its start, it was still competing with other popular genres of music, but it took off quickly, and several technological and economic factors may be attributed to its success: the new formats in which records were made available (singles and LPs); the new methods of distribution of records that made them available for sale in non-music outlets (such as one-stops and rack jobbers); the advent of multi-track recording; the creation of "pop song factories," most notably New York City's Brill Building at 1619 Broadway and Detroit's Motown Records; the making and distribution of records in stereo; the advent of Top 40 radio; the programming of pop-music television shows; the proliferation of pop and rock and roll labels; the running of rock and roll concerts; the exploitation of popular artists via merchandising, which oftentimes was creative and appealing for consumers; the popularity of jukeboxes with 45 rpm singles in diners and restaurants; and aggressive publicity efforts to secure coverage in the print and broadcast media. Of course, there was the quality of the music—from the mid-1950s through the end of the 1960s, the new genre of rock and roll and its offshoots were characterized by infectious songs, behind which were talented record producers who had an ear for making radio-friendly three-minute pieces of pop art (sometimes called "ear candy"). There were of course other factors such as the large number of teenagers in the 1960s resulting from the Baby Boom and the changing culture, as reflected on television and in movies, literature, and advertising.

Rock and roll started out pretty much as a singles medium to cater to radio airplay, and then the LP got a boost with the Beatles, whose albums generally contained all well-received songs, which fans could play without having to skip undesirable songs. Columbia rolled out the long-playing 33-1/3 rpm record (LP) in 1948, and the next year, 1949, RCA Victor launched the seven-inch 45 rpm single. These relatively lightweight vessels that embodied recordings were a significant improvement over the heavy 78 rpm discs that contained one or two songs on a side. These new record formats caught on quickly, and phonograph players were made to accommodate all three speeds (33 1/3, 45, and 78); inexpensive players for kids were also made, so when these 1950s youngsters became teens in the 1960s, their taste for popular music, which they had been weaned on, had already been developed.

The change to radio stations playing 45 rpm discs wasn't immediate or easy, however. By around 1954 record labels had established a pattern of phasing out 78 rpm discs to radio stations for promotional purposes and supplying 45 rpm records to stations. At first radio stations, most prominently WMCA and WNEW in New York City, resisted playing 45 rpm records because they didn't have the equipment to play them. It would require the stations to convert their turntables that played 78 rpm and 33 1/3 rpm discs to play all three speeds. By May 1954, however, record companies announced they would no longer be servicing stations with the 78 rpm discs, but the 45s. This caused a back log of orders for companies that manufactured the converters like RCA's Engineering Products Division. This change was accompanied by the public's own decline of purchasing 78 rpm records in favor of 33 1/3 LPs, EPs, and 45s. *Billboard,* in its July 17, 1954, issue, reported, "For the first five months of 1954, only 27 per cent [*sic*] of the dollar volume" of Columbia Records "was racked up by 78 disks, the rest was in 45s, EPs and LPs. Most firms had stopped turning out any albums on 78, and only singles are still pressed on 78s as well as 45s."

With the advent of the Todd Storz–credited Top 40 format on radio, rock and roll spread like wildfire. In most markets around the United States, there was at least one Top 40 station bringing rock and roll to youths. What was once referred to as the "hit parade" with essentially the most popular records of the day, was now Top 40, but with a high rotation of the most popular records—hot brand-new releases, hot current records already getting airplay, and hot recent releases—air personalities (deejays), and sundry promotions. Transistor radios were cheap and portable, so rock and roll had a funnel to bring it to the youth masses. But with the relatively new medium of television, rock and roll was brought into the living rooms of American homes around the country.

Many shows would bring popular music via TV to people starting in the 1940s. But the TV show that helped popularize rock and roll was *American Bandstand*, hosted by Dick Clark and broadcast nationally beginning on August 5, 1957, on the ABC-Television network (earlier versions of the show were broadcast on WFIL-TV in Philadelphia). On the show, teens danced to and rated the most popular records of the day; guest performers included the biggest rock and roll stars performing—well, mostly lip-synching—their hits. Viewers were treated to such acts as Bill Haley and His Comets with "Rock around the Clock," the Big Bopper with "Chantilly Lace," Paul Anka singing "Put Your Head on My Shoulder," The Silhouettes with "Get a Job," Jerry Lee Lewis with "Great Balls of Fire," and Chubby Checker with "The Twist." Other pop music television shows aired in the 1960s and 1970s, further promoting top artists and songs, such as *Where the Action Is*, *Shindig*, *Hullabaloo*, and *Soul Train*.

Like Tin Pan Alley had its row of publishing firms along 28th Street in Manhattan where songwriters wrote songs in small rooms, pop music had its own centralized locations where songwriters did what their Tin Pan Alley counterparts did. The most prominent one in New York City was the Brill Building, located at 1619 Broadway and 49th Street in Manhattan, where many young songwriters wrote pop tunes in their publishers' offices. Many hits of early rock and roll and pop emanated there from the hands of such talents as Carole King, Gerry Goffin, Cynthia Weil, Barry Mann, Ellie Greenwich, Jeff Barry, Neil Sedaka, Doc Pomus, Burt Bacharach, and Hal David. There were labels and recording studios and music stores in the building, too, so it was like its own pop music center all in one edifice.

In pre–rock and roll days, particularly during the Big Band era, it was the arranger who was the acclaimed behind-the-scenes contributor. There were such standout arrangers as Fletcher Henderson (Benny Goodman), Bill Strayhorn (Duke Ellington), Sy Oliver (Jimmie Lunceford, Tommy Dorsey), Alex Stordahl (Tommy Dorsey), Jerry Gray (Artie Shaw, Glenn Miller), and Bill Finegan (Glenn Miller, Tommy Dorsey). But with rock and roll, it was the producer who was the behind-the-scenes star, if not to the public then to artists and executives in the music business, with their services in demand.

The record producer's role is akin to that of the motion picture director—guiding the overall process of making the product—and they are responsible for the final outcome of the product. In the studio the producer starts with a song, which in its bare form is just words and melody, and with an arrangement and an assortment of musicians and singers, and an engineer handling all the technical work, makes that song come alive in a recording. He or she guides the musicians and singers in breathing life into that song as it becomes a permanently inscribed piece of art. Ever since the age of recording began, songs needed to be framed in ear-pleasing productions; it wasn't enough to just have a good song. The song had to be brought out with the right arrangement and delivery to catch on with the public. That need continues through today, but modern technology makes facilitating that process easier while at the same time demanding the producer be adept with the equipment and techniques at his or her disposal.

The producer has a plethora of responsibilities. Responsibilities may vary from producer to producer, as each have their own way of working, but responsibilities could be broken down in a general way: in pre-production record producers may plan the artistic direction of the artist and confer with the label about this, participate in the selection of songs, work with the artist in coming up with the desired structure and tempo of songs, and vocal delivery. They may also oversee the booking of studio time and the hiring of session musicians and singers, and handle related business responsibilities. During the sessions the producer oversees the recording of the tracks, guiding the artist, instrumentalists, and singers in their performances, and the engineer on how they want the music to be recorded. In the studio the producer needs to make sure everything flows along smoothly so the desired product can be achieved, which could mean creating an atmosphere of energy and excitement and encouraging the players in such a way as to draw out their best performances. In post-recording the producer may carry out or oversee the mixing and editing of the tracks as well as other post-production duties. Where an album or multiple songs have been recorded, the producer may discuss with the label what songs should be released as singles and in what order. A good producer can take a good song and make a great record out of it—after all, any song can be made into a bad or good record. The producer constructs an aural canvas that has a distinct personality and ambience that draws the listener in. The resulting aural portrait gives life to the song, and the listener is absorbed into the world created by that recording.

Notable rock and roll, country, and rock producers of past decades include Stephen Sholes (Elvis Presley), Lieber and Stoller (Elvis Presley, the Coasters, the Drifters, Sammy Turner, the Exciters, Jay and the Americans), Buck Ram (the Penguins, the Platters), Hugo and Luigi (Sam Cooke, the Isley Brothers, the Tokens, Little Peggy March), Phil Spector (the Ronettes, Crystals, Righteous Brothers, George Harrison), George Martin (the Beatles), Owen Bradley (Patsy Cline, Brenda Lee), Chet Atkins (Porter Waggoner, Hank Snow, Dolly Parton), Burt Bacharach (Dionne Warwick), Quincy Jones (Lesley Gore, Michael Jackson), Richard Perry (Barbra Streisand, Harry Nilsson, Carly Simon), Snuff Garrett (Johnny Burnette, Bobby Vee, Sonny and Cher, Vicki Lawrence, Pointer Sisters), Shadow Morton (the Shangri-Las, Vanilla Fudge, Janis Ian), Norman Whitfield (the Temptations), Holland-Dozier-Holland (the Supremes, the Four Tops), Peter Asher (Linda Ronstadt, James Taylor), Gus Dudgeon (Elton John), Nile Rodgers and Bernard Edwards (Chic, Sister Sledge), Billy Sherrill (George Jones, Tammy Wynette, Charlie Rich), Kenny Gamble and Leon Huff (the O'Jays, Three Degrees, Harold Melvin and the Blue Notes), Arif Marden (the Rascals, Bee Gees, Carly Simon, Judy Collins), and Phil Ramone (Bob Dylan, Billy Joel, Madonna).

Rock and roll and its scions such as rock, hard rock, and soft rock enjoyed immense popularity in the mid-1950s and 1960s, and a plethora of both new and established labels brought out records of these genres. In those days, it was possible to record a song quickly, promote it to radio right away, and score a hit if it got picked up by radio and got a lot of airplay, although quickie hits like that were usually only in the province of small independent labels. The "major" labels at the time had branch offices around the country and their own apparatus for distribution; planning and care went into their releases, whereas a small indie didn't have as much red tape to cut through and could move faster, although it lacked the clout of a major. Major labels might have various imprints for the release of certain kinds of music (such as country), or distribute the records of independent labels with whom they had distribution agreements. There were other independent labels not affiliated with a major that had their own independent networks for promotion and distribution.

For various reasons it was not uncommon for artists to have been on multiple labels during their career or to have their records issued by different labels via licensing agreements (some, after achieving success at a small label, would sign with a major for the greater fame, success, and money that could be earned there). There were rock and roll labels and R&B labels and pop labels and rock labels and more, and the roster of artists on a label indicated the genre of music in which it basically specialized. The independent labels in those days were often started by songwriters, producers, artists, and former executives in the music business, as well as by ambitious entrepreneurs, and many have fascinating lore associated with them.

Labels of yesterday and today are like brands, mirrored by the artists they put out and the artists mirrored by their labels. They represent a certain kind of music, sound, song, attitude, or style, and even within a single company there could be several labels, each representing a particular brand or kind of music. Although many consumers do not pay attention to the names of labels, some labels become famous for the recordings or artists they put out or for their logos (RCA Victor being an example with its picture of a dog peering into the external speaker of a record player; the trademarked logo is based on a painting titled "His Master's Voice" by Francis Barraud, and the dog's name was Nipper).

By the end of the 1960s numerous labels, from majors to small independents, released popular music (from Tin Pan Alley to rock, country, R&B, and Latin). The major labels at this time included RCA, Capitol, Warner Communications, CBS, and MCA (each with several well-known imprints, some of which released genres other than pop, and each owned by a large corporation). It was a day when labels' images were associated not only with their star acts but with their executives also, who through the glamour of the industry and media (if not public) interest had public profiles. Among the high-profile label executives were Alan Livingston at Capitol Records, Stan Cornyn at Warner Bros. Records, Clive Davis at Columbia Records, Herb Alpert and Jerry Moss at A&M Records, Mo Ostin at Warner/Reprise, Ahmet Ertegun at Atlantic Records, and Joe Smith at Warner Bros. Records and Elektra/Asylum Records.

In the 1950s and 1960s, deejays had the power to select what records they would play on the air. It was the job of record promoters to get their records on the air, and paying for airplay, or payola, was a practice that developed. Payola, which is a form of bribery, had actually been around in the music business since the earliest days of Tin Pan Alley when songwriters would pay entertainers to perform their compositions or share royalties with them, or song pluggers would give money or gifts to singers to put their songs on the singers' bills, or singers who brought songs to public attention would receive a songwriting co-credit—all to boost sheet music sales. For radio deejays, payola could be in cash or made in other ways. Some deejays wanted payment in the form of a piece of the publishing rights of songs they played on the air. Thus, they would earn revenues from songs' performance royalties for radio airplay and other public performances of them, mechanical royalties from sales of records containing the songs, royalties from sheet music sales, and revenues from other licensed uses of songs. Other illicit payments could come in the form of merchandise, company stock, loan of credit cards, paid vacations, drugs, and prostitutes. Although not limited to the music business, payola has been one of the negative factors of music business history.

7

DISCO FEVER AND MUSIC VIDEO FERVOR

Following the turbulence and various rights movements of the 1960s came the Watergate scandal, the resignation of President Nixon from office, the end of the Vietnam War, and the safe landing on Mars of the Viking unmanned spacecraft. The 1970s wouldn't be as tumultuous and transformative as the 1960s, but it would become culturally renowned for spawning a new genre of pop music. Just after the 1970s began, B. J. Thomas's recording of "Raindrops Keep Fallin' on My Head," Burt Bacharach and Hal David's jaunty ditty from the movie *Butch Cassidy and the Sundance Kid*, inherited the crown position on the *Billboard* Hot 100 from the 1960s' last pole inhabitant, Diana Ross and the Supremes' "Someday We'll Be Together." Over the next few months Thomas's record was succeeded in the number 1 position by the Jackson Five's "I Want You Back," Shocking Blue's "Venus," Sly and the Family Stone's "Thank You (Falettin Me Be Mice Elf Again)/Everybody Is a Star," Simon and Garfunkle's "Bridge over Troubled Water," the Beatles' "Let It Be," and the Jackson Five's "ABC" (Bronson, 1985). These quintessentially pop songs continued the pop scene of the 1960s, and few at the time would have imagined that in just a few years a new genre of music would become so popular that it would have a major impact on culture.

From rock and roll, the seminal new youth music of the 1950s and 1960s, emerged several sub-genres, hybrids and fusions such as rock, acid rock, hard rock, soft rock, Christian rock, heavy metal, and glitter rock. But in the 1970s came another style of youth music whose DNA strain emanated from mostly different forerunners in the popular music family, most notably Afro-Cuban, R&B, rock, and Latin, with its sundry dance styles ranging from the tango, rumba, sambo, and mambo to the cha cha chá, bossa nova, bugalú, and salsa. This energetic new hybrid of music was called *disco* because it was essentially launched in discotheques, stylized dance clubs with the French name (meaning "library of records"). It was characterized by a relentless beat, throbbing rhythms, electronic sounds, gliding strings, and a loud volume, and was intended for people to dance to.

As the rock and roll era got under way in the 1960s, nightclubs with dancing were popular, with such venues as the Peppermint Lounge in Manhattan and Whiskey a Go-Go in West Hollywood attracting much media attention. The Twist, Watusi, Jerk, Fly, Loco Motion, Hully Gully, Mashed Potato, and the Pony were some of the dance crazes in the early part of the decade. Around the early 1970s, a new dance movement developed underground in New York City that was populated by marginalized communities such as gays, Latinos, and African Americans and would spread nationwide. Before the middle of the decade, this dance music—disco—hit the mainstream of pop music, as, for instance, Love Unlimited Orchestra's "Love's Theme," a club favorite, bumped a quintessential pop ballad, Barbra Streisand's "The Way We Were," off the number 1 position on the pop singles charts in February 1974. Less than two months later, disco claimed two consecutive number 1 songs with the Hues Corporation's "Rock the Boat" and George McCrae's "Rock Your Baby." To put these disco entrées into pop mainstream perspective, when they topped the charts other songs in the top five included pure pop fare such as Gordon Lightfoot's "Sundown," Bo Donaldson and the Heywood's "Billy, Don't Be a Hero," Olivia Newton-John's "If You Love Me (Let Me Know)," John Denver's "Annie's Song," and Elton John's "Don't Let the Sun Go Down on Me." By the end of the year, Barry White's disco-danceable track "You're the First, the Last, My Everything" reached the penultimate position on the Hot 100 singles chart *of Billboard*. The next year, 1975, producer and writer Van McCoy released an album directed for club playing called *Disco Baby* with one of its tracks written as an eponymous dance tune for a popular club dance called the Hustle. "The Hustle," the record, was virtually ubiquitous in the club scene and was a staple on Top 40 radio, reaching the number 1 spot on *Billboard*'s mainstream singles chart.

Disco's success was soaring, but it didn't reach worldwide popularity until the release of the movie *Saturday Night Fever* and its disco soundtrack, which included several tracks by the Bee Gees, which became smash hits.

Discos were everywhere now, and where bars were once a popular location for single people to meet, discos were now not just a place to dance but a meeting place as well. Over the years, disco's audience had expanded from minority groups to all people, and so it was certifiably a mainstream genre of pop music. At a time when such artists as Grand Funk, Roberta Flack, the Carpenters, Tony Orlando and Dawn, the Captain and Tennille, Wings, the Eagles, Leo Sayer, Stevie Wonder, Glen Campbell, Fleetwood Mac, Marvin Gaye, and Anne Murray enjoyed immense popularity, numerous other disco songs placed high on the record charts in the decade: Gloria Gaynor's "Never Can Say Goodbye" and "I Will Survive," Abba's "Dancing Queen," Vicki Sue Robinson's "Turn the Beat Around," Tavares's "Heaven Must Be Missing an Angel," A Taste of Honey's "Boogie Oogie Oogie," Alicia Bridges's "I Love the Nightlife," C'est Chic's "Le Freak," Donna Summer's "Last Dance" and "Dim All the Lights," and the Village People's "Y.M.C.A.," "Macho Man," and "In the Navy," among others.

Disco reached national attention in the United States in 1974, and it lasted until the end of the 1970s. Its beats per minute, or BPM, a measure of the track's tempo, sped up after its initial success, going from 112 to more than 150. Disco was not just a different style of music, but with its club lifestyle (including drugs), flashy couture by clubgoers, glitter ball, strobe lights, disco visors, and other paraphernalia, it was a new kind of culture that was, in its way, an antecedent to future styles of club dance music.

Not all the major labels immediately jumped on the disco bandwagon, viewing this new form of dance music perhaps as a trend or passing fancy, so some independent labels or specialty labels distributed by a major were the main purveyors of disco early on. Midland International (its name was later changed to Midsong International) had big hits with Carol Douglas's "Doctor's Orders" and Silver Convention's "Fly, Robin, Fly"; Casablanca Records had not only disco diva Donna Summers (who became known as the Queen of Disco) but also the Village People and Lipps, Inc. (who had a major hit with "Funkytown"). Eventually the major labels embraced disco and established imprints to release records of that new genre.

Some disco artists were known for their signature vocal styles. Barry White, for instance, had a reputation of singing with a low male sensual style, and disco diva Donna Summer, thanks to her simulated orgasms on "Love to Love You Baby," was identified with orgasmic singing. Producers, who are usually not well known to the public, gained fame also. Donna Summer's producers Giorgio Moroder and Peter Bellotte, Gloria Gaynor's producers Freddie Perren and Dino Fekaris, Chic's Nile Rodgers and Bernard Edwards, and KC and the Sunshine Band members, writers, and producers Harry Wayne Casey and Richard Finch are among those who developed fame as creators and stewards of hit disco records.

The disco era was also notable for Tin Pan Alley songs or jazz tunes or even classical music motifs being arranged into disco records. One prominent example is Walter Murphy and the Big Apple Band's "A Fifth of Beethoven," which built a whole disco instrumental around the classical composer's famous motif in his early nineteenth-century *Symphony No. 5 in C minor* and became the number 1 record for the week of October 9, 1976 (Murphy adapted other classical melodies such as Rimsky-Korsakov's "Flight of the Bumble Bee" and called his disco version "Flight 76"). A studio group called A Wing and a Prayer had a hit single with the 1926 Tin Pan Alley tune "Baby Face" (coming from an album by the same name that was in the Top 50 pop album charts). And J. R. Bailey, a co-writer of the 1974 Grammy-nominated single "Everybody Plays the Fool" and a member of the 1950s doo-wop group the Cadillacs, released a disco version of Scott Joplin's "The Entertainer," which was resurrected to great popularity and a *Billboard* Hot 100 top five instrumental in May 1974 after its inclusion in the 1973 film *The Sting*.

In the disco era some songs were released as 12-inch singles. On the discs would be longer mixes of tracks for club play; shorter radio mixes would also be made available by labels of tracks released as singles.

As a result of the increasing popularity of discotheques in the mid-1970s came the record pool, service organizations comprised of disco deejays and disco operators that had a mutually beneficial relationship with record labels. The labels distributed to the deejays disco and dance records, and the record pools in turn gave the labels feedback on the records they supplied. The feedback was important because the records they supplied were often unreleased tracks, and the feedback could help the labels with their marketing campaigns. Great feedback on a record could result in heavy promotion and a large pressing, while poor feedback could result in the opposite, or the label remixing the record or perhaps not even releasing it at all. Feedback sheets would be supplied to members of the pools and they would write down the public reaction to the records they played as well as their own personal opinions. The information from the members' sheets would be compared and evaluate the overall response. This so-to-speak "free" marketing analysis helped labels make marketing decisions for their dance records.

At the same time the deejays and discotheque operators benefited by having a central source from which they could obtain the records they played. Otherwise, it would be time-consuming for them to get the records they wanted by contacting the labels individually or purchasing them from stores after they were released.

Members of record pools had to be working disco deejays in order for them to receive product. Potential members would be screened and their employment status would be periodically checked to make sure they were actually employed in that capacity. With the exposure in clubs and the potential increased record sales from patrons who purchased the records they danced to, artists indirectly benefited also as they stood to make more royalties. Moreover, it might be said that discotheque patrons benefited also by being exposed to dance tracks that might have otherwise escaped notice by the deejays and disco operators.

The record pool was actually more than just a record exchange service between labels and deejays and disco operators. They provided numerous other services for their members including supplying information about employment opportunities, demonstrating new skills to members, making artists available for autograph signing parties and guest appearances at discos (which would be used to promote new releases or tours), compiling charts of the most successful disco tracks in their area based on member feedback and furnishing them to radio stations and trade publications, providing information to discotheque operators on lighting and sound equipment, and printing newsletters that were distributed to members, labels, and record promoters.

Clubs like Copacabana and Studio 54 in New York City became famous in the disco era and attracted celebrities. But like many genres of popular music, disco's popularity eventually began to wane, although it set the pace for other new dance forms to come. Disco came in as the women's rights and gay rights movements were emerging on the national stage and psychedelic and other forms of rock were permeating pop music. With its sensuality and a dance form in which dancers let loose on the dance floor, disco was a welcome style of expression for the anxieties of the time. But one thing about the music business is that it is dynamic, and new genres come and go. Around the end of the 1970s, as the country moved out of the decade—the anti-war movement was over because there was no more war, women and gays had made their voices known, and hippies were relics of the past—the disco strobe lights began to fade as new pop music took its place in the public spotlight. Disco may have been a small revolution in the music business, but it wasn't the only one.

The phonograph player was the first means by which people could hear recorded music, and it was a durable mechanism whose popularity continued on and on. Then tape recorders and cassette players and eight-track players came along, which offered an alternative to record players. But none of them were portable in that they could be easily carried and music played as a person moved around. Not until, that is, Sony, in 1979, came out with the Walkman, a portable cassette player with headphones that people could use as they walked, jogged, or sat in a car or train or anywhere else. The Walkman caught on as a new form of hardware that could play pre-recorded music and enjoyed popularity for many years. Sony's iPod, a portable digital music player that was introduced to the commercial marketplace in 2001, offered another means by which to access desired songs and also enjoyed immense popularity for several years. Electronics manufacturers are always looking for new machines that can deliver music to consumers in unique and expeditious ways, and these machines are good for the music business in that they promote the sale or playing of music, which results in increased revenue for rights owners, artists, producers, and writers.

In 1982, just a few years after the Walkman debuted, compact discs (CDs) were introduced to the commercial marketplace. This new relatively small object, thin and about 4.7 inches in diameter, contained recorded music that had many advantages over the LP. With a push of a button users could go to any track on an album, whereas with a phonograph record a needle had to be lifted and placed down on a desired track, or, with a cassette player, the inserted tape had to be fast-forwarded or rewound to go to a desired track. CDs were generally more lightweight and portable than LPs or 45s, and could be played on home players, portable players, and car stereos. This new medium to carry recorded music would catch the fancy of many consumers and become the prevalent way in which people played music—for a while at least.

Songs are by their basic nature an auditory medium. They are sung and meant to be heard. But songs also tell stories or convey messages, so they paint pictures in listeners' minds and may also be deemed an audiovisual medium. Hence, the presentation of songs in audiovisual form has been a longtime dream of music visionaries. This dream was realized in the modern pop music era with the debut of a new television channel.

In June of 1981, *Raiders of the Lost Ark*, which would become one of the most popular movies of all time, was released. The next month, Prince Charles married Lady Diana Spencer at St. Paul's Cathedral in London. And in the following month another milestone cultural event took place. On August 1, 1981, MTV debuted, signaling a new era for the broadcasting and music industries, as it was a channel dedicated to airing programming true to its name—music television, or rather, music videos. At 12:01 a.m. the channel made its way into people's homes, and the first music video aired was of the English group the Buggles' "Video Killed the Radio Star." The video was essentially a concert presentation of the song being sung and lacked the imagination of future song videos.

The launch of MTV indeed brought in a new form of entertainment for the music business. People could now not just hear music but also see songs visually presented wherein the lyrics and emotions of songs could be acted out by the artist and others or portrayed in other ways. This new form of song presentation promised to enhance the enjoyment of songs and enable viewers to see performers' artistic visions for their songs. Songs tell stories, convey messages, and paint pictures in words, so it seems that videos were a natural way to present songs, and they veritably elevated the art of song presentation. Although songs are primarily a musical, or auditory, art form, they lend themselves to being presented visually also, and music videos are an excellent technology to deliver songs visually.

But actually, the idea of songs being presented visually was not new with the advent of MTV. Like many modern innovations, there are historical antecedents. The music video has its roots in the illuminated song slides of the late nineteenth century in what was the early days of Tin Pan Alley. Song slides were a forerunner to the later music video in which colored slides depicting different lines or elements of the story of a song were shone on screens, while a recording of the song played or a singer with musical accompaniment would lead the audience in a hearty sing-along of the song.

According to the Tin Pan Alley publisher Isadore Witmark, the idea for song slides came from George H. Thomas, who was the head electrician at the Amphion Theatre on Bedford Avenue in Brooklyn. Thomas conceived the idea in the 1890s when *The Old Homestead*, a play about a small-town farmer whose son left for New York, was running at the Amphion.

The play started out as a twenty-five-minute skit called *Joshua Whitcomb* by Henry Denman Thompson, a stage actor who was descended from an American colonist. Thompson expanded the sketch into a three-act play, and then, with George Ryer, extended it yet again to include another act. The four-act play opened in Boston in 1886 with Thompson starring in it, and its success made him a wealthy man. The play toured, and Thompson went on the road to continue starring in it.

In these days when songs in productions were interpolated into plays for effect but not necessarily to advance the plot was the Reverend Robert Lowry's 1877 song "Where Is My Wand'ring Boy Tonight?" a weepy number about a father at an alehouse who pines for his missing son, "The boy of my tend'rest care/The boy who was once my joy and light/The child of my love and pray'r." On stage, as the song was being sung, was a single roughly drawn song slide, and Thomas wondered why an entire song couldn't be similarly illustrated and successfully sought permission from the publisher of another tune, "The Little Lost Child" (lyrics by Edward B. Marks and music by Joseph W. Stern), and thus was born the song slide.

The song lent itself naturally to being illustrated. It was about a young girl who walks past a policeman and dries her tears and smiles.

The policeman tells her not to cry, for he will find her mama. He brings her to the stationhouse and asks for her name, and when she answers "Jennie," he exclaims, "At last of your mother I now have a trace/Your little features bring back her sweet face." In the song's chorus the policeman tells Jennie not to fear, "For you were a babe in arms when your mother left me one day/Left me at home, deserted, alone, and took you, my child away." It turns out the married couple had a quarrel and the wife left him. Then "suddenly the door of the station opened wide/'Have you seen my darling?' an anxious mother cried/Husband and wife then meeting face to face/All is soon forgiven in one fond embrace/Do not fear my little darling, and we will take you right home."

According to Witmark, after that time, the concept of illustrating songs in slides caught on and became a popular practice, with most of the illustrated songs being crying songs. Illustrated songs, featuring models who had posed, were commonly performed by singing acts, with someone running a projector. About fifty slide sets would be made for a song, with more if it proved especially popular. Special companies were hired by publishers to produce these slides, which they sent out around the country.

In the early twentieth century, the public craved amusement, and the relatively new motion picture, which the renowned inventor Thomas Alva Edison with his kinetoscope introduced to the public in 1894, filled the bill. At first, motion pictures were basically of people acting out in ways of ordinary life, then during the Spanish-American War films were made of soldiers in action (although so insatiable was the public appetite for this that filmmakers made fake footage that they tried to pawn off as real), and then came the story film. When these silent movies were exhibited in nickelodeons, usually converted theaters or auditoriums, in the early twentieth century, Tin Pan Alley publishers, always looking to stimulate sales of their sheet music, weren't far behind in promoting their latest releases in colored-glass song slides before or after the presentations of the movies. As the slides were projected onto a screen, a professional pianist would lead the audiences in singing the song, and the idea was for the song to stick in people's heads so they go buy the sheet music.

A Sears ad that ran around 1902 for the equipment to display this new form of song exploitation read as follows:

Our Great Illustrated Grapho Combined Outfit: Pictures in songs and songs in pictures for rendering and illustrating popular songs of the day. At the present time illustrated songs are the most popular means of entertaining the public and have been immensely successful in the various theaters in all the larger cities. The dramatic effect produced by illustrating the song in this manner is very marked and all audiences become greatly enthused over the vivid combination of the two. The views consist of pictures representing the most important incidents related in the song and are projected by the stereopticon. They are all hand painted and in each instance taken from life models, and when shown with the stereopticon, enlarged to life size, are exceedingly realistic.

The graphophone grand furnishes the music, delighting the ear, and the pictures are vividly projected onto the screen in view of the audience at the same time; while the comparative cheapest of this, the newest type of Grand machine, combined with its unapproachable musical excellence, enable us to place the outfit within the reach of our customers at a price hitherto unheard of. (Our Great, 1998)

By 1908, so great was the public demand for movies that thousands of nickelodeons were in operation across America, and each year the output of movies increased. Nickelodeons would be open from morning till night, and when motion pictures weren't playing, the public was being entertained with song slides. As the illuminated slides were flashed on a screen, a recording of the song would be played, or a singer, usually to the accompaniment of a piano, would lead the audience in singing some new Tin Pan Alley song. Patrons would heartily be led in singing the chorus, or catchy part of the song, over and over, in the song pluggers' hope that cash registers would soon ring up sheet music sales of the song to which the audience was just introduced.

One of the most successful examples of a song promoted via colored-glass slides was "Take Me out to the Ball Game," written by Jack Norworth and Albert Von Tilzer. Models were hired to portray the characters of the song and were posed in a ball field as an artist painted glass slides. The set of illuminated slides told the song's story: baseball fan Katie Casey was asked by her young beau on a Saturday if she'd like to go to a show, and she said no and told him what he could do. Then the song launches into the chorus with its title leading it off. The song swept the country with vaudeville singers performing it in small towns and large cities alike, and surely its illuminated song slides played a part in its great success. In fact, lyricist Norworth planned to sing it one night at a vaudeville theater, but so many other singers on the bill had already sang it that he had to drop it from his act that night.

Song slide popularity faded when radio and sound motion pictures came out but continued into the 1930s with organists at theaters playing, but not with pictures displayed on a screen but with the words to the songs. Still, in the 1920s and 1930s songs were sung on screen in a storytelling way—a good example of this is the Boswell Sisters singing "Rock and Roll" (referring to the effect of ocean currents on a small boat and not the future genre of music) in the 1934 motion picture *Transatlantic-Merry-Go-Round*—and some cartoons revolved around old Tin Pan Alley songs or classical pieces. But as movies headed deeper into their so-called "golden age" and captured the public's attention with their emotional content and escapes from everyday life—the Depression wasn't far behind—the public was not so much interested anymore in the old sing-alongs. Then Top 40 radio came along with high-energy danceable rock and roll exploding on the scene, and the public was more interested in hearing the latest releases broadcast over the air than singing sing-along songs in theaters.

But with the debut of MTV, audiovisual song presentations were to take a different form. The three-minute art form of pop songs would be translated into a three-minute audiovisual art form, with music videos increasing in artistry over time, not to mention portraying songs in salacious ways that reflected both their content and contemporary culture. Whereas song slides left stories to the imagination, music videos could use editing, animation, and special effects and all the other tricks of motion pictures to portray the content and vision of songs. One of the most classic examples is Michael Jackson's fourteen-minute horror lampoon, *Thriller*, which, more like a movie short, helped propel, along with other song videos from Jackson's album of the same name, the album into the second best-selling album of all time. (It was the best-selling album until 2018 when it was reportedly surpassed in sales and streams by a greatest hits album of the Eagles).

With a limited number of television sets broadcasting it when it was launched, MTV started out with a relatively small audience, but over time it was offered by more cable services, and its reach grew and the twenty-four-hours-a-day, seven-days-a-week channel had VJs, or video jockeys, host its shows, which sometimes played the same videos on high rotation. Then MTV aired different shows that featured different genres of music, and these also proved popular. But as audiences decreased, MTV began broadcasting other fare such as trivia shows and news programs, and then in 1992, it aired its first unscripted reality series, *The Real World*, and then the channel eventually focused on programming reality shows.

Music videos not only were a promotional tool for labels to get exposure for their product and sell records but also were a form of demo for unsigned artists to get record deals. Some artists would present themselves to labels with music videos to show their appeal and the potential of their songs in this form. The problem with making music videos for unsigned groups, however, was that they were expensive to make, and many could not afford to make them. Labels do provide funding for making music videos for signed groups, however, but that money is usually recouped from future royalties.

For new and upcoming artists, the Internet offers an opportunity to have them and their music exposed like nothing before. Getting a label deal has always been difficult, and those who were not able to either saw their careers ended in frustration or they ended up carving out a living playing bars or other small venues and selling their own recordings. With websites like YouTube, artists can now post videos of their music and promote themselves with or without a label deal, although with the many music videos posted, it is difficult for unknown acts to attract attention. But nevertheless there have been a number of artists who were discovered or broke through on the Internet with their music videos—Justin Bieber is a famous example—who may not otherwise have been discovered.

8

THE BOOM OF STREAMING

There's a remarkable Columbia Records publicity photo taken in 1948 of Dr. Peter C. Goldmark holding in his outstretched hands a small stack of LPs and standing next to the equivalent amount of shellac 78s that are piled neatly on the floor next to him and that rise way above his head and almost to the ceiling high above. The photo dramatizes the space-saving superiority of the new narrow-grooved 33 1/3 rpm long-playing record (LP) developed by a team of engineers led by Goldmark and William Bachman at CBS Laboratories over the previous heavy and brittle 78 rpm shellac discs, which generally embodied only one or two songs on a side. Lighter, thinner, and more durable, and able to contain many more selections than the turn-of-the-century-era 78, the LP promised to be a significant change in how people collected, played, and stored records.

Who would have ever dreamed at the time that one day—and not all that long after the introduction of the LP—that consumers would be able to hold in the palm of their hand a featherweight device that could give instant access to virtually *all* of recorded music?

What a difference technological progress makes! If the LP was considered a significant change for the record industry, digital audio files were certainly a seismic change.

The conversion of analog music into MP3 files and the distribution of these files to the public via streaming started to become widespread around the mid-1990s. Of course, companies and talent in the music business are always looking to monetize new ways music is used, conveyed, or distributed to the public, but the debut of this new technology was for the music industry rather inauspicious. The problem was one that in essence had plagued the music industry almost since its very beginning—unscrupulous or oblivious people, otherwise known as pirates, who seek to bring music to the public illegally and deprive the talent, owners, and purveyors behind it of their legal right to earn revenues from the music they wrote, recorded, own, or distribute.

Peer-to-peer file sharing was the bane of the music industry soon after the Internet became mainstream. Napster, Kazaa, Grokster, Morpheus, Pirate Bay, Aimster, iMesh, Mininova, and LimeWire were some of the P2P services that enabled members of a peer-to-peer network community access to the files on the hard drives of other members of the community. A person just needed to download a software program that other members of the community had, and he or she could then search the files of other members and download their files as well as have his or her files searched and shared by the community. Using these file-sharing sites, people in the networks shared music for free, and the sites were sued by record companies and music publishers for infringement of their sound recording and song copyrights. Illegal downloading was rampant, with new models constantly developing, and its financial effect on the industry was devastating. With the widespread P2P illegal file-sharing, some people even sounded the death knell for the recording industry.

The Recording Industry Association of America, the trade organization for record labels, vigorously went after peer-to-peer file sharing services and individual infringers, even if it meant bad publicity in that children, college students, and grandmothers could be among the alleged infringers and be pushed into litigation—the fine under the copyright law for willfully committing copyright infringement may result in damages of up to $150,000 per illegally downloaded track. Bad publicity indeed resulted in a public backlash against the RIAA (its campaign of litigation resulted in over 30,000 lawsuits), and although its aggressive litigation campaign didn't stop illegal file sharing, it was the position of the organization that it had launched a successful public relations operation that both scared and educated people about the ramifications of illegal downloading. One of the unpleasant side effects of it all, however, was that some larger labels, hurt financially by the calamitous effects of file sharing, imposed on their artists 360 deals, which essentially meant that in signing a 360 deal with a label, an artist basically agreed to share all or part of his or her entertainment revenues such as concert box office receipts, merchandising, music publishing, videos, games, books, and other products and services as long as he or she was contractually bound to the company.

Products of the digital technological revolution, online stores and streaming services on the Internet soon became popular means by which people obtained the music they wanted to hear. New models for making money were constantly coming up as entrepreneurs were constantly reinventing these digital stores and services (which still holds true today), but eventually various models for getting music to the public became prevalent: download sales and ad-supported content (which feature ads in addition to music and can be interactive or non-interactive) and the premium or subscription model (ad-free and interactive), for streaming sites.

In the beginning, download sales were the most profitable, as digital stores like Apple's iTunes offered millions of songs (some priced at $0.69, $0.99, and $1.29) and other services such as customized recommendations. Subscriptions were initially the least profitable for streaming services, as it appeared that people did not want to pay for music. So much content was available on the Internet for free that people resisted paying for music content; plus with radio having been a free entertainment medium since its beginning that many people were weaned on, their thinking was, *Why pay for music when I can get it for free?* But eventually, as streaming services expanded their catalogs offering millions of songs and added many features like curated playlists that enabled people to discover new music to their liking, many people came to embrace the subscription model, and the streaming services subsequently enjoyed growth with both nonpaying (freemium) users and paying (premium) subscribers. The major streaming services claim to offer users tens of millions of songs each.

Streaming services are a curious hybrid in the music industry. They offer to the public music content that plays continuously for free in real time, so in one sense they are like radio. They offer music content with other special benefits that can be paid for on a subscription basis, so they are in another sense like membership clubs. They also offer original content of artists and songs (at least for limited time periods); plus, some streaming services enable unsigned artists to upload their recordings, so in yet another sense they are like record labels and music publishers. But most of all, even with all their multiple hybrid forms, they are a completely new form of delivery of music to the public, a true newfangled modern mechanism of the digital era. Streaming services indeed are the first new major entertainment medium to come along since the advent of radio and television. They have been so massively embraced by the public—they offer songs that cannot be usually heard on terrestrial radio, users can create their own playlists, they offer many special features such as song lyrics, artist bios, and shuffle options, and they are an alternative to people who tire of hearing the same top-of-the-charts pop songs repeatedly on radio—that they have surpassed all other areas to become the number 1 source of revenue for the music business.

As consumers flocked to streaming and got their music for free or for nominal subscription prices, their new way of accessing music couldn't help but have a detrimental effect on other (traditional) areas of the music business. Consumers were less interested in purchasing CDs, so this naturally affected segments of the business involved in the sale of physical product. Consequently, as music streaming took off, the music business saw the demise of distributors, wholesalers, and brick-and-mortar chains as well as independent music stores. Handleman, Wal-Mart's rack jobber, got out of the music business due to declining sales by selling off its assets to Anderson Merchandisers (the rack jobber for such other outlets as Best Buy and Sam's Club); Alliance Entertainment, a major wholesale distributor of CDs and DVDs, was acquired by Super D; Sam Goody, Tower Records, Camelot Music, and Hastings Entertainment were some major CD/record retail chains that closed. Download sales, a big booster in the early digital era, have suffered, knocking out even the Internet's largest digital store, iTunes. Radio stations also have seen their audiences decline, and some industry pundits have even predicted the end of radio. Music streaming services as a major destination of choice for music listeners have indeed taken a toll on various traditional areas of the music business.

As bulk purveyors of music, streaming services offer vast amounts of tracks and thus need licenses from labels and music publishers to legally offer copyrighted music. There are two types of copyrights involved, and so they need licenses from two types of entities (or their agents). The two types of copyrights are the sound recording copyright (for the artist's recording of the song) and the song copyright (for the music and lyrics, if any). The former copyright is fairly modern, having first been provided for in the United States with the Sound Recording Amendment of 1971, effective February 15, 1972; the latter copyright came on February 3, 1831, in the first general revision of the U.S. copyright law, which protected musical works for the first time.

The sound recording copyright is usually obtained from the record label, and the song copyright is usually obtained from the music publisher, the owners, in each case respectively, of the underlying copyrights. Labels and artists earn royalties for the streaming of sound recordings, and music publishers and songwriters earn royalties for the streaming of songs (among other royalties, of course). Labels and artists do not earn performance royalties for broadcasts of their sound recordings on terrestrial radio, however. The reason for this is because Section 106(4) of the U.S. copyright law provides that the owners of certain types of copyrighted works have an exclusive right to perform their work publicly, but the category of sound recordings is not included here. Sound recordings are, however, covered in Section 106(6), which provides that the owner of copyright in a sound recording has the exclusive right to perform the sound recording publicly by means of a digital audio transmission—in other words, a streaming service legally needs a license from the owner of a sound recording to include it on its service.

Over the years as sheet music sales dwindled and music publishers found their major sources of income to be from licensing songs for reproduction on records and for performances on radio, the publishers, as owners of songs, essentially functioned as exploiters and licensors of songs rather than actual physical publishers. Likewise, as physical sales of CDs and vinyl have decreased, labels have increasingly become licensors of recorded tracks rather than manufacturers of physical product. Indeed, the streaming of music has increasingly relegated music publishers and record labels to be licensors of content, as streaming has become a major source of income for these companies. Music publishers and labels supply and license songs and recordings, respectively, for use by streaming services, and may get an advance for such licensing. Streaming results in royalties for these companies, and the royalty rates and methods of payouts may vary depending on whether the streams are non-interactive or interactive, and also according to the income and policies of the individual companies.

Streaming services are relatively new businesses that sprung into existence with technological advances and are profit-oriented businesses that license and deliver music to the public. The streaming business involves many parties and entities within the music industry. For the content there are artists and labels (for the sound recordings); songwriters and music publishers (for the songs); licensing organizations for the sound recordings (SoundExchange) and for the songs (ASCAP, BMI, SESAC, Global Music Rights). The background musicians and singers earn royalties based on agreements their unions have with the recording industry. Of course, there are the long-standing professionals around these parties such as personal managers and booking agents for artists, and trade associations for labels and music publishers. And then there are advertisers whose messages appear on streaming services. Streaming services are always tweaking their offerings, and of course, the goal of streaming services is to get as many paying subscribers as they can. This is advantageous to all the content contributors (labels, artists, music publishers, songwriters), as more subscribers mean more streams and consequently more revenues, and indeed, as the streaming platforms become more profitable, that could result in higher royalty rates.

There are non-interactive and interactive music streaming services. Non-interactive streaming is basically Internet (or webcast) radio where the user listens to selections without choosing them. In interactive (or on-demand) streaming, the user chooses what songs to play. A stream is deemed a performance of music, so like any performance of music except those allowed without permission from the owner as prescribed by the copyright law, a streaming service would need permission (a license) from the copyright owners of the sound recording and song to legally offer it, and consequently would pay performance royalties for streams. For interactive steams, where the user makes a selection, music publishers and songwriters collect a digital mechanical royalty in addition to a digital performance royalty.

The major streaming services have huge catalogs of songs (Spotify offers over 35 million songs, and Apple Music offers 45 million songs as of 2019) covering virtually every genre and subgenre of music and spanhing almost all time periods of recorded music. While each also offers other features to differentiate themselves from other services and attract users, their basic plans are similar. Streaming services typically offer a freemium model by which users can access music for free, but it comes with ads. There is also a subscription model where for a fee, such as $10 a month, users can get all the music the service offers without any ads, plus other features of the service; family plans (usually for up to six members) may run about $15 per month. Many users start off with the freemium model, and the streaming services try to convert them into being paid subscribers.

Despite streaming services typically having millions of monthly subscribers, it has generally become a struggle for them to become profitable. There are various reasons for this, including, most importantly, the high costs of licensing fees payable to labels, artists, music publishers, and songwriters. The sources of income for streaming services are essentially from subscription fees and ads. Because some streaming services are owned by companies with other, more profitable businesses, the parent companies can keep the streaming services going. Apple Music, for example, is owned by Apple Inc., which makes computers, iPhones, iPads, and Apple televisions and watches, among other products, and being able to offer music streaming with hardware products enables the company to cross-promote its products. Amazon Prime Music's parent company, Amazon, is involved in all types of Internet commerce and is one of the world's largest companies. The company's paid subscription service, Amazon Prime, offers eligible Prime members ad-free access to a large catalog of songs, personalized stations, and curated playlists (for a small monthly fee, they can access the full library).

In addition to the millions of songs they may offer, streaming services offer other features such as podcasts, curated playlists, personalized playlists, unlimited skips, voice recognition to facilitate searches of individual songs or playlists, biographies of artists, exclusive interviews with music stars, and content not found on other streaming services. Depending on the service, there may be other special features.

Since the inception of streaming, various services have gone out of business. Among the streaming services that have ceased operations are Guvera, Rdio (its intellectual property was sold to Pandora), Groove Music, iHeart Radio (an online radio station), and MOG (which was acquired and later closed by Beats Electronics, which itself was subsequently purchased by Apple). As of 2019, current international streaming services include Pandora, Spotify, Tidal, Google Play Music, Amazon Music Unlimited, Deezer, Apple Music, Napster, YouTube Music, SoundCloud, and Slacker Radio (which operates in the United States and Canada).

Pandora, an ad-supported service that was founded in 2000, is an example of a non-interactive streaming service. Users can choose stations from several different areas such as African, alternative, blues, chill, Christian and gospel, classical, country, dance/electronic, decades, dinner party, indie, instrumentals, jazz, K-pop, love songs, new music, pop, summer, today's music, women in music, workout, and world; users can also create their own customized radio stations according to their personal tastes. Song lyrics and artist biographies also appear on the site. As of 2018 Pandora offered three ways to listen to music on its service: free ad-supported radio ("Pandora free"); ad-free personalized radio with features such as unlimited personalized stations and unlimited skips and replays for $4.99 per month ("Pandora Plus"); and "personalized radio meets on-demand listening" in which subscribers can, without ads, search for and play songs they want to hear, create their own playlists, download songs to listen offline, and have unlimited skips and replays for $9.99 per month ("Pandora Premium"). Pandora started the personalized radio station, in which a user types in a box the name of a song, artist, or music genre, and a playlist of music comes built around that selection. For the year ending 2017, Pandora had about 75 million active users a month.

SoundExchange grants digital sound recording performance licenses to non-interactive streaming services, that is, online radio services like Pandora, as well as to satellite radio services like SiriusXM, and cable television, and distributes the collected license fees as royalties to artists and master-rights owners. SoundExchange entered the licensing arena for music publishing when it purchased the Canadian Musical Reproduction Rights Agency, a Canadian mechanical rights organization that represents Canadian music publishers for the licensing of their mechanical rights, in 2017.

YouTube has been harshly criticized in the music world for paying low royalties to artists and labels, and songwriters and music publishers. Many prominent people in the music industry spoke out against the streaming site including top-selling artists and heavyweights behind the scenes. The public seems to love YouTube, however, with its massive offering of music (and other types of) videos, with a billion-plus users that show the public embracing of it.

In December 2016 YouTube announced it had come to an agreement with the National Music Publishers' Association, a trade group that represents the owners of song copyrights, over royalties for songs on its service that were unpaid. YouTube claimed it could not locate owners of songs that were streamed or that the proprietary information it had was incorrect. The settlement provided an opt-in period for publishers to opt in to the agreement, after which YouTube would furnish to participating music publishers a list of songs for which it couldn't locate correct ownership information so participating publishers could claim ownership in and collect accrued royalties. Unclaimed accrued royalties would be distributed to publishers based on market share and royalties received for known usage on the site, and the rights of any music publisher or songwriter who chose not to opt in would not be affected by the agreement.

Streaming royalties are among many that a song may earn. Song royalties include a performance royalty for the public performance of a song on radio, television, concert halls, bars, and other venues in which the licensor (or music user) takes out a performance license (usually from the performing rights organization representing the songwriter and publisher and pays a fee for the license, which is later distributed to writers and publishers whose songs are performed by their PRO). A mechanical royalty for the sale of a recording (physical or digital) embodying a song that is paid by the label issuing the recording; print music royalty for the sale of printed editions of music compositions such as sheet music and songbooks, and band, orchestral, and choral arrangements of music compositions, which is usually paid by the print licensee (the printer/distributor of the print edition such as Hal Leonard Corporation), unless the music publisher itself prints and distributes its music; digital song performance royalty, which is paid for the streaming of a song by a streaming service (such as Spotify, Pandora, or Apple Music), usually to the writer's and publisher's PRO, which later distributes the fees paid by the streaming services to the writers and publishers of the streamed songs; digital mechanical royalty for an on-demand or interactive stream of a song; miscellaneous royalties for sale or product using the song in some way (such as posters with lyrics) or based on the song (such as a game). Among the sound recording royalties are a digital sound recording performance royalty for the stream of a sound recording paid to the label or other sound recording rights owner (which may be represented by a rights management organization such as SoundExchange, which collects royalties for non-interactive, or webcast radio, streams) and the artist; and a master recording royalty paid to the label, which in turn gives a portion to the artist for the sale of a recording such as a compilation album containing a licensed track. There are also synchronization licensing fees paid to songwriters and music publishers, and to labels and artists, when their song or sound recording, respectively, are used in conjunction with audiovisual content such as a motion picture, television show, television advertisement, or music video.

Artists and labels of course want to maximize their music business income, and to that end wish to have as many as possible interactive and non-interactive streams, paid downloads, and physical retail sales, as well as heavy radio airplay, all of which can contribute to their earnings. Radio airplay can promote album and singles sales, and if the artist is the writer or publisher of a song being aired, that can lead to performance royalties for that artist (or whomever the writer and publisher are). A mechanical royalty is paid for physical and digital sales of recordings embodying a song.

Back in the heyday of the Top 40 format, radio stations had playlists of the hits of the week. Listeners loved tuning into their favorite stations to hear the current hits and upcoming ones also. Top 40 was a prevalent format of radio for decades but waned with the proliferation of formats since that time and then later with the popularity of streaming, which caused a decline in radio listening. Streaming platforms, themselves, came to develop playlists, and these have proved to be massively popular with streaming service users. Like radio has programmers who determine which songs get onto their playlists (though the playlists are based on sales and other factors), streaming services have professional curators who create playlists and determine what songs get onto them. Data is used to determine which songs should be added onto a playlist as well as personal taste (or gut feelings). A new or unknown song that makes it onto a playlist of a major streaming platform can be catapulted into a hit. It's a difficult job to determine what gets on considering how many new songs playlist editors are sent on a daily basis. Given the fact of tight radio station playlists with mostly established artists getting slots on the playlists, it is difficult for unknown artists to get radio play. With streaming services, unknown artists can be heard, and if they get onto one or more playlists, they can receive attention that otherwise might have been difficult for them to receive. As *Digital Music News* reported in June 2018, Spotify's Today's Top Hits playlist has over 20 million followers, and songs on the playlist average about seventy-five days on it. Other Spotify playlists include Rap Caviar, Weekly Buzz, Discover Weekly, and Daily Mix. A song can get bounced onto other playlists that have more followers as it shows itself to be popular among the streaming service's users. For instance, a song that makes it onto the Today's Top Hits playlist has already virtually proven itself to be a bona fide people-pleaser (it can receive millions of streams on a daily basis), even if its popularity is limited to the streaming platform's users. Once a song is on a playlist, company workers track its performance with analytics, which provide various sorts of information about the song such as how often it is streamed, if it is skipped over or listened to in whole, or if it has been added to a playlist of a user. Streaming platform users can create their own playlists or use those developed by other listeners in addition to those of the curators. Apple Music has thousands of playlists. Amazon has voice-assisted devices (Alexa) that let listeners request tracks. It has been the practice of some artists to not release their music to streaming services right away; they hold it back to reap actual physical and digital sales (which yield much higher artist royalties) before they let it go on streaming services.

It is not unusual for a top ten record on the *Billboard* Hot 100 chart to amass tens of millions of streams. But despite the mass popularity of streaming, not all artists rush to put their music on online streaming sites. For many years the Beatles, one of the last major pop music-group holdouts, kept their music off streaming services, and it wasn't until December 24, 2015, at 12:01 a.m. local time anywhere that the group finally made its music available for global streaming on nine major services—Google Play, Amazon Prime Music, Tidal, Apple Music, Napster/Rhapsody, Microsoft Groove, Deezer, Slacker Radio, and Spotify. The group made known the announcement in the form of a thirty-five-second video that contained snippets of some of its most famous songs—"She Loves You," "A Hard Day's Night," "Help!" "Taxman," "Hey Jude," (the "nah nah nah nah" part), and "Let It Be." It wasn't until November 16, 2010, that the Beatles permitted iTunes to make available the band's catalog for download sales. According to *Billboard*, in the first week, 2 million individual Beatles songs were sold and 450,000 albums were sold.

Disputes over licensing and royalty payments have been common in the streaming world. Streaming embraces a complex system in which rights have to be obtained for both the sound recording and the song copyrights. Streaming services make available tens of millions of songs, and rights have to be cleared for the recordings' two copyrights. Licensing organizations represent the majority of copyright owners, but for those that aren't, that presents obstacles.

In early 2016 it was announced that Spotify settled a copyright infringement suit with the National Music Publishers Association. The suit stemmed over allegations that Spotify did not acquire mechanical rights for songs streamed on-demand. It was Spotify's contention that because there did not exist a central database for song rights, it could not find the copyright owners or determine which owners' claims were legitimate. It was reported that over $30 million was paid by Spotify to settle the dispute with remedies for music publishers to register claims on an online site and, if found to be legitimate, to be paid royalties owed to them. The Music Modernization Act, which was signed into law on October 11, 2018, aimed to address rights administration and royalty payments through the creation of a database of rights owners.

Streaming services not only have changed the music business but also may be regarded as one of its major boosters, if not saviors, in its history. The repeal of Prohibition on December 5, 1933, which sparked the opening of bars with jukeboxes and spurred the sales of records in the moribund industry, was an early instance. With the rampant piracy of the 1960s hurting legitimate sales of records, the Sound Recording Amendment of 1971 established a federal copyright for sound recordings and subsequently enabled labels and other owners of copyrighted sound recordings to sue pirates in federal court for copyright infringement and help stem the flow of illegitimate product, thus saving the industry from the deleterious economic effects of piracy. And streaming services have been heralded as saving the recording industry in the wake of the financially draining illegal peer-to-peer file sharing. They have infused record labels with substantial income, although the royalties they pay out are notoriously low. Still, with physical and digital sales having subsided substantially, streaming services, as the top choice of

music delivery for the general public, represent a vital source of revenue for labels and artists, and music publishers and songwriters.

9

THE RISE OF HIP HOP AND RAP

As the 1970s came to a close, disco, the breakout new music genre of the decade, was fading from mainstream popularity. End-of-the-decade hits such as Barbra Streisand and Donna Summer's "No More Tears (Enough Is Enough)" and Donna Summer's "Dim All the Lights" and "On the Radio" kept disco on mainstream singles life support, but for the most part this trendy form of dance music was on the way out, with its sales declining and interest in it diminishing. But as disco was gasping its last breaths, another music genre, hip hop, emerged onto the national and international scenes with the Sugarhill Gang's "Rapper's Delight," a catchy, rhythmic number essentially about dancing "to the rhythm of the boogie" in clean, innocuous language that created a sensation for hip hop (it perched at number 36 on the *Billboard* Top 100 and became a top ten hit on the UK singles chart). Although hip hop was the new kid on the block, so to speak, its success was marginal at first, and it would probably have been hard to believe at the time that it would one day push aside rock, R&B, country, and every other genre of pop music to dominate the charts and also to permeate society with its own inimitable brand of culture. It would take some time for hip hop to diffuse into the mainstream, and indeed, many of its future stars weren't even born yet!

Hip hop would follow many other genres of popular music to capture the public's fancy. In the early 1900s sentimental pop tunes and ragtime were the rage; jazz started to take off then, too, and Dixieland swelled, as popular songs and two-steps widely appealed to people in

the 1910s. The Roaring Twenties saw jazz-pop tunes become successful, even if some of them were launched in speakeasies. There was
swing music of the 1930s and 1940s with its bands of acoustic wind and
percussion instruments followed by rock and roll and its electrified
guitars and keyboards taking off in the 1950s, which in turn was followed by various scions of that genre. At the same time certain genres
such as rhythm and blues, country and western, and Latin were gaining
popularity outside of their respective markets and melding themselves
into the mainstream pop market. Disco's decade was the 1970s followed by not just pop fare but grunge and other assortments of hard
and alternative forms of rock. Pop music was evolving, as it is always
looking for new sounds and styles, wishing to break free from its con-
straints of the past and imbue itself with new energy and with novel
forms, trying to mold public taste to like it even if it was radically
different from what came before. And as the music changes, so too, do
certain aspects of the music business associated with it. By 2017, hip
hop became the best-selling genre of all popular music.

Hip hop is popularly said to have been born in the borough of New
York City known as the Bronx. Clive Campbell is credited with birthing
the genre on August 11, 1973, when he served as a DJ at a party jam his
sister sponsored celebrating the upcoming school year in a recreation
room at 1520 Sedgwick Avenue. Using two separate turntables to play
the same records, Campbell helped pioneer and popularize a technique
to keep the rhythmic beat going by moving back and forth between
records during the instrumental breaks during which dancers would do
acrobatic performances known as breakdancing. Campbell, known as
DJ Kool Herc, was eighteen years old at the time and born to parents
from Jamaica, and from his dexterous deejaying antics he ushered in a
revolution in music, even if unbeknownst at the time. The burgeoning
hip hop movement was aided by others at the time including such
pioneers as Lance Taylor, known as Afrika Bambaataa and Joseph Sadler, who used the moniker Grandmaster Flash.

Rapping, a rapid-talk style of performance that can be performed on
its own or as a component of hip hop, actually wasn't new in the 1970s,
as antecedents of this form of song-lyric delivery go back far, not only in
the lineage of popular music but also to related forms of message delivery such as street cries of the eighteenth and nineteenth centuries when
vendors would chant advertisements for their wares on public roads.

We could summon up the rapid-fire talk-sing delivery (with witty rhymes) of "I Am the Very Model of Modern Major-General" from the Gilbert and Sullivan 1879 operetta *The Pirates of Penzance*. Patter songs in musicals are not uncommon, and, in fact, have been quite popular with audiences (such as "Rock Island" from Meredith Wilson's 1957 Broadway Tony Award-winning show *The Music Man*). Rhythmic speaking in song can be found in the rock and roll and Tin Pan Alley eras, and a case may be made that it evolved from monologue recitation in song. Tin Pan Alley singer Sophie Tucker employed rhythmic speaking in her recording of the African American composer Shelton Brooks's "Some of These Days" and also her proto-feminist humor song "I Don't Want to Get Thin." A very close precursor to rap is Pigmeat Markham's 1968 Chess Records novelty recording of "Here Comes the Judge," in which his rhythmic vocal delivery is virtually undistinguishable from rap that people came to know later. But rapping, of course, is more than just rhythmic speaking, and these songs from previous musical eras generally didn't address the serious issues of poverty, racism, and life in the ghetto, among others, that can be found in hip hop.

Hip hop is essentially social conscious poetry set to music, its lyrics expressed verbally with a lilt or in interpretive cadences or intonations, with rhythmic phrasing, and with beats and sounds and melodies expressively played over, around, and between them. Rapping is the basic constituent of hip hop, and the genre is a blend of intoxicating speak-sing, rhythms, and a background of infectious music. Hip hop, with its rhythmic patter, is also a style of performance, in which the rapper smoothly, briskly, and cogently unravels words like a yo-yo spinning lickety-split.

The cadences, lilting, and rhythm of rapping to a beat has a natural appeal to the ear. A catchy background hook—instrumental or vocal—or altering the rap with a vocal hook, or varying the rappers and putting in special sound effects in the background can enhance the pleasure of the track. Videos are a common marketing tool for hip hop and rap, and videos tell the story visually as well as complement the recording.

Hip hop themes and lyrics have evolved over the years, generally becoming more graphic as time passed by. Whereas rock and roll's grand themes were about love and teenage angst, hip hop is largely about social and economic issues, embracing numerous themes such as the black experience in America and elsewhere, poverty, the ghetto, police, law enforcement, drugs, the legalization of marijuana, bling, gangsters, politics, lack of justice, anger, disrespect, inequality, the degradation of women, female empowerment, and black power. For some fans it is a mirror to society. With its stories and messages, it's literature and a manifesto rolled up into one. It's a musical op-ed, sober and contemplative, and for some its commentaries resonate long after a song of the genre has been listened to. As its lengthy lyrics are delivered, they paint pictures in the minds of listeners. They're dramatic paintings; they're artistic documentaries; they're action-packed films. Its lyrical content, style of performance, beats, and music can be seductive, pulling in listeners in a way that hooks of pop music generally do not. Its lyrics and rhymes, patterns and meters can be clever and creative. Its words are spoken with a cadence so that the song has a lyrical pulse. Lyrics can be delivered according to the artist's style, for instance, staccato or legato. It has its own lingo, which, for better or worse, can be obscene or sexist. Its themes can embrace violence or empowerment, depending on who is rapping. Hip hop is not stagnant; it is constantly evolving, if not reinventing itself, and like other genres, it is not a solitary form of music but can be fused with other genres such as R&B, rock, country, and hard rock. Some hip hop recordings use samples or instrumental lines from other recordings, or hooks, motifs, or sections of other songs. Some hip hop recordings feature rapping while a haunting melody is played in the background. Some hip hop recordings with powerful meanings have become anthems in the hip hop world.

Hip hop started as an underground genre of music and eventually spread out all over. "Rapper's Delight" was the match that started the fire. "Rapper's Delight" was followed by several milestones that gradually helped hip hop secure a place in mainstream music. In July 1982 Grandmaster Flash and the Furious Five's "The Message" was released by Sugarhill Records. It soon became a top ten mainstream singles hit in the UK when other top ten songs on the UK singles chart included the releases of Duran Duran, Dire Straits, Shakin' Stevens, and Survivor. Yet among this pop fare, "The Message" had a big impact with its real-life portrayal of life in the ghetto, or "jungle," as the rapper delineates: broken glass, urinating on the streets, rats, junkies—all making the rapper on the verge of losing his sanity. Diverging from the content of many previous rap records, "The Message" was among the first to employ themes about civil predicaments and difficulties. Two years later, in August 1984, Grandmaster Flash, Melle Mel, and The Furious Five had another UK hit with "White Lines (Don't Don't Do It)," which warned against using cocaine to get high.

On August 16, 1986, hip hop act Run-D.M.C.'s *Raising Hell* became the first rap album to hit the number 1 spot on the Top Black Albums chart of *Billboard*, and the disc, which received critical acclaim and was rap's first multi-platinum album, also climbed to the third position on the magazine's chart of the top 200 albums of every genre, a first for a rap recording to land in such a lofty atmosphere. This accomplishment sent a signal flare that hip hop was becoming mainstream. With "Walk This Way," Run-D.M.C. continued to make rap-rock hybrids of songs, this time hitting the number 5 spot on the mainstream singles chart in September 1986. In 1987 rap had its first album to reach the number one position on *Billboard's* Hot 200 album chart with the Beastie Boys' *Licensed to Ill*. Part of the reason hip hop caught on was because its fans saw themselves in its stories and messages and images; where they were invisible in other media, hip hop was a haven for their station in a difficult world.

As hip hop registered on the *Billboard* Hot 100 singles chart here and there in the 1980s, it should be remembered that pop reigned supreme at the time with artists such as Bruce Springsteen, Abba, Hall & Oates, Blondie, Elton John, Michael Jackson, David Bowie, Olivia Newton-John, Fleetwood Mac, Cyndi Lauper, Dan Fogelberg, Billy Joel, Rod Stewart, Stevie Wonder, Madonna, Whitney Houston, Lionel Richie, Bangles, Bon Jovi, Kool & the Gang, Gloria Estefan & the Miami Sound Machine, Stevie Winwood, George Michael, Billy Ocean, Cheap Trick, and Phil Collins having a commanding hold on the weekly chart. Even country music made a dent in the Hot 100, with artists such as Eddie Rabbit and Dolly Parton sometimes occupying the summit positions on the singles chart. Hip hop pitched its anchor into the pop mainstream, but it was more of a minor genre crossover at the time with questionable commercial potential.

Over the years, hip hop lyrics became more controversial, and its artists were criticized for exhibiting coarse behavior on stage. But the genre's popularity grew, as a steady stream of artists produced new and bolder recordings. In 1988 N.W.A. (the acronym for Niggaz With Attitude), a Los Angeles gangsta rap group, created controversy with its track "Fuck tha Police" (from the group's influential album *Straight Outta Compton*), which protested police brutality and incensed law enforcement, and was banned by radio stations, MTV, and public libraries. Indeed, in a letter dated August 1, 1989, Milt Ahlerich, the assistant director in the Office of Public Affairs of the Federal Bureau of Investigation of the U.S. Department of Justice, wrote to the National Promotions Director of Priority Records in Hollywood that

> a song recorded by the rap group N.W.A. on their album entitled "Straight Outta Compton" encourages violence against and disrespect for the law enforcement officer and has been brought to my attention. I understand that your company recorded and distributed this album and I wanted to share my thoughts and concerns with you. Advocating violence and assault is wrong, and we in the law enforcement community take exception to such action. . . . Music plays an important role in society, and I wanted you to be aware of the FBI's position relative to this song and its message. I believe my views reflect the opinion of the entire law enforcement community.

While hip hop artists may have expressed antipathy toward law enforcement, artists of the genre ignited their own internecine war, so to speak, around the mid-1990s, when a feud erupted between East Coast and West Coast rappers. A West Coast rap scene started to develop in the mid- to late 1980s when Ruthless Records formed in Compton, California, and the label released singles and the gangsta-rap album *Straight Outta Compton* by the group N.W.A. Other West Coast rappers, including former N.W.A. member Dr. Dre, released singles and albums (Dr. Dre's debut album, *The Chronic*, on his Death Row Record label, was critically acclaimed), and West Coast rappers earned a reputation as the leading rappers in America. Timothy Blair, a Bronx rapper who went by the name Tim Dog, released a single called "Fuck Compton," which besmirched West Coast rappers. The East Coast rap scene revitalized and the rivalry between rappers on both coasts intensified (the rivalry could be attributed to many factors including the West Coast rappers feeling they weren't given the same respect as the East Coast rappers by the media, radio disc jockeys, and the public as well as the ascendancy of West Coast rap slighting the feeling of East Coast rappers with hip hop originating in New York City), with West Coast rapper Tupac Shakur (also known as 2Pac) and New York rapper

The Notorious B.I.G. (whose real name was Christopher Wallace) feuding publicly and in recordings (Shakur was shot by robbers at a New York City recording studio in 1994 and accused B.I.G. and others of perpetrating that crime). The feuding continued, and in 1996 Shakur was murdered in Las Vegas, and the following year B.I.G. was fatally shot in Los Angeles. Following each shooting, a peace conference was held, and eventually the feud between the rappers on both coasts was ended. Despite the conflict, however, hip hop continued to grow in popularity.

In 1992 the hip hop duo Kriss Kross had the number 1 song for two months on the Hot 100 with "Jump," and their debut album *Totally Krossed Out* also topped the *Billboard* album chart. In 1995 hip hop claimed the number-1-selling single of the year with "Gangsta's Paradise," an MCA release by Coolio featuring L.V. Its haunting hook derived from Stevie Wonder's "Pastime Paradise," a song on his 1976 number 1 pop album and RIAA-certified diamond album *Songs in the Key of Life*. In 2017 hip hop became recognized with one of the highest mainstream honors of all when the Pulitzer Prize for music was bestowed on Kendrick Lamar for his album *DAMN*, the first time the award was given to a musician outside of the classical and jazz genres. And according to *Billboard*, Drake's 2018 LP *Scorpion* became the first album to garner 1 billion streams from around the world in a single week.

Hip hop music sales continued to excel into the twenty-first century. The genre's superstars included Drake, Rihanna, Fugees, Puff Daddy, Macklemore, Iggy Azalea, Eminem, Fetty Wap, Jay-Z, Kanye West, Dr. Dre, Run DMC, 50 Cent, Will I Am, Wiz Khalifa, Lil Wayne, Snoop Dogg, The Black Eyed Peas, Post Mallone, Kendrick Lamar, Nicki Minaj, Travis Scott, Cardi B, and Migos. Statistics regarding these artists' singles and albums put them in the company of the most successful artists of any genre of popular music. For instance, Drake's single "One Dance" garnered an astonishing 1 billion streams, and Puff Daddy's single "I'll Be Missing You," featuring singer Faith Evans, sold more than 8 million units around the world. Lauryn Hill's 1998 album *The Miseducation of Lauryn Hill* debuted in the number 1 position of the *Billboard* 200 (album chart), sold 19 million units around the world, and won the Grammy Award for Album of the Year, the first rap album to be honored with that accolade (other hip hop artists have also debuted on the top spot of *Billboard*'s album chart, such as Cardi B with her 2018 album *Invasion of Privacy*). Rap's popularity as a legitimate genre of popular music was ratified when in 1989 *Billboard* began publishing a rap chart.

Some hip hop producers became stars in their own right—at least to the music industry, if not so much to the public. They handle the usual functions of a record producer, overseeing a project from conception to completion but may also create the beats and suggest samples from a previous recording for a track, as well as collaborate with the artist in the writing of the songs being recorded.

Over the years, hip hop artists essentially upended the way traditional artists launched careers and sustained their success. In previous years, artists would make demos, shop for a record deal, land a deal, then go on tour to support their new album. At the same time, their label would be trying to get radio airplay for their singles, which would help promote the sale of their albums and attendance at their concerts. After their tour they would write new songs and go back into the studio to record their next album, and then go on tour again. And so forth. Budding hip hop artists have taken a different path: streaming. They upload songs—they could be demos or finished masters—to streaming services such as SoundCloud, and try to build a following. They promote their music on social media, too, and if they are fortunate enough to have attracted many fans, they may get picked up by a streaming service's playlist, which could have millions of followers and showcase their music to people who otherwise would not have known about it. They circumvent radio, which probably wouldn't play their music without a label deal, and also the expensive marketing campaigns of labels. They may collaborate with established artists in putting out new singles, and label and publishing deals may follow. Hip hop artists may release a steady stream of singles, get added to influential streaming service playlists, build a large following, and launch a successful career, which includes a label deal.

The process of hip hop artists creating recordings also differs markedly from the traditional manner in which pop artists made them. Hip hop musicians commonly download samples, or pieces of sounds previously made, and integrate them into their recordings. The samples they use can come from existing recordings, or they can get them from specialized music services that sell them (and pay royalties to the musicians who supplied them to the service). Sampling typically requires a license to use both the sampled sound recording (usually from the label) and song (usually from the publisher), although subscribers to specialized sampling music services may not have to pay any moneys beyond their monthly subscription fee. All types of sounds are typically available, and many music stars are known to use them in their recordings, and several singles with samples may at once be on the *Billboard* Hot 100.

The doom-and-gloom forecasts of the demise of the record industry of the late 1990s and early 2000s dissipated with the growing massive popularity of streaming by the second decade of the twenty-first century. Hundreds of millions of people around the world were by the 2010s subscribers or users of streaming services, and streaming revenues helped labels get back on their feet again (if not up to previous zenith levels) from losses to file sharing and the advent of music streaming when there were far fewer subscribers to streaming services, as well as the precipitous decline in physical sales. The comeback of the music industry coincided with the rise of hip hop and its becoming a mainstream force in the industry.

With hip hop the dominant genre of pop music in the 2010s, the major labels competed against each other to sign rappers whose videos went viral and who had a looming social media presence (labels have a history of avidly pursuing artists in the hottest new genre). Teenagers or artists in their early twenties whose names were largely unrecognized by the public could command million-dollar-plus advances from labels. Labels try hard to keep their market share by signing artists who can achieve high chart positions. Young hip hop artists became so much in demand that they were not only able to get high advances but negotiate other contract terms more favorable than those traditionally granted by labels. Some were even able to negotiate licensing deals in which they granted labels the right to distribute and promote their product for limited time periods without owning their masters or sound recording copyrights.

It's been the practice of many hip hop artists to use pseudonyms in their professional entertainment endeavors. Unlike most other industries where employees use their real names, show business has an intrinsic peculiarity in that entertainers adopt pseudonyms or stage names in place of their real names. Reasons for this range from it's better to have an alluring or unusual name that sticks out in the public mind to having a name that reflects the person's brand or artistic expression to avoid having a name that is close to and could cause confusion with another similar name in the entertainment industry. Indeed, the practice of using pseudonyms has a long history in the popular music business although it wasn't always this way. From the early 1900s to the 1930s, singers often used their real names like Bill Murray, George M. Cohan, Bessie Smith, and Ruth Etting, although some used anglicized versions of their real names or pseudonyms such as Fanny Brice (from Fania Borach) or Dolly Dawn (for Theresa Maria Stabile); some singers used "stage" first names with their real last names, such as Fats Waller (for Thomas Wright Waller) or Bing Crosby (for Harry Lillis Crosby). In the early 1900s, bands used colorful names such as Jelly Roll Morton and His Red Hot Peppers; Irving Mills and His Hotsy Totsy Gang; and the New Orleans Rhythm Kings. Bands in the rock and roll era had their share of distinctive names, such as Bill Haley and His Comets, the Crew-Cuts, the Four Aces, the Penguins, Nervous Norvus, Patience & Prudence, the Silhouettes, the Singing Nun, the Zombies, Herman's Hermits, Sam the Sham and the Pharaohs, the Mamas and the Papas, the Lovin' Spoonful, Paul Revere and the Raiders, the Temptations, the Grass Roots, the Classics IV, Vanilla Fudge, and Creedence Clearwater Revival; even individual singers tried to make their names more glamorous, such as Bob Dylan for Robert Zimmerman, Tom Jones for Thomas Woodward, Engelbert Humperdinck for Arnold Dorsey, Elton John for Reginald Dwight, and Drake (just the one name) for Aubrey Drake Graham. Some rappers like to use hyphenated pseudonyms such as Jay-Z for Shawn Corey Carter. But most commonly, individual hip hop artists use full-blown fanciful pseudonyms such as LL Cool J (for James Todd Smith), Eminem (for Marshall Bruce Mathers III), Flo Rida (for Tramar Lacel Dillard), or Cardi B (for Belcalis Marlenis Almanzar), although there are some common prefixes such as Lil (Lil Kim, Lil Xan, Lil Uzi Vert, Lil Pump, Lil Baby) or Ice (Ice-T, Ice Cube).

With its success in supplanting the longtime genre-pillars of pop music, hip hop presents itself as a case study of a new form of music that can change popular taste and become a dominant force in the music world. Why did hip hop take off and have staying power whereas disco (and other genres) had a quick rise to fame and then faded?

At first, hip hop had a limited audience and was essentially a subculture, but as its popularity grew, it became a full-fledged culture. Clothes, hair, the way of carrying oneself, speaking, dancing, and much more made hip hop part of people's daily routines. These elements turned out to be not just trends but a way of life for its fans. Hip hop artists are known for being social justice activists or for taking part in charities, for illuminating perceived injustices in the criminal justice system, and for raising money to rectify them. Its artists are known for building their brands, being entrepreneurial, and having their own companies that become well known to their fans—clothing, perfumes, sneakers, shoes, headphones, beauty products, jewelry, wines, and vodka, not to mention labels, music publishing companies, and management firms; you name it, there's a hip hop artist who's mining that kind of company or lending his or her name to a particular product. They branch out into other entertainment fields such as television, motion pictures, and radio; they not uncommonly amass hundreds of millions of streams. When CD sales plummeted with illegal streaming in the late 1990s, labels needed to derive revenue from other sources, so they increased their efforts in developing their artists' brands, which could possibly result in additional revenue from licensing and physical and digital sales. With the rising popularity of hip hop and its attendant culture, hip hop artists were especially suited for brand building and marketing arrangements. *Billboard* recognizes the genre with its R&B/Hip-Hop Airplay chart.

Musically speaking, many factors can account for hip hop's ascendancy and staying power: its universal themes of poverty, life in the ghetto, substance abuse, the police, the difficulties of life; its catchy beats and melodies; its poetic words that transcend forgettable or hackneyed lyrics and resonate in the minds of listeners; its clever rhymes; and themes, such as empowerment, that seem to speak to its fans. As more or less social commentaries, hip hop changes with the times, making it a dynamic music genre that just doesn't change its sounds but also keeps up to date with the oppressed, distressed, maltreated, destitute, suppressed, or those who harbor these feelings. Of course, rap has earned a reputation of being controversial with its use of profanity or degrading lyrics or of being violent with the criminal backgrounds or actions of some of its artists or with the murders of two of its biggest stars, Tupac Shakur in 1996 and The Notorious B.I.G. the next year, but it has survived all that to not just continue as a viable music genre but also even grow more in popularity.

Despite negative aspects of its reputation, hip hop has managed to surpass other genres and become a powerful force in the music industry. But if there's one thing about the music industry, it's that new artists, songs, and sounds are always catering to new fans as previous fans age out of the desired demographic target audiences of artists and labels. Like dynasties that have ruled nations for long periods of times, music genres eventually fall also, as the next big thing takes over.

10

A NEW AGE OF POP STARS

The date November 30, 1982, may be regarded as an epoch of the music business, for it was on this date that Michael Jackson's *Thriller* album was released to the world. What enshrines this date as a landmark juncture in the annals of music business history is not just the stratospheric sales of the album—it went on to become one of the best-selling albums of all time—but also that it ushered in a new kind of pop star.

To be sure, Michael Jackson was a pop star before the release of *Thriller*, but with the release of the album, Michael Jackson the person arguably became more important than the music of Michael Jackson, setting in motion a music business dictum that would become prevalent for future pop stars; that is, it's as much or more about the person than the music. Sure, an artist's music is of paramount importance and to a great extent defines the artist, but Jackson set the tone for the burgeoning modern age where the artist's looks, costume, hair, image, personality, and interaction with fans are all part of the mix of factors for achieving and sustaining pop stardom.

With the release of *Thriller*, Michael Jackson became a brand. He developed a public image that was part music, part sartorial, part choreographic, part personality. He was known for catchy pop dance tunes. He had different wardrobes for different tours, videos, stage appearances, and albums he promoted, becoming known for his front-zipper jackets or jackets with metal epaulets on the shoulders, his black fedora, white sox, tight-fitting pants, and his crystal-studded white glove. He had visually alluring choreographic moves that showed off his limber legs and famous back-gliding moonwalk. He even had a signature pre-dance stance of bended knees, arched back and head titled forward. Jackson was soft-spoken and owned a chimpanzee that he kept on his famous Neverland Ranch, leading some people to say he was quirky or eccentric. It was all part of his brand (or public persona or image). But whenever he appeared in public, he carried himself as a star with his striking raiment. Elvis and the Beatles (especially in their *Sgt. Pepper's Lonely Hearts Club Band* album) may have pioneered pop star fashion, but MJ, AKA the "King of Pop," branded it as an integral part of a pop star's identity.

While Jackson personified the pop star image of a new age, the transition from pop star of the 1950s, 1960s, and 1970s to pop star of the 1980s, however, cannot be attributed solely to the branding of artists. The beginning of different types of identities that were not the typical pop star archetype can be attributed to a host of other factors including technology and the changing tides of culture and society. Jackson's *Thriller*, the debut of MTV, the introduction of CDs, the popularity of mixtapes, and developing computer technology that would give the world the Internet were all part of a confluence of factors that gave way to a new phase in the evolution of the music business and of pop stars. Indeed, the pop star image would be fluid as new technologies and new cultural developments came into being.

Curiously, Michael Jackson may have ushered in a new era of pop stars, but the parade of pop stars who followed him were predominantly female—an illustrious queue that includes Madonna, Whitney Houston, Tiffany, Debbie Gibson, Belinda Carlisle, Taylor Dayne, Paula Abdul, Janet Jackson, Mariah Carey, Toni Braxton, Jewel, LeeAnn Rimes, Alicia Keys, Christina Aguilera, Britney Spears, Amy Winehouse, Miley Cyrus, Beyoncé, Taylor Swift, Katy Perry, Rihanna, Selena Gomez, Nickie Minaj, Lady Gaga, Adele, Lana Del Rey, and Ariana Grande. Actually, the volume of female pop stars who burst onto the scene is not all that surprising given the fact that the ongoing women's liberation movement was opening minds and opportunities for females and that women had always tried to break through the male-dominated music business but encountered resistance. Female artists had always been an integral part of the music business, from Billie Holiday to Aretha Franklin, from Patti Page to Janis Joplin, but their numbers were relatively small, and in this new age of pop stars, pioneering women artists would break down barriers for new generations of females to come into the limelight like never before.

On September 6, 1983, Cyndi Lauper's "Girl's Just Wanna Have Fun" was released, and the accompanying video of the buoyant song helped not only etch her brand in the shrine of female pop stars but also inaugurate the dauntless, independent, secure female of a new pop era. The video shows Lauper wearing a cool hat over big hair, earrings, a dress, fingerless gloves, and sunglasses—the perfect costume for a young woman of the 1980s—rebelling against parental authority and bonding with other "girls" where they all end up dancing, partying, and having, well, fun! The video perfectly reflected the spirit of the song, which hit the number 2 position on the *Billboard* Hot 100, but also helped brand Lauper as a spunky musical artist and feminist.

Following Lauper in the new procession of female pop stars was Madonna Louise Ciccone, who the world came to know by her first name and who earned the regal sobriquet of the "Queen of Pop." Madonna's long string of hits began in 1984, and she virtually perfected the concept of music branding. As a female pop artist, she was daring in the way she dressed and presented herself in concert, the music she wrote and recorded, the provocative book she wrote called *Sex*, and the way she carried herself and spoke. With her immense commercial success and becoming a cultural icon, she opened the floodgates of music business opportunity for women in her wake to pursue their artistry in open and boundary-pushing ways. Among the themes Madonna explored in her songs were (with subjective interpretations) being driven crazy by unsettled love ("Borderline," 1984), how the right love can make one surrender her chastity ("Like a Virgin," 1984), good fortune comes with the right person ("Lucky Star," 1984), just make physical contact with me and my reaction will show you how I feel about you ("Crazy for You," 1985), faithfulness comes with the right love ("True Blue," 1986), girls grow up and are entitled to make their own choices ("Papa Don't Preach," 1986), secrets will eventually be revealed ("Live to Tell," 1986), there's no escaping from that special someone ("Who's That Girl," 1986), dream where you wish to be ("La Isla Bonita," 1987), we could be exciting together if you let it happen ("Causing a Commotion," 1987), and your pull on me is blissful ("Like a Prayer," 1989). Madonna carved out her stellar brand from her music, fashion, videos, film acting, books, and much more, and was famous for changing her image with the times, a strategy to stay relevant as culture progresses that was exemplified by the Beatles.

Not all the new pop stars of the 1980s were female, of course. Another pop star who had several hits in the decade was Prince, born Prince Rogers Nelson, who put out songs that were often dark, metaphoric, cryptic, or lascivious. The themes of his 1980s songs (interpretations again subjective) include: I'm broke, but I want to give you all my love ("I Wanna Be Your Lover," 1980); you're fast and experienced, but you need someone like me who can tame you and give you long-lasting love ("Little Red Corvette," 1983); in the year 2000 it could be all over, so let's party like it's the year before ("1999," 1983); I get so crazed when I'm around you that I need you to relieve me ("Delirious," 1983); I may ask too much of you, and you never seem to be happy, but when we fight we sound like weeping birds ("Doves Cry," 1984); I'm sorry for hurting you—you belong where life is grand, dignified, and peaceful (characteristics symbolized by the color purple) ("Purple Rain," 1984); live your life to the fullest because none of us lasts forever ("Let's Go Crazy," 1984); you may not understand me because I am your inner voice, but no matter how bad you are, I'll do anything for you ("I Would Die 4 U," 1985); life can be cool when it's artsy ("Pop Life," 1985); when you've got nothing going, someone can walk into your life and change everything ("Raspberry Beret," 1985); I don't need beauty, wealth, or coolness, just a woman to give me her body all day ("Kiss," 1986); the world is full of bad news that can be upsetting, so let's love each other and start a family ("Sign O' the Times," 1987); you attract me in a way that makes me want to love you and have sex with you ("U Got the Look," in 1987); I'm going to that place to make it with the first girl I encounter ("Alphabet Street," 1988); if criminal thoughts make one guilty, then I deserve the electric chair, so if I'm the devil, let's just keep dancing ("Batman," 1989). Prince's band, the Revolution, played with him on such best-selling albums as *Purple Rain*, *Around the World in a Day*, and *Parade*, and was known to have female musicians.

Although alternative rock, country, heavy metal, and rap landed in the top echelons of the national singles or albums charts in the 1980s, the decade started with "poppy" singles in the top five and ended with "poppy" singles in the top five, influenced in part by MTV and its music videos, moving from Rupert Holmes's "Escape (The Pina Colada

Song)," the Captain and Tennille's "Do That to Me One More Time," Stevie Wonder's "Send One Your Love," and Kenny Rogers's "Coward of the Country" in January 1980 to Billy Joel's "We Didn't Start the Fire," Phil Collins's "Another Day in Paradise," Linda Ronstadt's (featuring Aaron Neville) "Don't Know Much," Soul II featuring Caron Wheeler's "Back to Life," and Taylor Dayne's "With Every Beat of My Heart" in December 1989.

Pop still dominated the mainstream music turf, but with artists like Jackson and Madonna, the seeds had been planted for pop to move in an edgier direction. They presented a more rebellious or debauched attitude of pop star to the public. Indeed, with national television as a common means of exposure for chart-making artists, it would be hard to imagine a pop star of the 1960s or 1970s executing crotch grabs as Michael Jackson did or for a female singer wearing nipple cones as Madonna did on her 1987 Who's That Girl World Tour. Although artists and songs of previous generations pushed the limits of so-called decency in performance and music, some 1980s artists seemed to prepare the mainstream mind for shocking changes in music to come. Other artists who scored hit singles in the 1980s, a time of the latchkey generation and the AIDS epidemic, included Van Halen, Guns N' Roses, Motorhead, New Kids on the Block, Bananarama, Pet Shop Boys, Expose, Billy Idol, George Michael, Iron Maiden, Whitesnake, Def Leppard, and Bon Jovi. While pop still ruled the charts, clearly hard rock was making inroads.

While dance pop enjoyed popularity in the 1980s, teen pop (perhaps a redundant term since all pop may be deemed teen pop) was in vogue in the 1990s. Catchy pop confections were turned out by such artists as Britney Spears, Christina Aguilera, Hanson, Backstreet Boys, New Kids on the Block, N'SYNC, Jessica Simpson, and the Spice Girls. The music of these artists was indeed aimed at tweens and teens and, indirectly, their parents, as their parents might accompany them to concerts of these artists as they would accompany their children, say, to a Disney movie. In this way there was a sort of commercialization of pop where kids were targeted to be consumers of a certain product, like, say, sugary cereal.

Britney Spears, who was a cast member of *The Mickey Mouse Club* in the early 1990s and would be dubbed the Princess of Pop, would tour shopping malls to promote her . . . *Baby One More Time* album; all five

Spice Girls had different personalities and different "Spice" nicknames that ended in "Spice" (Posh, Ginger, Sporty, Scary, and Baby). Hanson, with hits like "Mmmbop" and "I Will Come to You" specifically oriented their concerts for teens (they were teens themselves at the time). At the same time, female pop artists commonly marketed their music to female youths with the songs having empowering themes for girls. Some of these songs, staples on girls' music empowerment online lists, are TLC's "Unpretty," the Spice Girls' "Wannabe," Britney Spears's "Stronger," No Doubt's "Just a Girl," Alanis Morrissette's "You Oughta Know," Salt 'N Pepa's "None of Your Business," and Destiny's Child's "Bills, Bills, Bills."

While pop ruled the singles charts in the 1990s, other genres also had hits. For instance, grunge made an impact with Nirvana's "Smells Like Teen Spirit" (the group also had hits in England with "Come as You Are" and "Heart-Shaped Box"), and hard rock crossed over into the mainstream, with groups like Guns N' Roses and Foo Foo Fighters having numerous hit singles.

The late 1990s were a time of rampant peer-to-peer file sharing and a precipitous decline of CD sales for the music industry. But while it would take years for the industry to spearhead the taking down of P2P file-sharing sites and stem the flow of P2P revenue losses, the first decade of the 2000s was a time of streaming service growth and Internet commerce, especially with iTunes (which started in 2001), as well as marketing with social media such as Facebook (which launched in 2004), Twitter (2006), and Instagram (2010). There were numerous online sites where budding talent could upload videos, and such artists as Justin Bieber, on YouTube, and Charli XCX, on MySpace, were famously discovered in this way.

Artists of the twenty-first century use websites and social media to showcase their brand, expand their fan base, and drive consumers to their recordings, concerts, and merchandise, as well as inform them of any special interests they may have such as particular causes or charities. Indeed, it's almost unthinkable today that a hit artist wouldn't use these tools to stay relevant. Fans want to know everything about their favorite artists, from announcements of tours and releases to what they're doing or their reactions to current events, which is why artists, for instance, regularly send out tweets and post on Facebook and Instagram, supporting the rule that in today's world it's more about the person than the music. Indeed, in our 24/7 world of social media and Internet communication, today's pop stars could not exist without the mediums that deliver them.

Female artists would continue to be music stars in the first two decades of the twenty-first century with Taylor Swift, Katy Perry, Beyoncé, Rihanna, Selena Gomez, Nickie Minaj, Lady Gaga, Adele, Lana Del Rey, and Ariana Grande, among others, consistently hitting the top of the national singles or album charts, or both. Another star of the first decade of the 2000s was Kelly Clarkson, who rose to fame from the contest-television show *American Idol*, showing not all stars gain their fame in the traditional way. Moreover, not all mainstream artists began as pop artists. Katy Perry started out in gospel and Taylor Swift in country, but they later crossed over onto the mainstream charts. Indeed, the goal of many non-pop artists, it seems, is to cross over into the pop mainstream, to land on the *Billboard* Hot 100, so as to broaden their popularity and audience and consequently their revenue from sales, streaming, and merchandising, as well as to open up opportunities in such areas as film, television, commercials, and touring by having a wider fan base.

A plethora of other artists hit the Hot 100 in the 2010s—Bruno Mars, Halsey, Ed Sheeran, Post Malone, Imagine Dragons, Marshmello, Travis Scott, Sam Smith, J. Cole, Cardi B, Maroon 5, Dua Lipa, Khalid, Charlie Puth, Demi Lovato, Blake Shelton, Lil Pump, Ellie Goulding, Billie Eilish, Florida Georgia Line, and Camila Cabello, to name but a few. Unfortunately, in the popular music world there are seemingly countless artists who are talented but don't make the charts or climb very high on them, yet are adored by fans and critics alike. The pop music world is like a Darwinian universe, a "survival of the fittest" world where only the most successful artists thrive and survive. In this case, *fittest* is often determined not just by the music and brand of the artist but also by the support behind the artist, particularly in the areas of promotion and distribution, with such muscle most ably supplied by labels with financial backing, which of course are the major labels (Universal, Sony, and Warner).

The songs of this new pop era differed from the pop songs of the 1950s, 1960s, and 1970s. They can be earworms just like their predecessors, but they incorporated new genres and sounds, beats, samples, and styles of singing.

Sampling has become a common means of constructing songs, and is sometimes obvious and sometimes not. It might be said that there is even a gray area between a sample (which can be as small as a snippet) and an interpolation, where a section of a previous recording (or melody of a song) that is not tiny has been inserted into the new recording. The title hook of Cardi B's 2018 "I Like It" uses the hook from Pete Rodriguez's 1967 recording of "I Like It Like That." Ariana Grande's 2019 "7 Rings" uses the melody of Rodgers and Hammerstein's "My Favorite Things," a song from the musical *The Sound of Music*. Some hit recordings use samples that listeners are not even aware of.

The structures of contemporary pop songs are often more complex than the erstwhile conventional AABA or ABAB pop song structures. Take, for example, the structure of Megan Trainor's 2014 number 1 pop single, Grammy Award–nominated, diamond-certified worldwide hit, "All about That Bass": ABCDAEDAAA. The song has a bounteous four different sections before there is any repetition, and then it goes on to a new fifth section before repeating its D section and ending with three repeats of its main (A) section, leaving listeners stuck with that catchy title-hook in their heads (repetition of the main theme or hook of a song has always been the staple of pop song structures).

In the ever-evolving music business, radio airplay is not as crucial as it used to be for making a hit. Streaming service playlists have become an influential factor in what recordings streaming service users listen to. They are less democratic than the charts, since the choices of numerous people determine chart rankings, including radio station program directors who aim to put on their station playlists recordings that listeners in their market would most want to listen to; consumers, whose purchases of physical and digital recordings are tracked; and users of streaming services, whose song selections are tracked. Streaming service playlists are curated by music professionals, whose job it is to select the songs of a particular genre that would most likely appeal to listeners. The curators are akin to radio programmers, station employees who determine what tracks the station will play. With the financial benefits that could result from a song being selected for a playlist on a streaming service, the competition to get tracks on them is quite fierce, with many labels, artists, personal managers, and others submitting material. To get on, curators review data that show a song's plays and important other information about it. A playlist can have millions of followers from around the world, and its influence can spread to radio programming decisions and ultimately to the music charts. Playlists for certain genres attract more listeners; hip hop, for example, has enjoyed immense popularity with Spotify's RapCaviar playlist. A streaming service can have thousands of curated playlists, and a playlist can have millions of daily streams. Nielsen Music, which tracks online streaming, sales, and radio airplay, counts 1,500 streams as the equivalent to the buying of on album. The artist royalty for an album (perhaps 10 to 20 percent of the retail price of the album) is substantially more than for a single stream (a fraction of a penny depending on the streaming service), but huge hits can generate hundreds of millions of streams (even over a billion streams), which can add up to big royalties for the artist.

As much as sounds have changed over the years, what is old is often new again, just in different forms. With boy groups like the Backstreet Boys and N'SYNC and girl groups like the Spice Girls, the 1990s was the decade for these types of music artists. But these groups weren't the first of their ilk. Boy bands, which came into vogue in the post-rock-and-roll age beginning in the 1980s by their literal member-makeup, were nothing new. After all, the Beatles and Rolling Stones in their heyday were all composed of young males, as well as earlier groups such as the Teenagers and Danny & the Juniors. Indeed, in its literal sense, boy bands go all the way back to male ensembles of the early days of the music business. But the term in a more contemporary sense became applied to all-male groups of teenagers or young adults who specialized in singing songs with pleasant vocal harmonies and whose repertoire largely consisted of romantic ballads; the members were typically not featured playing musical instruments. New Kids on the Block, Boyz II Men, the Backstreet Boys, N'SYNC, and One Direction are some of the so-called boy bands who topped the charts.

Similarly, girl groups are characterized by their all-female members singing in engaging harmony. Girl groups may be notably traced back to the World War II–era Andrews Sisters, who had such hits as "Boogie Woogie Bugle Boy" and "Rum and Coca-Cola"; 1950s groups like the McGuire Sisters with "Goodnight, Sweetheart, Goodnight," "Sincerely," and "Picnic"; 1960s groups such as the Ronettes with "Be My Baby" and "Walking in the Rain," the Shangri-Las, whose biggest hits included "Remember (Walking in the Sand)" and "Leader of the Pack," Martha and the Vandellas with "Dancing in the Streets" and "Quicksand," the

Marvelettes with "Please Mr. Postman" and "Don't Mess with Bill," the Chiffons with "One Fine Day" and "He's So Fine," the Murmaids with their only hit "Popsicles and Icicles," the Supremes with numerous hits such as "Baby Love" and "Where Did Our Love Go?" the Pointer Sisters with "Slow Hand" and "I'm So Excited"; and through the 1990s and after with Expose, En Vogue Cover Girls, Wilson Phillips, Seduction, and Red Velvet. For predecessors of 1990s manufactured groups like the Spice Girls and boy bands like the Backstreet Boys, one only need to look to the Monkees of the 1960s, who were also assembled like these later-year groups.

In this new era of pop, music festivals soared in popularity, regularly attracting thousands if not hundreds of thousands of people to these events. Among the well-known music festivals that have been sponsored are Coachella, Lollapalooza, Outside Lands, Governors Ball, Afropunk, Summerfest, Firefly, Panorama, Impact Music Festival, Bonnaroo Music & Arts Festival, Seven Peaks Music Festival, Bumbershoot, and Mountain Jam. The headliners at music festivals are typically major acts, and the supporting artists could be well-known names or rising acts or artists who had hit records in the past. Festivals may cover multiple genres, or particular genres, and some are seasonal, such as occurring during the summer months. Festivals are multi-day fan-fests usually bringing together large numbers of like-minded fans who come to celebrate the music and artists they enjoy and to revel in the spirit of the event. In open-field festivals, attendees often camp outdoors, and there is an earthy, convivial nature to these outdoors music celebrations.

In the popular music field concerts and music festivals have been held as both money-making events and for activist causes. Indeed, social consciousness has been a perennial concern of musical artists, and many pop and rock artists have weighed in on this. In 1971 Beatles' guitarist George Harrison and Indian musician Ravi Shankar sponsored the Concert for Bangladesh at Madison Square Garden in New York City to help war refugees. Musicians Bob Geldof and James Ure promoted the Live Aid benefit concert in 1985 to raise money for famine relief in Ethiopia. Also, in 1985, numerous pop superstars, collectively using the name USA (United Support of Artists) for Africa, recorded the song "We Are the World," written by Michael Jackson and Lionel

Richie, to raise money for humanitarian relief in African nations. The Tibetan Freedom concerts beginning in 1996 were held to help the Asian nation of Tibet gain independence. Many well-known musicians participated in these benefit concerts, which raised millions of dollars for their causes. Interestingly though, despite the many famous musicians who selflessly gave their time for good causes, few modern-day concerts have matched some nineteenth-century concerts in terms of the sheer volume of musical participants.

To commemorate the end of the Civil War, in 1869 (four years after the southern and northern army generals Robert E. Lee and Ulysses S. Grant, respectively, signed the terms of surrender at Appomattox Court House in Virginia), Patrick Gilmore, the renowned American bandmaster who emigrated to the United States from Ireland, organized a "National Peace Jubilee" in Boston with eight hundred orchestral musicians and ten thousand choral vocalists. Three years later, in 1872, a second peace festival called the International Peace Jubilee was held in Boston but on a grander scale. This time, the chorus consisted of twenty thousand singers and two thousand musicians formed the orchestra, and the event took place in a venue that held fifty thousand concert-goers (distinguished vocalists, bands from other countries, and Johann Strauss, famous for such waltzes as "The Blue Danube" and "Tales from the Vienna Woods," also participated in the Jubilee).

But it's been non-benefit, or profit-making, concerts that have been the staple of live popular music over the years. Concerts are electrifying events that bring fans together to see their favorite artists perform on stage, and what could be more exciting for fans than to be packed in a venue with tens of thousands of other screaming fans watching artists they deeply admire perform songs they genuinely enjoy? Concert-goers listen to the music, sing along, stand on their seats, dance, and engage in other ways, even if not always harmless; moshing became popular in the 1980s, a practice in which those daring enough would enter a so-called mosh pit and collide with each other or engage in other physical encounters, which could lead to injury.

For concert promoters, the entrepreneurs who put on the musical events, concerts can be lucrative, although they may be financially risky. Concert promoters engage musical acts to perform at concerts they produce. They may be individuals or large companies. In the rock era of the 1960s, 1970s, and 1980s, certain established promoters would dominate the big venues in their cities by producing concerts by the big touring acts in these venues. Some of these promoters specialized in acts of a certain genre. Later, national companies pretty much took over promoting concerts in large cities, putting some local promoters out of business, as it was hard for local promoters to compete with large companies that could act as a one-stop promoter who could handle booking tours on a national basis. Today, some large companies dominate the concert business, booking tours for major acts and booking them into large venues, which they may own. The major concert promoters are AEG, or Anschutz Entertainment Group, and Live Nation. AEG handles concert promotion, touring, festivals, and merchandise as well as produces sports events and owns venues all over the world. Its primary ticket agent is AXS (which is owned by AEG), and its secondary ticket agent is StubHub (which is owned by eBay). Live Nation, formerly a division of Clear Channel Radio Network, is involved with concert promotion, artist management, and ticket sales. Its primary ticket company is Ticketmaster (which is owned by Live Nation), and its secondary ticker agent is TicketsNow. There is also Another Planet Entertainment, which promotes hundreds of events per year. Major concert venues include Barclays Center (Brooklyn, New York City), Madison Square Garden (New York City), Staples Center (Los Angeles), Greek Theatre (Berkeley, California), Bill Graham Civic Auditorium (San Francisco), and Fox Theater (Oakland, California).

Music festivals, multi-day events where hordes of fans gather to hear artists perform at outdoor locations or venues, may trace their rock roots to the famous Woodstock festival that took place in Bethel, New York, from August 15–18, 1969. An estimated 400,000 to 500,000 people attended the multi-day concert at which some of rock's biggest stars performed, including Janis Joplin, Jimi Hendrix, Creedence Clearwater Revival, Arlo Guthrie, Crosby, Stills & Nash, Melanie, Joe Cocker, Santana, Joan Baez, and Jefferson Airplane. But Woodstock may also be regarded as the pioneering event for setting the untamed counter-culture and even spiritual lifestyle that is associated with modern pop festivals. So many teens and young adults converged on Max Yasgur's 600-acre Sullivan County dairy farm that cars and buses, some brightly painted in the art-style of the hippie movement, were left abandoned in the roadways. Fans camped out on the grounds and waded in the mud. There were drugs and nudity and sex, and handwritten signs and songs protesting the Vietnam War. There was one birth and one lethal drug overdose during the rockfest, yet it was all peaceful. As Woodstock guitarist-singer Richie Havens famously stated, "Woodstock was not about sex, drugs and rock and roll. It was about spirituality, about love, about sharing, about helping each other, living in peace and harmony" (https://www.azquotes.com/quotes/topics/sex-drugs-and-rock-and-roll.html).

Almost four months after Woodstock, the Altamont Speedway Free Festival was held in northern California. Unlike Woodstock, this concert, featuring artists such as the Grateful Dead, Santana, Crosby, Stills, Nash and Young, and the Rolling Stones, was marred with bedlam, with one attendee being stabbed to death by a Hells Angel member when he moved toward the stage, plus a few accidental deaths and several auto thefts. But a violent concert wasn't enough to keep fans from live musical extravaganzas, and in subsequent years organized music festivals were sponsored and were successful and are now a regular part of the music business.

11

A HIERARCHY OF POPULAR SONGS

If we consider popular music the realm of all musical styles outside of classical and serious music that is directed for appreciation by mass audiences, then the term applies to songs from long ago through today and includes many genres or styles of music. We may not consider a long-ago song "pop," as we consider a pop song today, but it may have been pop for those times, just like what we consider pop today may not be considered pop in a hundred years. By taking this conception of popular music into account (in terms of both a song's past or present style and popularity), we may devise a hierarchy for popular, or pop, music as follows (with the term *pop* used below in a general sense, and not the specific genre of pop music as some may regard it):

HISTORIC POPULAR MUSIC

This category would include songs going back long ago—including those from the time of the exploration and settlement of America, songs from colonial America, mountain songs, pioneer songs, cowboy songs, lumberjack songs, sea chanteys, spirituals, traditional folk songs, college songs, and tunes brought in from Latin and South America.

Following the founding of Jamestown by English settlers in 1607, people from other lands such as Spain, France, and Germany came to the shores of America bringing with them tunes from their native lands. During America's colonial days such songs as "Comin' through the

Rye," "The Campbells Are Coming," "O, Dear, What Can the Matter Be?" "Auld Lang Syne," "Believe Me, if All Those Endearing Young Charm," and "Loch Lomond" were sung in villages and cities. Patriotic songs inspired the American colonists during the Revolutionary War, and after America gained its independence from England, music was a beloved pastime in the American states. As the United States developed, songs became employed by people in various ways.

There were songs, for instance, that were popular among sailors, such as "Rocked in the Cradle," "Blow the Man Down," and "Haul on the Bowlin'"; among pioneers who traveled to the west of America in covered wagons, such as "Sweet Betsy from Pike," "Ben Bolt," and "Wait for the Wagon"; among mountaineers, such as "Sour Wood Mountain" and "Little Mohee." There were songs associated with armed conflict, such as these American Civil War songs: "The Battle Cry of Freedom," "Just Before the Battle Mother," "Tenting Tonight on the Old Camp Ground," "When Johnnie Comes Marching Home," "Tramp, Tramp, Tramp the Boys Are Marching"; from the Crinoline days, such as "Old Folks at Home," "Jeannie with the Light Brown Hair," and "Massa's in De Cold, Cold Ground"; there were songs associated with merriment, such as "For He's a Jolly Good Fellow" and "Three Blind Mice." In the nineteenth century, college glee clubs, commonly composed of males, were a popular attraction with their crooning of pop-like tunes and may even be likened to what is referred to today as "boy bands." In their repertoire were such crowd-pleasing and catchy ditties as "Good-Night Ladies," "My Last Cigar," "The Bull-Dog," and "Polly Wolly Doodle." Folk tunes and dance songs from the Caribbean, Latin America, Mexico, and South America were brought northward, and new lyrics were written for them, as their previous words about life in their homelands didn't apply to life in America. Again, these songs may not fit people's conception today of what pop songs are, but they had mass appeal in their day, which, arguably, makes them popular, or pop songs, of their day.

TIN PAN ALLEY (OR VINTAGE) POPULAR MUSIC

Songs that were published for commercial purposes by the centralized music industry that formed in New York City in the latter part of the nineteenth century are the bedrock of this category. Many famous pop songs and songwriters came from this era, which is said to have supplied the material for the "Great American Songbook." Tin Pan Alley pop may be considered the time period from 1880 to the end of the 1940s, when Tin Pan Alley tunes predominated but other styles of music were also part of the era. Such other styles included ragtime, Dixieland (including New Orleans and Chicago styles), waltzes, foxtrots, tango music, patriotic (World War I) songs, "Broadway" music, swing (or Big Band), rumba, "Hollywood" songs, hillbilly, Western swing, boogie-woogie, middle-of-the road songs, bluegrass, bop, and cool.

In this era, Tin Pan Alley songs, or what may be called vintage pop songs, were being cranked out in the cubicles of New York City music publishers, but other genres of popular music found national audiences, too. One of these was the unsophisticated tunes about life in the backwoods produced in rural areas of the southern United States, called hillbilly music, later to be called country and western or country music. Ralph Peer, an executive of the Okeh Recording Company, in the mid-1920s recorded hillbilly artists such as the Hill Billies, Vernon Dalhart, and Ernest Stoneman, and helped hillbilly music gain popularity; he later worked for the Victor Talking Machine Company and formed Southern Music Publishing Company, and recorded some of country and western music's seminal artists and published some if its greatest songs. At the Grand Ole Opry, beginning in 1925, country music began being broadcast over the radio, expanding the genre's audience. From the 1920s through the 1940s, the stars of country music included Jimmie Rodgers, the Carter Family, Hank Williams, and Ernest Tubb. In the 1930s and 1940s, a style of country music combined with jazz called western swing (with vocals and instrumentation that included piano, fiddles, and slap bass) that people danced to was popular, with Bob Wills and the Texas Playboys and the Light Crust Doughboys among its stars. Bluegrass, an offshoot of hillbilly music, differentiated by its vocal style and instrumentation (such as a guitar, fiddle, mandolin, and banjo) and its themes commonly of love and family, received widespread attention around the mid-1940s.

There are various categories of jazz, which is generally an upbeat form of music played in combos with instruments such as piano, clarinet, trumpet, trombone, and drums, or piano alone, and is considered indigenous to America. Ragtime, with its syncopated rhythms in the melody and written mainly for piano, developed around 1890 and was boosted in popularity by composer Scott Joplin, whose works such as "The Maple Leaf Rag" and "The Entertainer" were popular. Other forms of jazz developed, including Dixieland (around the early 1900s) and swing (which enjoyed popularity in the 1930s), followed by boogie-woogie (mainly a piano style), bop (or bebop), and cool jazz around 1949.

From the 1920s into the 1940s, dance bands enjoyed immense popularity and of course they caught the Alley's eye. Leaders of dance bands such as Ted Weems, Vincent Lopez, Ben Selvin, and Fred Waring played on the radio, in theaters and clubs, at restaurants, and released records, and while the leaders and their orchestra members wrote some of their songs, many of their hits were supplied by established tunesmiths of Tin Pan Alley. In the 1930s the Big Band era was in full bloom with bands such as those led by Duke Ellington, Glenn Miller, Benny Goodman, Harry James, Woody Herman, Count Basie, Jimmy and Tommy Dorsey, Cab Calloway, and Artie Shaw. These bands often featured female vocalists who achieved fame such as Billie Holiday, Helen Forrest, Ella Fitzgerald, Ethel Waters, Doris Day, and Helen O'Connell.

Around 1914 a syncopated dance music played in 2/4 or 4/4 time in which dance partners glided and executed twisting steps and low dips that was called the tango became popular in the United States. Other popular forms of Latin music, which came out of various Caribbean and South American countries, followed, including the rumba, which enjoyed widespread popularity in America in the 1930s. In the 1930s and 1940s, folk music, which had sundry traditional forms such as chanteys, cowboy songs, spirituals, and mountain songs, started coming into the mainstream with radio now a means to get it heard by many people, and folk artists such as Woodie Guthrie and Burl Ives were among its most prominent exponents.

Some of the prominent songs from the Tin Pan Alley pop era include "Give My Regards to Broadway," "You're a Grand Old Flag," "By the Light of the Silvery Moon," "Alexander's Ragtime Band," "Peg O' My Heart," "St. Louis Blues," "I Love a Piano," "Swanee," "April Showers," "I'm Sitting on Top of the World," "Baby Face," "Bye Bye Blackbird," "My Blue Heaven," "Strike up the Band," "I Got Rhythm," "I've Got the World on a String," "Blue Moon," "I Only Have Eyes for You,"

"Winter Wonderland," "I'm in the Mood for Love," "My Heart Belongs to Daddy," "I Don't Want to Walk Without You," and "Sentimental Journey."

Tin Pan Alley was a product of its own time, and its end was inevitable. Its writers rose to the occasion of writing great songs, songs that the public loved and songs that endure, laying the foundation of pop music, not to mention establishing basic industry practices. The popular music of the Tin Pan Alley era, which had various forms, found its main audience in those who were youngsters during the Great Depression, often referred to as the Greatest Generation.

ROCK AND ROLL

Out of the vat of popular music, most prominently its genres of rhythm and blues, jazz, country and western, gospel, rockabilly, blues, and vintage pop, came rock and roll in the late 1940s and early 1950s when records that may be characterized as rock and roll were released. Its ingredients percolating over time, it emerged like a stew in a crucible with some ingredients hotter, spicier, more palatable than the others (most prominently R&B) that had been cooking and cooking until one day the whole stew took a form that was its final incarnation. The name *rock and roll* was put to it in the early 1950s, and it became the music for a new generation of youths. It was characterized by a driving beat, strong vocals, simple chord progressions, and musicians who played piano, lead guitar, and bass guitar. From rock and roll would evolve a plethora of rock music forms, but rock and roll was the epoch in the history of modern youth music, and its biggest stars would become music icons as founders and progenitors of pop scions of that new youthful music.

By around the mid-point of the twentieth century, the young people of the day yearned for a music of their own. The popular music of the 1920s, 1930s, and 1940s was old and square, and they wanted a kind of music that they could relate to. And what they wanted was almost there. It was called rhythm and blues, and it had a number of musical styles, usually vocal with a driving beat, and evolved from black folk music, southern rural blues, and various jazz idioms. With its bluesy vocals, sexy wailing saxophone, and rapid tickling of the high notes on the piano, R&B drew to it young people—whites as well as blacks. It made them want to move, to dance, to snap their fingers and move their legs. But it was music made by African Americans, and African American music at the time was mainly directed for African Americans, and for white society it wasn't white enough yet. Indeed, there were songs by African American artists that could be labeled rock and roll, but they didn't gain mass acceptance for that genre. Rock and roll, as an official new pop music genre, was just waiting for the right song by the right white artist to bring it to the mainstream, meaning white teenagers, as society at the time segregated white music from black music and would label whatever music black musicians came up with as rhythm and blues. It wouldn't be exactly R&B; it would, as it evolved, synthesize other genres and styles, too, such as blues, country, western swing, jazz, ragtime, honky-tonk, spirituals, folk, and traditional pop. But it needed a Big Bang.

Rock and roll records hit the singles charts in the early 1950s and competed with other genres; some people indubitably doubted its long-term success, thinking it was just a temporary youth craze, but the genre may be said to have been officially crowned as a bona fide new genre that had mass appeal when it had its first number 1 song, "Rock around the Clock," in July 1955 (an early release of the record failed to climb high on the charts, but its success now was propelled by being in the soundtrack of the movie *The Blackboard Jungle*). The next year, rock and roll became a dominant new force of popular music when Elvis Presley, the future "King of Rock and Roll," burst onto the scene with multiple records reaching the summit position of the singles charts. The Big Bang of "Rock around the Clock" gave way to Elvis Presley leading the expansion of the rock and roll universe.

Other popular styles of music in this fleeting era included the cha cha cha, the plena/bomba/merengue, and doo-wop. Its time period was relatively short—it lasted until the late 1950s or early 1960s—but its impact was explosive, lighting the fire for a plethora of pop music genres and subgenres for new generations. With Tin Pan Alley pop before it, and rock (and all other kinds of popular music) after it, rock and roll was like the demarcation line between vintage pop and modern pop. Rock and roll laid the foundation for the divergent styles that followed and is comparable to the First Viennese School of classical composers with its iconic pioneers of Mozart, Haydn, and Beethoven. Rock and roll's icons included Presley, Chuck Berry, Little Richard, Bill Haley and His Comets, Carl Perkins, Buddy Holly, and Jerry Lee Lewis. It was a ripe time for a new youthful music. Hollywood had for years become bolder, releasing films that featured drugs, exploitation, and erotic scenes such as *Assassin of Youth* (1937), *Child Bride* (1943), and *The Outlaw* (1943), but popular music was still stuck in Tin Pan Alley, essentially producing feel-good saccharine songs (risqué songs were released, but the Hit Parade was mostly high-spirited love songs). Music lagged behind other forms of culture, but with rock and roll and its scions, it would come roaring back, although it would take time—even the Beatles' early songs such as "I Want to Hold Your Hand," "I'm Happy Just to Dance with You," and "And I Love Her" were fairly innocent. Examples of songs from the rock and roll era are "Rock around the Clock," "Maybellene," "Why Do Fools Fall in Love," "Ain't That a Shame," "See You Later, Alligator," "The Great Pretender," "Cherry Pink and Apple Blossom White," "Heartbreak Hotel," "Blue Suede Shoes," "Hound Dog," "Be-Bop-A-Lula," "Blueberry Hill," "Singing the Blues," "In the Still of the Night," "Young Love," "Little Darlin'," "Party Doll," "All Shook Up," "That'll Be the Day," "Bye Bye Love," "Jailhouse Rock," "Silhouettes," "At the Hop," "Great Balls of Fire," "My Special Angel," "Peggy Sue," "Sweet Little Sixteen," "Tequila," "Witch Doctor," "Tea for Two Cha Cha," "Stagger Lee," "Charlie Brown," "Personality," and "Sleep Walk." The core contemporary audience for rock and roll was the first-born of the Baby Boomers, those born between 1946 and 1964, and teens and young adults of the time period.

THE FIRST WAVE OF MODERN POP

Pop music is not stagnant; it is ever-evolving, and out of rock and roll came a new form of pop that was also intended for youths. This would be the first wave of modern pop to evolve from rock and roll, and it was a more sophisticated form of pop music with sleeker productions that used strings, horns, and new electronic instruments. From the early 1960s to the early 1980s, this era of pop, which was known in a general sense as "rock," included numerous genres such as surf, British pop, bubblegum, protest songs, folk rock, salsa, Mozambique, bugalu, bossa nova, country, soul, funk, soft rock, hard rock, acid rock, heavy metal, glitter rock, progressive rock, punk rock, and disco.

The stars of this first descendant of rock and roll started dominating the singles charts in the 1960s and included the Beach Boys, the Beatles, the Rolling Stones, the Dave Clark Five, the Who, Simon and Garfunkel, Janis Joplin, Sly and the Family Stone, Elton John, David Bowie, Bruce Springsteen, Queen, and Billy Joel. It was a creatively fruitful era that had both "pop-zations," where distinct genres of popular music became more pop-sounding, and "mold-breakings," in which rock music strayed into territory that was less mainstream. In this era country and western music began edging over to pop with several of its songs crossing over onto the pop charts. At the same time other styles of rock emerged, some played at high decibel levels where melody was subservient to screaming vocals and howling guitar riffs (heavy metal) or where performers on stage, with spiky hair or mohawks, would act out the protests of their songs by engaging in offensive antics such as plunging pins into their faces or making themselves throw up (punk rock).

In this wave, some R&B music continued its move into the mainstream with Motown artists such as the Miracles, the Temptations, Stevie Wonder, the Marvelettes, Martha and the Vandellas, and the Supremes all reaching the highest echelons of the mainstream charts. While classic R&B continued its ascent, over the years there had been many black artists who crossed over into the mainstream such as Duke Ellington, Billie Holiday, and Ella Fitzgerald, followed by Nat "King" Cole, Sarah Vaughan, Sammy Davis Jr., and the Platters and the Motown artists. Their music may be deemed pop (in the pure sense of its musical meaning) but because it was made by black artists it was often tagged as R&B, showing the myopic racial lens through which the music business and society view music products.

The first wave of modern pop songs include "All Day and All of the Night," "Baby, I'm Yours," "Ferry Cross the Mersey," "(I Can't Get No) Satisfaction," "King of the Road," "The Name Game," "You've Lost That Lovin' Feelin'," "California Dreamin'," "The 'In' Crowd," "Ticket to Ride," "Your Song," "Ain't No Sunshine," "Happy Together," "Papa Was a Rollin' Stone," "The Fool on the Hill," "How Can You Mend a Broken Heart," "Magical Mystery Tour," "Bridge over Troubled Water," "Reach Out (I'll Be There)," "Sugar, Sugar," "Mrs. Robinson,"

"Ain't No Mountain High Enough," "Tie a Yellow Ribbon Round the Old Oak Tree," "Goodbye Yellow Brick Road," "Dancing Queen," "One Tin Soldier," "Alone Again (Naturally)," "Just the Way You Are," "You Make Me Feel Like Dancing," "The Air That I Breathe," "Hopelessly Devoted to You," and "You May Be Right." The Baby Boomers were the main audience for this first wave of modern pop, but it also included, to a lesser extent, Generation X, those born between 1965 and 1979.

THE SECOND WAVE OF MODERN POP

It might be said that Michael Jackson and his 1982 *Thriller* album ushered in a new kind of pop, making it a second wave of pop. It was pop, to be sure, with many of its songs dance tunes, but not 1960s pop, 1970s pop, or disco. It had a crisp new feel to it, with different kinds of catchy hooks. Although some of the iconic rock stars of previous years continued to burn up the charts during this era, in the wake of *Thriller* came a new generation of pop artists such as Culture Club, the Eurythmics, Prince & the Revolution, Madonna, Van Halen, Bananarama, New Edition, Billy Ocean, Wham!, Whitney Houston, Sade, Janet Jackson, Bon Jovi, Tiffany, Debbie Gibson, Cheap Trick, New Kids on the Block, Taylor Dane, Fine Young Cannibals, Guns 'N Roses, Bangles, Milli Vanilli, Motley Crue, Gloria Estefan, M. C. Hammer, Billy Idol, James Ingram, Mariah Carey, Amy Grant, Nirvana, Boyz II Men, En Vogue, Kris Kross, TLC, Dr. Dre, 2Pac, the Cranberries, Toni Braxton, Jon Secada, Ace of Base, LL Cool J, Brandy, Goo Goo Dolls, Gin Blossoms, Spice Girls, Babyface, Puff Daddy, Celine Dion, Backstreet Boys, Jewel, Hanson, N'SYNC, Christina Aguilera, Destiny's Child, and Britney Spears. Examples of the second wave of modern pop songs include "Billie Jean," "Beat It," "She Drives Me Crazy," "Express Yourself," "Shoop," "I'll Make Love to You," "Creep," "Take a Bow," "Gangsta's Paradise," "Vision of Love," "Emotions," "Jump," "End of the Road," "I Will Always Love You," "Un-Break My Heart," "Can't Nobody Hold Me Down," "Hypnotize," "I'm Too Sexy," "I Want It That Way," "Truly, Madly, Deeply," "Waterfalls," and "Baby One More Time." This second wave of modern pop had its core audience with Generation X and millennials, those born between 1980 and 1994.

THE THIRD WAVE OF MODERN POP

In the early 2000s, a third wave of popular music started evolving, owing largely to the rise of women and rap in pop. There were several second wave female pop artists who were successful, but this subsequent wave produced female superstars in abundance including Beyoncé, Taylor Swift, Katy Perry, Ariana Grande, Lady Gaga, Rihanna, Ellie Goulding, Nicki Minaj, Kacey Musgraves, Meghan Trainor, Lorde, Cardi B, and Billie Eilish. Some of the stars of this era, such as Miley Cyrus, Selena Gomez, and Demi Lovato, got their start on kids' television shows before launching careers as music artists (the same may be said of stars of the previous wave such as Britney Spears, Alanis Morissette, and Justin Timberlake).

In this third wave, country music continued its decades-long traverse into pop music terrain—a number of country songs became pop hits in the 1960s, and in 1969 country artist Glen Campbell's *By the Time I Get to Phoenix* became the first country disc to win one of the pinnacle Grammys, "Album of the Year." Country artists such as Taylor Swift, a Nashville transplant from Pennsylvania who crossed the Mason-Dixon line of popular music after much success as a country songwriter, singer, and crooner and became a bona fide mainstream pop music superstar, may be regarded as the premier example of the country crossover migrant in this wave. Other country artists also went beyond their country roots—such as Florida Georgia Line, who had a smash country single in 2012 with "Cruise"—and incorporated other influences as they did with a remix of "Cruise," featuring the Grammy Award–winning rap artist Nelly.

In this wave, country music continued to embrace the genre's stereotypical redneck themes of drinking, trucks, honkytonks, and male camaraderie in recordings performed with southern drawls, fiddles, and twangy guitars, and while it was all a far cry from the yodels and themes that were inherent to the genre's primordial commercial days, its assimilation into mainstream pop veered further, with, depending on the artist, pop-like hooks, retro-rock-sounding records, and the use of beats and sounds that might be identified as hip hop and disco, respectively. Like with other specialty genres, streaming was a factor in bringing country music to audiences outside of its core.

Lyrics and song themes in this third wave became more prurient, profane, and underground than ever before, in some part due to the themes and lyrics embraced by rap and hip hop songs. Controversial lyrics have for a long time been a concern to the music industry, such as those that contain obscene words, descriptions of illegal drugs, graphic descriptions of sexual acts, descriptions of violence, and references to physical features of people or religion or ethnicity, and, as an FCC memorandum in August 1971 mentioned, "the pressing problems of crime, race relations, war, violence, drug abuse, and poverty," which it said listening audiences demand stations not shun and stay informed on.

Controversial lyrics even have a history of the songs from which they came being banned from airplay by radio stations. Pursuant to complaints about lyrics making illegal drug use sound desirable, on March 5, 1971, and also on April 16, 1971, the Federal Communications Commission issued statements about its concern over some radio station licensees playing records that "promote or glorify the use of drugs," informing broadcasters (which are licensed by the FCC) that they have a responsibility for their programming, although it didn't specify certain types of records that are prohibited from airplay. The Kingsmen 1963 hit "Louie Louie" reportedly has the F-word in it as a result of the drummer dropping his drumstick, which sparked an FBI investigation and led to many radio stations banning the record from airplay. Suggestive lyrics on Rolling Stones songs such as "Honky Tonk Women" and "Brown Sugar" also generated controversy. Randy Newman's 1977 "Short People" was banned by some radio stations for its alleged insult for those who were the subject of its title, and Barry McGuire's "Eve of Destruction" was banned as an anti-war song.

But times and musical genres change, and what was considered controversial in previous decades would be considered tame in later ones. Rap and hip hop brought in a whole new era of controversy with its use of profanity and themes of anti–law enforcement and misogyny among other controversial themes. In 2010 CeeLo Green had a huge hit with "Fuck You," a record that surely would have been banned by radio in previous decades; a sanitized version titled "Forget You" was subsequently released to make it more radio-friendly. While this third wave has its share of traditional-style pop songs, many of its hits would not even have been released in previous decades.

Although its roots go back decades, during this era electronic dance music (EDM) surged in popularity with a plethora of genres and sub-genres such as techno, trance (with subgenres including tech trance and vocal trance), house (electro and progressive), dubstep and drum and bass (ragga jungle, techstep, and liquid funk), jungle, UK garage, and grime. K-Pop, or Korean pop which incorporates elements of EDM, R&B, and hip hop and whose roots go back to the 1990s, also became a worldwide pop phenomenon in this era.

Traditional-type pop artists likewise enjoyed stellar success in this era, with artists such as Justin Bieber, Imagine Dragons, Bruno Mars, Maroon 5, and Ed Sheeran tearing up the charts, but traditional pop in this third wave of pop became usurped in terms of commercial success. Hip hop, gradually growing mainstream over the years, by the 2010s became the best-selling genre of popular music. The third wave of modern pop songs includes "In Da Club," "Lose Yourself," "Should've Said No," "You Belong with Me," "Swagga Like Us," "Gold Digger," "Viva la Vida," "Poker Face," "Drunk in Love," "Teenage Dream," "Super Bass," "California Gurls," "Raise Your Glass," "Flawless," "Hips Don't Lie," "Umbrella," "Sorry," "Moves Like Jagger," "Bodak Yellow," "Closer," "Thank U, Next," "Rolling in the Deep," "All about That Bass," "Can't Stop the Feeling!" "Love on the Brain," "See You Again," "Grenade," "Miss Movin' On," "Fancy," "Hello," "Happier," "Despacito," "Uptown Funk," "Psycho," "This Is America," and "God's Plan."

With the World Wide Web, the internationalization of pop music arguably manifested more in this wave than ever before. Sure, countries around the world had long embraced popular music—English troubadours came to America in the nineteenth century and performed popular tunes around the country; the tango enjoyed immense popularity in the country in the early 1900s. The Manhattan Transfer's "Chanson D'Amour" in 1977 and Falco's "Rock Me Amadeus" in 1986 are just some examples of foreign language songs that landed on the charts. And the Swedish group ABBA was a worldwide phenomenon of pop music with their string of hits in the 1970s. Although western hits have long permeated the charts in foreign countries, in this third wave countries around the world have been exporting pop groups like never before. In 2012 the Korean artist Psy hastened worldwide circulation of the term *K-pop* (Korean pop) with his 1 billion YouTube views (the first recording to achieve that humongous number) mega-hit "Gangnam Style."

The multi-billion YouTube-viewed "Despacito," released in 2017, brought heightened international interest in Latin pop. Although Cantonese-language pop music, or Cantopop, whose roots may be traced back to the 1970s and which has enjoyed popularity in Asian countries, has had good years and bad in terms of sales, it's still around, and Cantopop artists are still performing and releasing recordings in an effort to keep alive this native form of pop music. Russia, France, Denmark, and other countries have been exporters and importers of contemporary pop music, too. All in all, the internationalization of pop shows pop music to truly be an international language.

This third wave of modern pop has as its core audience Gen Z, those born around 1995 to 2015, and to a lesser extent, millennials. Of course there will be new waves of modern pop as new generations of youths come of age to create new permutations of pop music, and young fans look for a new music that speaks to their generation. With the vast catalog of existing pop music to build on, the advent of new forms of pop music promises to be exciting.

12

POP GOES THE FUTURE

What is the future of the pop song in the burgeoning digital music business?

As always, songwriters ply away, trying to find new ways to express, in verse and melody, the human experience. But the digital revolution is changing the way pop songs are written, recorded, marketed, distributed, tracked (on radio, streaming services, and social media), listened to, shared, recommended, streamed, sold, and otherwise monetized. Some of the technology and innovations that have ushered the pop song into a new age are digital audio workstations (DAWs); streaming services; curated playlists; social media; smartphones; ringtones; online distribution platforms; satellite radio; television and club track monitoring services; streaming service playlist tracking companies; and analytics.

For many years the primary factors in ranking recordings of songs in the trade charts have been their retail sales and the radio airplay they received. Then new technologies moved in to improve the methodologies of ratings. As modern technology evolved even further and social media and streaming platforms proliferated, new measurement techniques developed, and data is now used in all sorts of ways by the music business. Consequently, the industry can track people's online music listening habits as well as their purchases of recordings and concert tickets, the numbers of streams of songs on streaming services, the number of fans songs get on streaming services, radio station playlists, and much more. Indeed, numerous aspects of songs' performances can be measured, and in turn analytics (using data to discern consequential patterns and predict possible outcomes) may affect decisions made by various companies and individuals in the commercial marketplace. Analytics are used to predict how songs may commercially perform and even which new songs may become hits.

Modern technology has immersed the pop song in a mass of data that is constantly ongoing and can measure myriad angles of its activity and popularity. Clicks, hits, views, likes, posts, comments, and tweets on electronic devices are micro-analyzed so that virtually every facet of a song's performance becomes a statistic. In this respect songs are a true commercial product, analyzed matter-of-factly like cereal and candy for consumer appeal. Although songs may be differentiated from grocery goods and other products for their emotional and aesthetic appeal, in our technological age songs are veritable commercial goods and analytics are used to gauge and predict various aspects of songs' performances, and in turn these could have repercussions for the people who create music and who commercially release it.

There are numerous companies that serve to supply data that is of interest to the music industry—labels, artists, radio, songwriters, music publishers, streaming services, radio stations, and retailers, in particular—and the public. Nielsen Audio tracks people's radio listening habits and gives stations information on how many people are listening to their station out of their market's population (rating) and out of all listeners in the market tuned into all stations in the market (share), when they are listening, and the demographics of their listeners. Nielsen Sound-Scan is a data system that tracks the sales of songs and albums (as well as music videos) at their point of purchase at brick and mortar stores and online in some forty thousand outlets in the United States and around the world. Recorded music product is issued with a Universal Product Code, or UPC (barcode), and International Standard Recording Code (or ISRC, which provides international identification of sound recordings), which are machine-read, to indicate recorded music sales (the ISRC is also used for rights administration and royalty collection). SoundScan reports give labels and other industry professionals insight into what music is being purchased and the locations of the purchases, which can have ramifications for marketing. *Billboard* uses information supplied by SoundScan to compile some of its charts. For example, its album chart, the *Billboard 200*, uses a combination of actual sales as well as Track Equivalent Albums (TEAs; presently ten song downloads to equal one album purchase) and Streaming Equivalent Albums (presently 3,750 audio streams on free-tiers, 1,250 streams on premium tiers, or 3,750 video streams to equal one album purchase). Since singles became available for downloading, enabling consumers to avoid purchasing albums where many of the songs wouldn't be to their liking and they could instead purchase only songs they like, TEAs offer an alternative means for calculating what would be an album sale. Similarly, with people not purchasing albums because they could stream the same music for free or for a nominal fee from a streaming service subscription, TEAs offer an alternative means for calculating what would be an album sale. Nielsen Broadcast Data Systems, or BDS, tracks airplay of songs on radio and television, and plays of songs on Internet radio. It uses digital pattern recognition so that when a track is played, it is identified by the system's technology. Mediabase is a subscription-based information service owned by iHeart Media that monitors airplay on radio. Mediabase publishes charts of the top-ranked songs on radio stations of numerous formats so the movement of these songs may be monitored. Radio stations use Mediabase charts and information in their programming. They provide charts of the top tracks in many countries around the world, including the United States. Next Big Sound is a service that enables artists to see how they are performing on Pandora. Artist profiles include such information as their lifetime Pandora streams, unique listeners, weekly Pandora radio spins, and artists' audience engagement rating. Next Big Sound's information is used to compile Pandora's charts, such as its Trendsetters Chart, which shows which twenty artists Pandora users have focused on to compile the greatest number of stations over the most recent week. Nielsen Ring-Scan tracks weekly ringtone point of sales. Its ringtone reports are on polyphonic, voice, and master ringtones, and they are used by *Billboard* for its ringtone chart. Shazam is a mobile app that tells users the titles of songs that are playing. A Shazam user activates the app when music is playing, and the app creates a digital fingerprint of the song and matches it with the millions of songs in the Shazam database; the song title is then identified and related information may appear such as the song's lyrics. Shazam also offers users a way of discovering new music by enabling users to follow artists and listen to tracks these artists are listening to.

So what does this all mean for the songwriter?

Since the days of Tin Pan Alley, tunesmiths have striven to write songs that could become hits in the commercial marketplace. It's nice to write songs, but if one wanted a career from it, it was necessary to make money from it. Moderate sheet music sellers would bring in income, but the writers and publishers wanted hits (just like today). Hits in the Alley's early days would lead to million-selling sheet music sales and later on to huge phonograph record sales as well, all of which could make the writers and publishers of the hits wealthy. If a certain kind of song struck it big, then other writers would imitate the style or subject of the hit. Creators followed trends. Indeed, some writers tried to cash in this way, although other writers pressed on with originality that pioneered new forms and sounds. In any case, the songwriters of this age only had sheet music and record sales information to go on, and publishers, labels, artists, and producers used their ears and instincts in deciding what songs to sign, record, and release into the commercial marketplace.

If artists and others write songs based on targeting specific audiences or demographics on online platforms, then it may be said that songs could be "manufactured" for the commercial marketplace, although it might be argued that such a process wouldn't actually be a new phenomenon, as songwriters since the days of Tin Pan Alley, as just mentioned, have been writing tunes with the idea of selling as many copies of sheet music or records as possible, often following trends. But by using metrics and analytics to predict song success, songwriters could "micro-tailor" and fine-tune their work for specific audiences. Indeed, singles and whole albums could be tailored in this way.

While songwriting has long been a collaborative process, in recent years it has been common for numerous writers to take part in the writing of a song. Writers who specialize in certain aspects of songwriting such as creating hooks or bridges or samples may be called in to help the songwriting process. This may be akin to, say, baseball, which has specialists such as pinch hitters, pinch runners, and closers.

As streaming services become even more dominant in the delivery of music, CD and vinyl sales decline further, and, as some have prognosticated, radio becomes a less important source of music delivery, what will that mean for the fate of the song? Will tunesmiths be penning songs for the myriad curated streaming playlists? Will songs be written for both broad and niche markets? Will attitudes expressed about artists and songs on social media influence how writers pen songs? Will people try to enter the music business based on their analysis of data and try to engineer their way to success based more on statistics than a genuine love of music?

Today, there are myriad opportunities for the tunesmith. There are the traditional revenue streams such as radio airplay and other public performances, recorded music sales, motion picture and television syncs, advertisements, and printed music sales. Digital technology offers revenue from sources such as streaming and ringtones. Although writers complain the royalties in these areas are low, with social media songs can become known to more people than ever before, as some songs have garnered over 1 billion streams on the major streaming services. According to a report in December 2018 by the online international music industry publication *Music Business Worldwide*, the five most streamed pop songs of the twentieth century were Queen's "Bohemian Rhapsody" followed by Nirvana's "Smells Like Teen Spirit," Guns N' Roses' "Sweet Child O' Mine," Guns N' Roses' "November Rain," and a-ha's "Take on Me," all with over 1 billion streams ("Bohemian Rhapsody" had at that time 1.6 billion streams, no doubt aided by the then recent release of the biopic of Queen with the same title). In July 2017, NPR reported that within six months of its release. "Despacito," the Spanish-language Latin pop tune recorded by Daddy Yankee and Luis Fonsi, a January 2017 release with an April 2017 remix version featuring Justin Bieber, garnered 4.6 billion streams. While undoubtedly some people stream a song multiple times, that staggering number of a billion-plus streams for an individual song may be seen in perspective by comparing it with the world's population, which as of May 2018 was estimated to be 7.6 billion people. With the sundry online platforms, there are many places for songs to be heard today, not to mention that it is easier than ever to record songs in a professional manner.

In previous years, songwriters would make demos by going into a professional studio and making recordings of their songs. The demos could be simple, perhaps just a vocal rendition of the song with either a guitar or keyboard accompaniment, or maybe they would be more elaborate with a rhythm section and background singers. In any case, studio time was usually expensive with costly hourly rates, and not all writers could afford to demo their songs in a studio. As computer technology advanced, songs could be recorded on home equipment relatively cheaply, and recordings could be made at home that actually sounded like professional masters. The quality of these digitally home-made recordings could be so good that they actually matched or surpassed that of professional recordings made in previous decades such as the 1940s, 1950s, 1960s, and 1970s. All that is needed to record at home is a computer; a digital audio workstation (DAW) or application software such as Pro Tools, GarageBand, Logic Pro, or Renoise; a microphone; cables; and instruments. With the relatively inexpensive technology now available, anyone, even children, can make recordings from their bedrooms, living rooms, or garages, and use online music distribution services (such as Bandcamp and SoundCloud), social media, and streaming services to post and publicize their songs. With technology enabling anyone to record a pop song he or she writes, this may result in more songs being written and recorded than ever before, yet at the same time with the increased number of songs, it can become even more competitive for songwriters to license their works and earn a living from their craft.

There are sites like Songtradr that list song needs for TV shows, movies, advertisements, and other uses. Songwriters can upload their recordings and with a click submit their work for whatever need is listed, but with calls sometimes running several days, they can also create and record music they think will fit a particular need and submit it. While their work has to compete with many other submissions, the overriding point here is that with digital technology they are now able to have a chance of getting their music in professional and big-time productions that previously were offered only to seasoned professionals, with neophytes having virtually no chance of having an opportunity for their work to be considered.

Technology aside, the future of pop songs is indubitably bright, as history has shown popular music is an art form that people like, want, and need. From calamitous times like war to dire times like economic depressions, songwriters have been productive creators of popular songs, and consumers have been avid followers of popular music. Even when peer-to-peer file sharing economically hurt the record industry and some people predicted its end, songwriters continued to bountifully put out new music, and many consumers eventually became paying subscribers to streaming services, helping the record industry to bounce back from its economic throes.

It used to be said that music industry executives shaped public taste, but in the digital age with metrics influencing signing and airplay and streaming curator decisions, and with unsigned artists able to put their music out there and let the public judge its worth through streaming, it may be said that the public now has a greater role than ever in shaping the music industry. In that sense, with public taste all over the place, the music business is in an "anything goes" mode. Artists and writers can put out their material and use social media, touring, and other means to help them find an audience, and the public can respond as it wishes. Artists don't have to follow trends; they can follow their hearts. The commercial marketplace is now a vast arena of sundry music genres and styles, with the *Billboard* Hot 100, once a bastion for pop songs (in the narrow traditional pure sense), now, in its top echelon, a haven for whatever musical style is dominant at the moment. In the late 2010s hip hop has occupied the top slots of the singles chart with Drake its premier exponent. Latin-pop numbers such as Camila Cabello's "Havana" and Cardi B, Bad Bunny, and J. Balvin's "I Like It" have been sensational worldwide hits. As old-style pop becomes less a factor in the commercial marketplace and factionalized genres become more mainstream, the term *pop* music becomes more inclusive than ever as an umbrella term for any style of music that captures the public's attention. *Billboard* issues around the end of the year a list of the top artists, songs, albums, and labels for the country, rock, R&B/hip hop, rap, Latin, Christian, Gospel, and dance/electronic genres for the year and generally don't even list "pop" as a separate category (although the Grammy Awards have categories for "pop").

With the future of the album questionable and 45s essentially a product of a bygone era, it may be argued that the song is more important than ever. There has been a trend for artists to continually release singles into the marketplace, hoping to catch streaming activity, and with that, album cuts and 45 B sides may become relics of the past. Another trend has been for artists to release singles and remixes featuring another (often well-known) artist. This could enable an artist of one genre to cross over into another genre (or mainstream) with a featured artist of that other genre.

Indeed, in the evolving digital age with culture changing at a rapid pace, people of different countries more closely connected than ever before, diversity becoming pronounced, and more music than ever available, it's a whole new world for pop songs.

The story of pop music is not an American story, nor is it a British or French story or that of any other nationality. Pop music is not indigenous to any nation, and its evolution came about as an amalgamation of the folk tunes and rhythms of many lands. Sure, a genre such as rock and roll may have its launch in one country (America), but its roots may be traced back to blues and spirituals and beats of other countries. Today, many countries have their own pop charts, although some hits are international and may become popular on foreign charts as well as their domestic charts. With the Internet and streaming services, there is an internationalization of pop music like never before, and modern technology threatens to break down the erstwhile and existing national divisions of pop music further.

The music business has always been dynamic. Culture is always changing, and as popular songs reflect culture, writers are always crafting new kinds of songs. Technology changes, and so, too, do the methods of recording music and delivering it to the public. Likewise, business practices change, and ways in which the public pays for music change, too. But in our digital age, never has the pace at which the music business changes been so rapid, practically on a daily basis. Indeed, today's music business may look different from the way it will be in three years, five years, and so forth.

We live today in one of the most exciting—and arguably *the* most exciting—times of the music business ever, so dynamic is it that it must be considered in context. There have been many watershed moments of the modern music industry: the birth of Tin Pan Alley, the beginning of radio, the emergence of the first popular music superstar (Al Jolson), the repeal of Prohibition sparking the resurrection of the floundering music business, the use of electronic instruments in making music, the creation of LPs and 45s, the emergence of rock and roll, the advent of Top 40 radio, the rise of Elvis Presley and the Beatles, the running of the iconic pop music festival Woodstock, the Sound Recording Amendment creating a copyright in sound recordings to help protect against piracy, the rise of disco and rap and hip hop, the launching of MTV, the creation of CDs, MP3s, and iPods, and iTunes and smartphones. But before the launch of social media and streaming services, never had virtually the whole catalog of recorded music been available to the world instantly and for free or for a nominal price. And now as technology increases at a record pace with all sorts of innovations previously thought to be fictional, the possibilities for making and delivering music to the public are virtually endless.

Music is a vital and ubiquitous part of the twenty-first-century cultural landscape. It's on the radio, on streaming services, in stores and shopping malls, in concert halls, in dance studios, on buses, on phone holds, in schools, in doctors' waiting rooms, on smartphones and computers and other devices via streaming services, in movies, on television, in advertisements, in theaters and arenas, in clubs and concert halls. It's in our cars, and we can hear it when we walk or run. It's in our kitchens and by our beds. Music is part of the tapestry of daily life. Songs are everywhere. And that's good, of course, for songwriters and the music business.

A song makes money from being licensed. There are many ways a song can be licensed, and consequently there are many ways a song can make money, but licensing is a short and simple way of summarizing how a song is legally disseminated to the public and has the potential to generate revenue.

As a copyrightable work—songs fall under one of the eight categories of copyrightable works in Section 102 of the U.S. copyright law— the owner of a song has the exclusive right, subject to certain limitations, to reproduce, adapt, distribute, publicly perform, and display his or her work, or to authorize others to do so. This means that if anyone wants to use a copyrighted song in ways protected by the copyright law, permission must be obtained from the copyright owner, or the owner's agent. In commercial practice permission is granted in the form of a written license, which generally means the licensee must pay fees or royalties for uses or sales of the owner's song in whatever form it was licensed. The moneys collected for these uses or sales is the income for the song, which the copyright owner, usually a music publisher, splits with the song's writer in accordance with their contract.

In what ways may a song be licensed? Licenses to use a song in accordance with the exclusive rights granted to the owner of a copyright under the copyright law are many and varied and include the following:

radio airplay; television broadcasts; streaming; performances in concert halls, bars, arenas, and dance studios; reproduction in CDs, vinyl, and cassettes; digital downloads; video games; motion picture and television synchronization; music boxes; commercial announcements; sheet music and other printed editions of the work such as band, orchestral, and choral arrangements; ringtones; and reproduction of the lyrics in posters and other items.

Every licensed use of a song has the potential to earn money for its copyright owner and writer. License fees or royalty rates are negotiated between the music user and the copyright owner or the owner's agent, although under the U.S. copyright law the compulsory license provision for making and distributing phonorecords in effect sets a limit to the royalty a record manufacturer must pay to be the copyright owner of a song (the parties are free to negotiate a lesser royalty). The kinds of fees and royalties a song generates often have particular kinds of names in the music business. There are many different kinds of royalties in the music business, and technology seems to be increasing them. With technology continually evolving and the forms of delivery of music changing and expanding, the potential for copyright owners to derive revenues from new and varied sources is considerable.

When it comes to the law, it doesn't matter what a song's genre is— hard rock, grunge, country, hip hop, jazz, reggae, bluegrass, Latin, electronica, punk, or folk—or how good or bad it is. All songs in which copyright protection subsists are equal under the law and have the same right to be licensed and to earn money. The quality of a song, however, may determine how popular it becomes and how many and what kinds of licenses are issued for it and what fee or rate and how many sales or streams it will have. A popular song could earn substantial money from being licensed in many different ways, not only from the initial sound recording, where a new song usually starts life, but also from subsequent recordings and licenses issued during its entire term of copyright protection, which, if it was written on or after January 1, 1979, and is not a work for hire, endures for the life of the author plus an additional period of seventy years. It is generally up to the copyright owner (music publisher) to exploit the song and maximize its number of licensed uses and income.

The story of a record is that it will be issued by a label, and if it catches on, with everything from radio airplay, streaming, and word of mouth influencing sales and plays, it may land on the charts. It will have a limited duration there—as new product is constantly coming out, and after a while people will get tired of it—but its duration on the charts can be long, and it can even fall off and come back on again. The story of a song is somewhat different, as it can be covered by artists of the same or other genres, and be on the charts at the same time or a later time. A record can fall off the chart and another artist's recording of the same song can land on the same chart a year later or five or ten or fifty years later. But once an artist's recording falls off, then it usually doesn't come back on again, although there are exceptions, an example of which would be a perennially popular holiday recording or the use of the recording in a popular TV show or film. Of course, just because a recording doesn't come back on a chart doesn't mean it's the end of that recording. It can be issued in albums or appear in TV shows or movies, as well as, of course, being played on the radio or streamed. All these different uses of a recording and song earn royalties or license fees in different ways for the copyright owners (labels for the recording and music publisher for the song) and the artist and songwriter.

Indeed, songs and sound recordings are not just sources of musical entertainment but are intellectual properties with many potential revenue streams that have to be properly exploited, marketed, and administered to reach their full economic potential. That the song is an intellectual property whose owner has the right to authorize and profit off its uses is rooted in the copyright law, which has undergone several revisions over the years and will indubitably continue to undergo revisions that further define the rights of owners of intellectual properties such as songs. The music business professional looks at songs not just as sources of entertainment, but as intellectual properties whose purpose, in addition to their aesthetic and cultural impact, is economic, meaning, to make money for all the participants involved.

The pop song business today is one of licensing. It's an exciting time, this burgeoning digital age, where songs can reach more people quicker than ever before, and the potential for a song to be used in many different ways has never been greater.

Indeed, songs have numerous potential revenue streams, and song owners, the music publishers, function to get songs used in as many areas as possible and maximize the revenues in each of those areas. They try to think creatively, finding novel uses for their songs that will consequently result in new revenue streams. With CD sales having diminished since streaming took off, it is incumbent on publishers to find other sources of revenue and also to promote their music copyrights in every way.

Today, music is ubiquitous, as it can be accessed essentially anywhere from so many different devices. But in its essence, the music industry is still the same as it was in the days of the horse and buggy. In our age of driverless cars and sophisticated machinery that responds to voice-activated commands and in which technology is evolving at an ever-fast pace, it is difficult to say where the music industry will be in ten or twenty or fifty or one hundred years from now, but it is safe to say that what will keep it going is great songs and, just the same as it was in Tin Pan Alley, bringing them to the public as efficiently and affordably as possible.

With technology having vastly changed the world since 1976, when the fourth general revision of the U.S. copyright law was signed (which became fully effective on January 1, 1978), the U.S. copyright law has been sorely in need of reform. At the time of the 1976 law's enactment, there were no CDs in the commercial marketplace, no online retailers of recorded music, and no streaming services. Since that time, recorded music sales declined precipitously, the death knell has been sounded on terrestrial radio, and the world and the music business have become immersed in the streaming era.

On October 11, 2018, President Donald Trump signed into law the Music Modernization Act. Consisting of three areas of legislation, the act helps make sure that songwriters get paid a fair market value for their songs in the digital era. It creates a governmental mechanical licensing collective for the purpose of forming a database of song information that streaming services can use to remit royalties to songwriters (ameliorating the difficulty of locating song rights' owners for obtaining streaming performance licenses). The Copyright Royalty Board, which decides certain royalty rates, was permitted by the act to determine a song's royalty rate based on the open market, which it could not do before, which means songwriters should see increased royalties in areas such as webcast radio. The performing rights organizations, ASCAP and BMI, had their legal cases decided by the same judges at the U.S. District Court for the Southern District of New York, which has not always worked out favorably for them. The act provided that a rotating panel of judges would hear the cases of these organizations, which license the non-dramatic performance rights of songwriters and music publishers.

The Music Modernization Act, while beneficial to songwriters but not a panacea to their perceived song-royalty ills, was just the latest of a long line of legislation addressing musical composition income, and of course there will be more needed legal enactments pertaining to this area in the years ahead. And like the chain of copyright legislation, new generations of songwriters will undoubtedly fight for and become beneficiaries of laws pertaining to songs. Each new generation of songwriters carries on the genetic material of their predecessors. No matter what kind of music they write, no matter what genre their songs are in, new-generation songwriters are like members of a family chain who sprout up to create music for public enjoyment. Indeed, future songwriters will carry on the DNA of a long line of songwriters that include Stephen Foster, Scott Joplin, George M. Cohan, George Gershwin, Cole Porter, Irving Berlin, Hank Williams, John Lennon, Paul McCartney, Bob Dylan, Carole King, Elton John, and Stevie Wonder, whose songs, like those of so many others, will live on forever.

Pop music is an ever-growing organism. It doesn't stay stagnant. It's like a tree with many branches, and with new ones growing out of old ones. It is a tree that will never stop growing, no matter which direction its branches go. It will continue to grow and have many dynamic branches, but they will all be part of one family tree.

What is the future of the music business? Technology and business practices are always changing, but insofar as the music business is concerned, from radio airplay to streaming, from concerts to movie themes, in the end, it all comes down to the song. Future generations will inherit the task of supplying music to the public, and while styles and genres may change, there's one thing you can be sure of: as long as there's love and heartbreak, friendship and loneliness, joy and jealousy, there will always be great pop songs.

APPENDIX A

100 Years of Hit Songs: A Select List

Following is a list of hit songs from 1919 to 2019. First appears the year in which the song was written or a hit (as songs could be recorded many times over the years, the year listings here may refer to when the song had its biggest hit). Then follows the title and the writer(s) of the song in parentheses (gleaned, where possible, from the physical recording's printed credits). Next is a short summary of the song's lyrics. As all lyrics are open to interpretation, the summaries shouldn't be taken as definitive descriptions of the songs, but rather just the author's interpretations. For songs from the 1950s on, the name of the artist or artists who had a hit with the song that year follows the short summary, as these artists today are closely associated with those songs. A preponderance of these hit songs come from the 1960s, a decade characterized in this book as a "golden age of pop." The list presented here is a select one, and does not include many songs that were hits in these years, nor does it include instrumentals. Of course, songs could have been hits in other years than the ones listed here, but the year indicated is usually the first year they were hits or when they were written.

- *1919*—"A Pretty Girl Is Like a Melody" (Irving Berlin): Just like you can't free your mind of a haunting melody, you can't get a pretty girl out of your head.

- *1919*—"Swanee" (George Gershwin and Irving Caesar): Singing birds, strumming banjos, my own mammy calling me from home—I'd give anything to be back in Dixie by the Swanee with the old folks there.
- *1919*—"How Ya Gonna Keep 'Em Down on the Farm after They've Seen Paree?" (Joe Young, Sam Lewis, and Walter Donaldson): After the boys return home from the war and having seen Paris, how are they going to want to rake and plow when they'll want to go to Broadway and paint the town?
- *1919*—"Love Sends a Little Gift of Roses" (John Openshaw and Leslie Cooke): Love is a gift of roses in which your heart grows more tender and your eyes glow with love's splendor.
- *1920*—"My Mammy" (Joe Young, Sam Lewis, and Walter Donaldson): The further away from home you get the more lonely you could be, so you might find yourself saying, "No matter how far apart we are, Mom, I'd walk all the way home just to see your smile."
- *1920*— "Avalon" (Al Jolson, Vincent Rose, and B. G. DeSylva): I dream all day of the love I left in a place by the bay called Avalon.
- *1920*— "I'll Be with You in Apple Blossom Time" (Albert Von Tilzer and Neville Fleeson): You told me that when the apple tree blossoms you'd be mine, so spring is coming and we'll be together and we'll be wed.
- *1920*—"Whispering" (Vincent Rose, Richard Coburn, and John Schonberger): Your whispers of love cheer me.
- *1920*—"Look for the Silver Lining" (Jerome Kern and B. G. DeSylva): When sadness comes, try to look on the bright side of life.
- *1920*—"When My Baby Smiles at Me" (Harry Von Tilzer, Andrew B. Sterling, Billy Munro, and Ted Lewis): I'm in heaven when my sweetheart smiles at me.
- *1921*—"I'm Just Wild about Harry" (Eubie Blake and Noble Sissle): I just want to plainly make it clear that my man and I are just crazy about each other.
- *1921*—"April Showers" (Louis Silvers and B. G. DeSylva): Life's not always easy so when bright days give way to rain, don't worry—flowers will soon bloom.
- *1921*—"Second Hand Rose" (James Hanley and Grant Clarke): Woe is me! Everything I have is second-hand from my father's

second-hand store, and even the man I love was married once before!

- *1921*—"Ain't We Got Fun" (Richard A. Whiting, Gus Kahn, and Raymond B. Egan): The bill collectors come for us because we can't pay the rent or the grocery bills, but we've got each other plus the stork just delivered twins so "ain't we got fun"?
- *1921*—"My Man" (Jacques Charles, Maurice Yvain, Albert Willemetz, and Channing Pollack): My man isn't that good looking, he's no hero, and he's got lots of girls, but I'm lost without him, and when he embraces me everything is bright, so I will always be his.
- *1921*—"Ma, He's Making Eyes at Me" (Con Conrad and Sidney Clare): All the guys wanted little Lilly, but she resisted them all, and when a guy would try to get romantic with her, she would cry out to her mother that "he's making eyes at me."
- *1922*—"I'll Build a Stairway to Paradise" (George Gershwin, Ira Gershwin, and B. G. DeSylva): Learn the right moves and take the right steps, and you will have a staircase to heaven.
- *1922*—"Way Down Yonder in New Orleans" (J. Turner Layton and Henry Creamer): With "those beautiful queens" in New Orleans that place of "dreamy scenes" is heaven.
- *1922*—"My Buddy" (Walter Donaldson and Gus Kahn): Ever since you went away my days are long, I miss everything about you, and I just want you to know that "your buddy misses you."
- *1922*—"Toot, Toot Tootsie! (Goo' Bye)" (Gus Kahn, Robert King, Ted Fiorito, and Ernie Erdman): I'm so sad to have to leave you and I'll always write, but if you don't get a letter from me then you'll know I've been locked up.
- *1922*—"Carolina in the Morning" (Walter Donaldson and Gus Kahn): Carolina mornings are a glory to be with my sweetie.
- *1923*—"That Old Gang of Mine" (Billy Rose, Mort Dixon, and Ray Henderson): I'll never forget my buddies—I'd give anything to be with "that old gang of mine."
- *1923*—"Who's Sorry Now" (Harry Ruby, Ted Snyder, and Bert Kalmar): I cried each time you broke your vow, but I warned you, so I'm happy that you're feeling sorry now.
- *1923*—"Barney Google" (Billy Rose and Con Conrad): He thought he had it all, that cad Barney Google with the "goo-goo-

googaly eyes," but when he tried to enter heaven he was told to "Go to the other place."

- *1923*—"Charleston" (Cecil Mack and Jimmy Johnson): That new dance, the Charleston, was made in Carolina, which may not be able to do the two step or fox trot, but the Charleston will put Carolina on the map.
- *1924*—"It Had to Be You" (Isham Jones and Gus Kahn): For all your faults I could only love you.
- *1924*—"The Man I Love" (George Gershwin and Ira Gershwin): I dream that one day the man I will love will come along.
- *1924*—"I Want to Be Happy" (Vincent Youmans and Irving Caesar): I can only be happy if I make you happy like you make me happy.
- *1924*—"All Alone" (Irving Berlin): I wait alone "by the telephone" for you to call.
- *1924*—"California, Here I Come" (Al Jolson, Joseph Meyer, and B. G. DeSylva): I'm going back to California, which is my favorite place to be.
- *1924*—"Everybody Loves My Baby, but My Baby Don't Love Nobody but Me" (Spencer Williams and Jack Palmer): All the other girls might love my man, but I know he only loves me.
- *1924*—"Fascinating Rhythm" (George Gershwin and Ira Gershwin): I've got this captivating rhythm in my head that's driving me crazy and everybody wants to know why I'm hoofing and strutting, so please, take some time off, so I can be "the girl I used to be."
- *1925*—"Five Foot Two, Eyes of Blue" (Sam M. Lewis, Ray Henderson, and Joe Young): If you happen to see a five-foot-two gal with a nose that's turned up and hosiery that's turned down, you can be sure that the fur and diamond ring she has aren't hers; have you seen her?
- *1925*—"I'm Sitting on Top of the World" (Joe Young, Sam M. Lewis, and Ray Henderson): My honey's going to marry me so I feel like I'm as high as I can be.
- *1925*—"Who" (Jerome Kern, Oscar Hammerstein II, and Otto Harbach): Who has my heart and makes me dream dreams that can't come true? Just you.

- *1925*—"A Cup of Coffee, a Sandwich and You?" (Billy Rose, Joseph Meyer, and Al Dubin): I don't need the romance of movies and magazines; "a cup of coffee, a sandwich and you" will do!
- *1925*—"Always" (Irving Berlin): I will always be there for you.
- *1925*—"If You Knew Susie, Like I Know Susie" (Joseph Meyer and B. G. DeSylva): People may think they know my sweetie, but nobody knows her like me.
- *1925*—"Sometimes I'm Happy" (Vincent Youmans, Irving Caesar, and Clifford Grey): Whether I'm happy or not depends on you.
- *1925*—"Sweet Georgia Brown" (Maceo Pinkard, Ben Bernie, and Kenneth Casey): Wherever she goes that sweet Georgia Brown just slays them.
- *1925*—"My Yiddishe Momme" (Jack Yellen and Lew Pollack): I may not have grown up in paradise but I was a treasure for my mother, who cared nothing for material things; even though I made her cry, I now need her more than ever.
- *1926*—"Bye Bye Blackbird" (Ray Henderson and Mort Dixon): Goodbye, black bird, I'm going home tonight to somebody who understands and waits for me.
- 1926—"Mountain Greenery" (Richard Rodgers and Lorenz Hart): It's spring so it's time to get away from the city and go to the country, which is blessed with "mountain greenery."
- *1926*—"Are You Lonesome Tonight?" (Roy Turk and Lou Handmand): Like a stage play we acted like lovers, but you lied when you told me you loved me, and now that the stage is empty, I wonder if you're lonesome tonight.
- *1926*—"Gimme a Little Kiss, Will Ya Huh?" (Maceo Pinckard, Roy Turk, and Jack Smith): You have nothing to lose, and I'm not asking for much, so why don't you give me a little kiss?
- *1926*—"Baby Face" (Benny Davis and Harry Akst): You're so cute that when I'm with you I'm in heaven.
- *1926*—"Someone to Watch over Me" (George Gershwin and Ira Gershwin): I don't care if he's handsome; I'm just longing for someone to look out for me.
- *1926*—"When the Red, Red Robin Comes Bob, Bob, Bobbin' Along" (Harry Woods): Even if I'm blue, I can wake up and be happy and feel like a kid again when that red robin comes along chirping that wonderful old song of his.

- *1927*—"I'm Looking over a Four-Leaf Clover" (Harry Woods and Mort Dixon): The leaves of my four-leaf clover are sunshine, rain, and roses, but the last one, the one I've overlooked "is somebody I adore."
- *1927*—"Side by Side" (Harry Woods): We don't need much money and the world can come tumbling down, but it doesn't matter if we can move along singing right next to each other.
- *1927*—"Ol' Man River" (Jerome Kern and Oscar Hammerstein II): We go through life sweating and straining, but the earth keeps moving, saying nothing, but must know something.
- *1927*—"Can't Help Lovin' Dat Man" (Jerome Kern and Oscar Hammerstein II): My man's got a lot of faults, but like creatures of the world do their natural thing, I can't help loving him.
- *1927*—"The Varsity Drag" (B. G. DeSylva, Ray Henderson, and Lew Brown): Forget what they teach you in school; learn how to dance the "Varsity drag."
- *1927*—"Thou Swell" (Richard Rodgers and Lorenz Hart): You're sweet, witty, pretty, and grand—you're swell.
- *1927*—"Me and My Shadow" (Billy Rose, Al Jolson, and Dave Dreyer): It's evening and I'm sad and alone as couples are out having fun, so I'll stroll along, just "me and my shadow."
- *1927*—"My Blue Heaven" (George Whiting and Walter Donaldson): Like lovebirds returning to their nests at night, I rush to my own nest where Mollie and our baby are happy in our "blue heaven."
- *1928*—"Shortnin' Bread" (Clement Wood and Jacques Wolfe): Mama's baby sure loves that shortnin' bread.
- *1928*—"Crazy Rhythm" (Joseph Meyer, Irving Caesar, and Roger Wolfe Kahn): I'm a high brow and that crazy rhythm's a low brow, and it's to blame for making me a "no brow" and now I'm "crazy too."
- *1928*—"You're the Cream in My Coffee" (Ray Henderson, Lew Brown, and B. G. DeSylva): You're everything to me and without you I'd be lost.
- *1928*—"Love Me or Leave Me" (Gus Kahn and Walter Donaldson): I only love you, so if you don't love me, then leave me, as I only want to be with you.

- *1928*—"I'm a Ding Dong Daddy from Dumas" (Phil Baxter): I may be a country bumpkin, but just watch me sashay.
- *1928*—"Sweet Sue, Just You" (Victor Young and Will Harris): The stars in the heavens and the moon in the sky know, just as my heart does, that you're the one I love.
- *1929*—"Stardust" (Hoagy Carmichael and Mitchell Parish): In the twilight of my years, we may be apart, but I am reminded of the music of our love in the haunting melody "in the stardust of a song."
- *1929*—"Singin' in the Rain" (Arthur Freed and Nacio Herb Brown): It may be cloudy and dark, but I'm raring to love, so I've got sunshine in my heart and I can burst with song even when the rain comes down.
- *1929*—"With a Song in My Heart" (Richard Rodgers and Lorenz Hart): Every time we meet it's like the first time, so when I gaze into your face and the heavens open when I hear your voice, I meet you with my heart fluttering a melody.
- *1929*—"Ain't Misbehavin'" (Thomas "Fats" Waller, Andy Razaf, and Harry Brooks): When we're apart, I'm staying faithful to you.
- *1929*—"Moanin' Low" (Ralph Rainger and Howard Dietz): My man is mean but he needs me and I'm going to lose him, so I'm lamenting low.
- *1929*—"More Than You Know" (Edward Eliscu, Vincent You-mans, and Billy Rose): No matter where you wander or if your friends turn away from you or if you don't succeed at what you want, I could never live without you, and I need you so much that you can't even imagine it.
- *1929*—"Tip-Toe thru the Tulips with Me" (Al Dubin and Joe Burke): Come walk quietly with me in the flowers of the garden where the rain will stay away, and I'll kiss you in the moonlight.
- *1929*—"What Is This Thing Called Love?" (Cole Porter): Love flew into my life and then went; it's a mystery and made a fool of me, so I ask, what is it?
- *1929*—"Louise" (Richard Whiting and Leo Robin): Every little thing reminds me that I love you, but how can it be that someone like you loves me?

- *1929*—"Puttin' on the Ritz" (Irving Berlin): When you're sad and don't know where to turn, go to where the rich and famous sit, "puttin' on the ritz."
- *1930*—"Ten Cents a Dance" (Richard Rodgers and Lorenz Hart): From seven to midnight I dance with tough guys and rough guys for a dime as saxophones and trumpets burst my eardrums and patrons step on my toes.
- *1930*—"I Got Rhythm" (George Gershwin and Ira Gershwin): I've got music, rhythm, and a man, and I couldn't ask for anything more.
- *1930*—"On the Sunny Side of the Street" (Jimmy McHugh and Dorothy Fields): Don't walk in the shade with the blues, but cross over to the sunny side of the street where "the happy tune is your step" and life is sweet.
- *1930*—"Cheerful Little Earful" (Harry Warren, Ira Gershwin, and Billy Rose): No matter what life's downs are, a "cheerful little earful" is "I love you."
- *1930*—"Fine and Dandy" (Kay Swift and Paul James): With you, everything is "fine and dandy."
- *1930*—"You Brought a New Kind of Love to Me" (Sammy Fain, Pierre Norman, and Irving Kahal): Everything in life is better because you're loving me like I've never known before.
- *1930*—"Just a Gigolo" (original Austrian version: Leonello Casucci and Julius Brammer; English lyrics: Irving Caesar): I don't have anyone and I'm sad and lonely because I'm just a gigolo.
- *1931*—"Love Letters in the Sand" (Nick Kenny, Charles Kenny, and J. Fred Coots): We used to write love letters in the sand just like today, and I cried every time the tide washed them away, but you broke your promise, and now my heart aches when the waves break like when it used to wash our letters away.
- *1931*—"All of Me" (Gerald Marks and Seymour Simons): When you left me you took my kisses and my love, and now I'm just a remnant, so take my lips and my arms because I'll never use them again; so since I'm not complete alone why don't you just take my whole self?
- *1931*—"Dream a Little Dream of Me" (Gus Kahn, F. Andre, W. Schwandt): May you have sweet dreams as the stars shine brightly

in the night sky, but no matter what your dreams are, have sweet dreams of me.

- *1931*—"Got a Date with an Angel" (Jack Walter, Sonny Miller, Clifford Grey, Joseph Tumbridge): I'm heading to heaven where I'll hear bells ring and choirs sing because I'm meeting a heavenly girl.
- *1931*—"As Time Goes By" (Herman Hupfeld): Time may move on but there will always be kisses and sighs and expressions of love.
- *1932*—"Forty-Second Street" (Harry Warren and Al Dubin): On 42nd Street there's plenty of dancing, sexy women, underworld characters, and the elite, so I'm bringing you to that avenue.
- *1932*—"Try a Little Tenderness" (Harry Woods, Jimmy Campbell, Reg Connelly): The way to a young girl's heart is to be tender with her.
- *1932*—"It Don't Mean a Thing if It Ain't Got That Swing" (Duke Ellington and Irving Mills): It can be sweet or hot, but if it doesn't have rhythm, it ain't got it.
- *1932*—"Isn't It Romantic" (Richard Rodgers and Lorenz Hart): When you're in love everything's romantic.
- *1933*—"Love Is the Sweetest Thing" (Ray Noble): Nothing is sweeter than love because when you've got love you've got everything.
- *1933*—"Smoke Gets in Your Eyes" (Jerome Kern and Otto Harbach): They questioned if my love was true, and I said my feelings cannot be doubted, but since my love left me I now know that when your heart is ablaze, your vision is clouded.
- *1933*—"Inka Dinka Doo" (Ben Ryan and Jimmy Durante): That melody of mine is a symphony and a masterpiece and it goes "inka dinka doo."
- *1933*—"Easter Parade" (Irving Berlin): In the Easter Parade I'm taking you to, everybody will be looking at you in your beautiful Easter bonnet.
- *1933*—"Did You Ever See a Dream Walking?" (Harry Revel and Mack Gordon): When you're in my arms I'm in heaven, so in my dreams you're walking and talking and dancing and romancing.
- *1933*—"It's Only a Paper Moon" (Harold Arlen, Billy Rose, E. Y. Harburg): Nothing is real without your love, and so the moon is

paper and the sea is cardboard, but it all wouldn't be unreal if you loved me.

- *1934*—"Love in Bloom" (Leo Robin and Ralph Rainger): It's not that trees are filling the air with sweet scents or that spring is bringing starlight to us; it's the blossoming of love.
- *1934*—"Blue Moon" (Richard Rodgers and Lorenz Hart): When I found true love the moon turned from blue to gold.
- *1934*—"I Only Have Eyes for You" (Harry Warren and Al Dubin): My vision is obscured because my heart sings only for you.
- *1934*—"For All We Know" (Sam Lewis and J. Fred Coots): Let's not say goodnight until we have to because—who knows?—we may never see each other again.
- *1934*—"Anything Goes" (Cole Porter): The past was the past but now? Whoo, anything goes!
- *1934*—"The Very Thought of You" (Ray Noble): My world is a daydream and I see you in everything just by the mere idea of you.
- *1934*—"Santa Claus Is Comin' to Town" (Haven Gillespie and J. Fred Coots): Better be nice because Santa is checking off who is and who isn't and he's coming here.
- *1934*—"The Object of My Affection" (Pinky Tomlin, Coy Poe, Jimmy Grier): My whole outlook on life changes when the one who has my heart holds me and says I'm his.
- *1935*—"I'm in the Mood for Love" (Jimmy McHugh and Dorothy Fields): Just being near you puts me in a loving state of mind.
- *1935*—"Zing! Went the Strings of My Heart" (James Hanley): I could never sing but when you came along a symphony started in me and my heart and my heartstrings played rapidly.
- *1935*—"Summertime" (George Gershwin and DuBose Heyward): Don't despair, it's the peacefulness of summer now and you'll be safe with your folks watching over you until you rise up.
- *1935*—"I'm Gonna Sit Right Down and Write Myself a Letter" (Joe Young and Fred Ahlert): I'm going to write myself a letter with sweetness and kisses and pretend it came from you.
- *1935*—"It Ain't Necessarily So" (George Gershwin and Ira Gershwin): What you're led to believe in life is not necessarily true.

- *1936*—"The Way You Look Tonight" (Jerome Kern and Dorothy Fields): If I'm ever feeling low I'll just think of how you look tonight and I'll feel a special glow.
- *1936*—"I've Got You under My Skin" (Cole Porter): You're a deep part of me and no matter what my inner voice warns me, it has no effect because you're embedded in me.
- *1936*—"I'm an Old Cowhand" (Johnny Mercer): I may be an old rancher but I don't know any of the stuff cowboys do because I ride the trails in a car and listen to cowboy songs on the radio.
- *1936*—"The Glory of Love" (Billy Hill): Love may at times break your heart and make you cry, but that's the great way love works.
- *1936*—"In the Chapel in the Moonlight" (Billy Hill): I'll wait for you in the chapel in the moonlight until the organ turns to rust and the roses turn to ashes.
- *1936*—"The Whiffenpoof Song" (Rudy Vallee, Tod Galloway, George Pomeroy, Meade Minnigerode): We're just pushovers who have drifted.
- *1937*—"Harbor Lights" (Hugh Williams and Jimmy Kennedy): From the shore I saw you on the ship and the harbor lights told me we were breaking up.
- *1937*—"Thanks for the Memory" (Leo Robin and Ralph Rainger): Even though we separated over a trifle thing, for the memory of everything we shared together, thank you.
- *1937*—"Whistle While You Work" (Larry Morey and Frank Churchill): You can work more efficiently if you just whistle a happy tune.
- *1937*—"In the Still of the Night" (Cole Porter): In the quietness of the night when the world is asleep, I am consumed with you.
- *1938*—"My Heart Belongs to Daddy" (Cole Porter): I may date others but it's just a pretense and I couldn't be naughty because that man has my heart.
- *1938*—"You Must Have Been a Beautiful Baby" (Harry Warren and Johnny Mercer): From the way you look now you must have been a pretty child driving all the boys crazy.
- *1938*—"Jeepers Creepers" (Harry Warren and Johnny Mercer): When you turn on those big eyes of yours they entrance me.

- *1938*—"Heart and Soul" (Frank Loesser and Hoagy Carmichael): When you held me and kissed me I lost control and fell completely in love with you.
- *1938*—"A-Tisket A-Tasket" (Ella Fitzgerald and Van Alexander): I dropped the basket I bought for my mother and if the little girl who picked it up doesn't return it I'll fall apart.
- *1939*—"God Bless America" (Irving Berlin): May this sweet land of America be blessed and guided and championed by the Lord.
- *1939*—"Over the Rainbow" (Harold Arlen and E. Y. Harburg): If you are brave enough to make your dreams come true, you can soar like the birds who fly over that colored crescent in the sky.
- *1939*—"We're off to See the Wizard (the Wonderful Wizard of Oz)" (Harold Arlen and E. Y. Harburg): If you follow the golden road, your dreams can come true.
- *1939*—"I'll Never Smile Again" (Ruth Lowe): I love you so much that since we're over I could never smile or love again unless it's with you.
- *1939*—"Strange Fruit" (Abel Meeropol): Hanging from trees in the South are bloody black bodies with contorted faces and the stench from being set on fire, and they make "strange fruit." (artist: Billie Holiday)
- *1940*—"Because of You" (Arthur Hammerstein and Dudley Wilkinson): Everything in my life is wonderful now because having you is like being in paradise.
- *1940*—"How High the Moon" (Morgan Lewis and Nancy Hamilton): When love is absent the music is faint and the moon is high, and until love arrives, my heart will be still and the moon will be high.
- *1940*—"When You Wish upon a Star" (Ned Washington and Leigh Harline): Anything you wish for can come true, for fate comes to those whose heart is truly in their hopes and desires.
- *1940*—"Beat Me Daddy, Eight to the Bar" (Eleanor Sheehy, Hughie Prince, Don Raye): Nobody plays piano like the guy who plays boogie woogie so cool he hypnotizes everybody.
- *1941*—"I Don't Want to Walk without You" (Jule Styne and Frank Loesser): You broke my heart when you left me, and if I can't be with you then I just want to be left alone.

- *1941*—"Chattanooga Choo Choo" (Harry Warren and Mack Gordon): Shoe shine boy, polish my shoes because I'm getting on board the Chattanooga Choo Choo where someone special at the station is waiting for me.
- *1941*—"Blues in the Night" (Johnny Mercer and Harold Arlen): Beware of the two-faced man, as he'll leave you crying when the evening comes on.
- *1941*—"Bewitched" (Richard Rodgers and Lorenz Hart): Since love struck me I'm entranced, anxious, and bowled over.
- *1942*—"That Old Black Magic" (Harold Arlen and Johnny Mercer): I'm under the spell of love, "that old black magic."
- *1942*—"Praise the Lord and Pass the Ammunition" (Frank Loesser): Freedom comes to fighters who bless the Lord.
- *1942*—"White Christmas" (Irving Berlin): Like the happy snowy Christmases of my past, I'm wishing you a bright white Christmas.
- *1942*—"Don't Sit under the Apple Tree with Anyone Else but Me" (Charles Tobias, Lew Brown, Sam Stept): I've been true-blue to you so don't go off with anyone else or charm anyone else or relax with anyone else if it's not me!
- *1942*—"At Last" (Harry Warren and Mack Gordon): Since you are finally mine, I am no longer lonely and my dream has come true.
- *1943*—"You'll Never Know" (Harry Warren and Mack Gordon): Since you left me you cannot imagine how much I care for and miss you.
- *1943*—"Oh, What a Beautiful Mornin'" (Richard Rodgers and Oscar Hammerstein II): Everything around me seems blissful, so I have this fabulous feeling that it's going to be a beautiful day.
- *1944*—"Swinging on a Star" (Jimmy Van Heusen and Johnny Burke): You can reach your potential by not being stubborn or rude or lazy but by being dazzling, in which case you'll have rewards to take home.
- *1944*—"Saturday Night Is the Loneliest Night of the Week" (Sammy Cahn and Jule Styne): Until you come back, Saturday night, when we used to dance closely, will be the week's loneliest night for me.

- *1945*—"Let It Snow! Let It Snow! Let It Snow!" (Sammy Cahn and Jule Styne): When everything is cozy inside and you love me, it doesn't matter if it keeps on snowing.
- *1945*—"It's Been a Long, Long Time" (Sammy Cahn and Jule Styne): We haven't kissed for a long time, so please keep on kissing me!
- *1945*—"If I Loved You" (Richard Rodgers and Oscar Hammerstein II): It would be hard for me to find the words to tell you I love you if I really did.
- *1945*—"You'll Never Walk Alone" (Richard Rodgers and Oscar Hammerstein II): When life seems bleak, fill your heart with hope, and you won't be alone.
- *1946*—"Zip-a Dee-Doo-Dah" (Allie Wrubel and Ray Gilbert): The bluebird of happiness is on my shoulder, so I feel it's going to be a marvelous day.
- *1946*—"There's No Business Like Show Business" (Irving Berlin): For the applause and thrills that it brings, nothing can beat show business.
- *1946*—"Anything You Can Do" (Irving Berlin): I can top you at anything you do.
- *1947*—"A Fellow Needs a Girl" (Richard Rodgers and Oscar Hammerstein II): For getting through distressing days or talking or for comfort when things go wrong, as well as to share good news, a man needs a woman.
- *1948*—"Red Roses for a Blue Lady" (Sid Tepper and Roy Brodsky): Listen up, my florist, my girl and I had a senseless spat and she's upset now, so I'd like to order some red roses for her, and if they get us back together, I'll be back to buy an orchid for her wedding dress.
- *1948*—"It's a Most Unusual Day" (Jimmie McHugh and Harold Adamson): I can do whatever I want now—sing or fall in love or not worry—because this is not my usual day.
- *1948*—"Since I Fell For You" (Buddy Johnson): After falling in love with you and then you leaving me, I know the pain love brings, so it's best to let love go, but you're in my heart, so I'm blue all the time.

- *1948*—"The Night Has a Thousand Eyes" (Jerry Brainin and Buddy Bernier): Don't utter false feelings about me because the truth comes out at night.
- *1948*—"Once in Love with Amy" (Frank Loesser): Once you're in love with her you'll always be in love with her.
- *1949*—"Some Enchanted Evening" (Richard Rodgers and Oscar Hammerstein II): You may see a stranger or hear her laughing from afar, and when she calls you, you should run to her side when it happens on an unpredictable magical night.
- *1949*—"Rudolph the Red-Nosed Reindeer" (Johnny Marks): Like Rudolph, the reindeer with the red proboscis, everyone has a special quality that when it shines will bring the person love.
- *1949*—"I'm Gonna Wash That Man Right out of My Hair" (Richard Rodgers and Oscar Hammerstein II): If someone is on a different wavelength than you, don't try to make it right; just get rid of him right away!
- *1949*—"Baby It's Cold Outside" (Frank Loesser): You say you should be going, but the air outside is frigid and your eyes are shining and your lips look tasty, so maybe you should stay.
- *1949*—"Bibbidi-Bobbidi-Boo" (Mack David, Jerry Livingston, Al Hoffman): When you put things that don't make sense together, with some magic they can come together.
- *1950*—"If I Knew You Were Comin' I'd've Baked a Cake" (Bob Merrill, Clem Watts, Al Hoffman): You dropped in out of the blue, but if you'd let me know, I would have secured a band and a ballroom and baked you a cake.
- *1950*—"A Bushel and a Peck" (Frank Loesser): I love you heaps even though you mess up my life.
- *1950*—"Be My Love" (Sammy Cahn, Nicholas Brodsky): Only you can end my yearning for love, so be mine.
- *1951*—"Hey, Good Looking" (Hank Williams): Hey, cutie, I've got a recipe for us to have fun, so why don't you cook up something with me?
- *1951*—"A Kiss to Build a Dream On" (Harry Ruby, Bert Kalmar, Oscar Hammerstein II): If you kiss me, then when I'm alone I can use my imagination to create wonderful stories of romance in which we're together.

- *1951*—"I Whistle a Happy Tune" (Richard Rodgers and Oscar Hammerstein II): You can overcome your fears and be as brave as you want by whistling a cheerful melody and believing you're fearless and brave.
- *1951*—"Getting to Know You" (Richard Rodgers and Oscar Hammerstein II): Since ancient wisdom holds that students can teach teachers, I'd like to get to know you.
- *1952*—"I Saw Mommy Kissing Santa Claus" (Tommie Connor): She thought I was fast asleep last night, but I crept down the stairs and saw Mommy under the mistletoe kissing Santa Claus.
- *1952*—"Hi-Lilli, Hi-Lo" (Bronislau Kaper and Helen Deutsch): Love songs can be sad songs, but I hope to sing a love song again.
- *1952*—"Hold Me, Thrill Me, Kiss Me" (Harry Noble): When you embrace me and send me into delirium with your kisses, that makes me fall in love with you. (artists: Karen Chandler, Muriel Smith, Mel Carter, Bobby Vinton, Johnny Mathis, Gloria Estefan)
- *1953*—"Ebb Tide" (Carl Sigman and Robert Maxwell): Like when the tide is at its low point and the sea is still, I come for your embrace and feel serenity. (artists: Frank Chacksfield, The Righteous Brothers)
- *1953*—"That's Entertainment" (Arthur Schwartz and Howard Dietz): Everything we experience can be seen on a screen to make people laugh and cry, and that can be captivating.
- *1953*—"How Much Is That Doggie in the Window" (Bob Merrill): I'm taking a trip so I'd like to purchase that waggly tailed dog for my lover so he won't be alone. (artist: Patti Page)
- *1953*—"I Believe" (Ervin Drake, Al Stillman, Jimmy Shirl, Irvin Graham): I believe there is hope for everything because I have faith. (artists: Jane Froman, Frankie Laine)
- *1954*—"Oh! My Pa-Pa" (Paul Burkhard, Geoffrey Parsons, John Turner): I miss my father, who had so many wonderful qualities. (artist: Eddie Fisher)
- *1954*—"Stranger in Paradise" (Robert Wright and George Forrest): For a mortal like me, being next to an angel like you in paradise, we don't need to be strangers if you open your arms to me. (artist: The Four Aces)

- *1954*—"That's Amore" (Harry Warren and Jack Brooks): You know you're in love when everything seems like you've had too much to drink. (artist: Dean Martin)
- *1954*—"Young at Heart" (Johnny Richards, Carolyn Leigh): Anything you dream of can come true if you are young-minded. (artist: Frank Sinatra)
- *1954*—"Three Coins in the Fountain" (Sammy Cahn, Jule Styne): Three starry-eyed lovers threw a coin in the fountain, and with only one that will be blessed, I hope it's mine. (artist: The Four Aces)
- *1954*—"Hernando's Hideaway" (Jerry Ross, Richard Adler): You can look and talk to me with love at Hernando's Hideaway, where no one will know you and you can stay as late as you want. (artist: Archie Bleyer)
- *1954*—"Sh-Boom" (James Edwards, James Keyes, Carl Fester, Claude Fester, Floyd McCrae): If you let me know I'm your only love, we can journey to paradise and "life could be a dream." (artist: The Chords)
- *1954*—"Goodnight, Sweetheart, Goodnight" (James Hudson, Calvin Carter): I'm sorry to part now, but it's 3 am, so goodnight. (artists: The Spaniels, The McGuire Sisters)
- *1954*—"Shake, Rattle and Roll" (Charles Calhoun): If you thaw your heart, you can come alive if you move your body to the music. (artist: Bill Haley and His Comets)
- *1954*—"Papa Loves Mambo" (Bix Reichner, Al Hoffman, Dick Manning): Mama and Papa love to swing, dancing the mambo. (artist: Perry Como)
- *1954*—"Mister Sandman" (Pat Ballard): I hope to meet my dream man in my dreams. (artists: The Chordettes, The Four Aces)
- *1955*—"Teach Me Tonight" (Gene de Paul, Sammy Cahn): Tonight teach me the A-B-C's of love. (artist: The De Castro Sisters)
- *1955*—"Earth Angel (Will You Be Mine)" (Curtis Williams): You're an angel on earth, and I always love you. (artist: The Penguins, The Crew Cuts)
- *1955*—"Tweedle Dee" (Winfield Scott): For my happiness, for your love, for my luck and your kisses, I sing from my heart "Tweedle Dee." (artist: LaVern Baker)

- *1955*—"Sincerely" (Harvey Fuqua, Allan Freed): I say I love you, "sincerely." (artists: The McGuire Sisters, The Moonglows)
- *1955*—"The Ballad of Davy Crockett" (George Bruns, Thomas Blackburn): A story song of a Tennessee-born fighter. (artists: Bill Hayes, Fess Parker, Tennessee Ernie Ford)
- *1955*—"Unchained Melody" (Alex North, Hy Zaret): For a long while, I've been craving for your love. (artist: Al Hibbler)
- *1955*—"Whatever Lola Wants" (Richard Adler, Jerry Ross): Lola gets whatever she wants, and she wants you lock, stock, and barrel. (artist: Sarah Vaughan)
- *1955*—"Rock around the Clock" (Jimmy De Knight, Max C. Freedman): We're going to rock all day, and with each hour that strikes we're going to shout for the band to keep up the beat, feel ecstatic, continue rocking, and then take a quick breather before we start all over again! (artist: Bill Haley and His Comets)
- *1955*—"Ain't That a Shame" (Antoine Domino, Dave Bartholomew): I wept when you left me and that's a shame. (artists: Pat Boone, Fats Domino)
- *1955*—"The Yellow Rose of Texas" (Don George): A soldier left a Texas woman, breaking the heart of the most charming woman he knew, and now he's going back to look for her. (artists: Mitch Miller, Johnny Desmond)
- *1955*—"Maybellene" (Chuck Berry): Maybellene in her Cadillac racing me in my V8 Ford, that's my Maybellene. (artist: Chuck Berry and His Combo)
- *1955*—"Love Is a Many-Splendored Thing" (Paul Francis Webster, Sammy Fain): Love is a multi-faceted thing that makes life worth living. (artist: The Four Aces)
- *1955*—"Sixteen Tons" (Merle Travis): Doing the heavy work just gets you older and more in debt. (artists: Tennessee Ernie Ford, Frankie Laine)
- *1955*—"The Great Pretender" (Buck Ram): People think I'm doing well because I pretend I am, but you broke my heart, and I'm lonely even though I pretend we're still together. (artist: The Platters)
- *1956*—"Blue Suede Shoes" (Carl Perkins): You can hurt me in any way if you want, but my blue-suede shoes (my pride and joy) are off limits. (artists: Carl Perkins, Elvis Presley)

- *1956*—"Hot Diggity" (Dick Manning, Al Hoffman): Wow, you have such a great effect on me that I never thought my life could be so great. (artist: Perry Como)
- *1956*—"Heartbreak Hotel" (Mae Axton, Thomas Durden, Elvis Presley): When your heart is broken, you can hole up in the Heartbreak Hotel, where you can be lonely even though it's crowded there. (artist: Elvis Presley)
- *1956*—"The Poor People of Paris" (Rene Rouzaud, Marguerite Monnot, Jack Lawrence): Oh, pity those Parisians, who only know from dancing, finding romance, and singing. (artist: Winifred At-well)
- *1956*—"The Wayward Wind" (Stanley Lebowsky, Herb New-man): The wayward wind broke my heart because he broke his promise to be faithful to me and wandered. (artist: Gogi Grant)
- *1956*—"I Want You, I Need You, I Love You" (Ira Kosloff, Maurice Mysels): Please be mine because everything about me has to have you. (artist: Elvis Presley)
- *1956*—"Be-Bop-a Lula" (Gene Vincent, Tex Davis): I'm certain that that woman who knows how to move her feet is my love. (artist: Gene Vincent)
- *1956*—"Whatever Will Be, Will Be (Que Sera, Sera)" (Jay Livingston, Ray Evans): No one knows the future, so whatever happens happens. (artist: Doris Day)
- *1956*—"My Prayer" (Jimmy Kennedy, George Boulanger): As our hearts glimmer together after the twilight, I pray that we'll always be together and that you'll be there after I pray. (artist: The Platters)
- *1956*—"In the Still of the Night" (Fred Parris): Before darkness turns to light, embrace and pledge you'll be together forever in the evening's serenity. (artist: The Five Satins)
- *1956*—"Hound Dog" (Mike Stoller, Jerry Leiber): You're just a good-for-nothing philanderer who doesn't deserve me. (artist: Elvis Presley)
- *1956*—"Love Me Tender" (George Poulton, Vera Matson, Elvis Presley): Cherish me and I will always love you. (artist: Elvis Presley)
- *1956*—"Singing the Blues" (Melvin Endsley): Since you left me all I do is cry my heart out. (artists: Marty Robbins, Guy Mitchell)

- *1957*—"Blueberry Hill" (Vincent Rose, Larry Stock, Al Lewis): Though you broke your promise to me and we're not together anymore, I'll never forget how you swept me off my feet when we met on Blueberry Hill. (artist: Fats Domino)
- *1957*—"All Shook Up" (Otis Blackwell, Elvis Presley): When you're in love you become rattled in so many ways. (artist: Elvis Presley)
- *1957*—"(Let Me Be Your) Teddy Bear" (Bernie Lowe, Kal Mann): Like the stuffed toy animal that can be lovable, that's what I want to be to you. (artist: Elvis Presley)
- *1957*—"Bye Bye Love" (Felice Bryant, Boudleaux Bryant): Since my baby left me for someone else, it's so long ecstasy, greetings empty-heartedness. (artist: The Everly Brothers)
- *1957*—"It's Not for Me to Say" (Al Stillman, Robert Allen): It's up to you to tell me what I long to hear. (artist: Johnny Mathis)
- *1957*—"Diana" (Paul Anka): Our age difference doesn't matter to me; I just want you to be mine. (artist: Paul Anka)
- *1957*—"Whole Lotta Shakin' Goin' On" (Dave Williams, Sunny David): Over here, baby, we're really moving, so get over here. (artist: Jerry Lee Lewis)
- *1957*—"Happy, Happy Birthday Baby" (Margo Sylvia, Gilbert Lopez): I would like to wish you a happy birthday even though I am no longer in the picture, although I wish I were. (artist: The Tune Weavers)
- *1957*—"Chances Are" (Al Stillman, Robert Allen): Just by the way I smile and lose my bearing when we're together, there's little doubt that you know I love you. (artist: Johnny Mathis)
- *1957*—"Silhouettes" (Frank Slay Jr., Bob Crewe): When I walked by your house last night and saw the silhouettes of two lovers at the window, I lost my mind and furiously knocked on the door but was told I was at the wrong house, and afterward I promised myself we would be two silhouettes like the lovers I just saw at the window. (artists: The Rays, Herman's Hermits)
- *1957*—"You Send Me" (Sam Cooke): Whenever we're together you delight me. (artist: Sam Cooke)
- *1957*—"Jailhouse Rock" (Jerry Lieber, Mike Stoller): All the inmates in the country jail were jammin' when the jailkeeper made a party. (artist: Elvis Presley)

- *1957*—"Rock and Roll Music" (Chuck Berry): I only dance to rock and roll music. (artist: Chuck Berry)
- *1958*—"At the Hop" (John Medora, David White, Artie Singer): When the music starts playing at the dance, you can move in any way you want. (artist: Danny and the Juniors)
- *1958*—"Do You Want to Dance" (Robert Freeman): How about dancing with me? (artist: Bobby Freeman)
- *1958*—"Chantilly Lace" (J. P. Richardson): Everything about you drives me to act nutty and empty my wallet on you. (artist: The Big Bopper)
- *1958*—"Lollipop" (Julius Dixon, Beverly Ross): Because my baby is so sweet, my nickname for him is "lollipop." (artist: The Chordettes)
- *1958*—"Nel Blu Dipinto Di Blu (Volare)" (Domenico Modugno, Franco Migliacci): I soar with your love, so let's fly to the clouds and sing. (artists: Domenico Modugno, Bobby Rydell)
- *1958*—"Dizzy Miss Lizzie" (Larry Williams): I'm so wild about you that I'm punch-drunk and reeling. (artists: Larry Williams, The Beatles)
- *1958*—"The Book of Love" (George Malone, Warren Davis, Charles Patrick): The Book of Love has all the answers, so I need to find out who wrote it. (artist: The Monotones)
- *1958*—"Tears on My Pillow" (Al Lewis, Sylvester Bradford): You left me and broke my heart, and now my pillow has my tears. (artist: Little Anthony and the Imperials)
- *1959*—"Sixteen Candles" (Luther Dixon, Allyson Khent): It's your sixteenth birthday, and I want you to know I love you and will always love you. (artist: The Crests)
- *1959*—"The Battle of New Orleans" (Jimmy Driftwood): It's the War of 1812 and the Americans are fighting the British. (artist: Johnny Horton)
- *1959*—"A Teenager in Love" (Mort Shuman, Pomus): When we argue, it makes me afraid you'll leave me, so I look up to the heavens and ask why must I be in love. (artist: Dion and the Belmonts)
- *1959*—"Lipstick on Your Collar" (Edna Lewis, George Goehring): You lied to me about where you were going, and I know because the evidence is on your collar, and to make matters worse you said

it was mine, but I know it's not because it's not the color I have on. (artist: Connie Francis)

- *1959*—"Poison Ivy" (Jerry Lieber, Mike Stoller): You may think she's sweet, but if you let her get to you, she'll infect you. (artist: The Coasters)

- *1959*—"Put Your Head on My Shoulder" (Paul Anka): Let's do the things that lovers do: kiss, whisper in ears, and put heads on shoulders. (artist: Paul Anka)

- *1960*—"Teen Angel" (Red Surrey, Jean Surrey): I dragged you out of your car, but then you went back to the railroad track to get my ring, and now I wonder if you can see or hear me. (artist: Mark Dinning)

- *1960*—"Stairway to Heaven" (Neil Sedaka, Howard Greenfield): You're heavenly and I'll climb as high as it takes to reach you. (artist: Neil Sedaka)

- *1960*—"Swingin' School" (Dave Appell, Bernie Lowe, Kal Mann): School's cool at this wild school. (artist: Bobby Rydell)

- *1960*—"Alley Oop" (Dallas Frazier): Alley Oop, that comic strip guy from the cave man days, is the coolest dude there is. (artist: The Hollywood Argyles)

- *1960*—"Itsy Bitsy Teenie Weenie Yellow Polka Dot Bikini" (Paul Vance, Lee Pockriss): She put on a tiny bikini that she never wore before and was shy to let anybody see her. (artist: Brian Hyland)

- *1960*—"Only the Lonely (Know the Way I Feel)" (Roy Orbison, Joe Melson): The only people who can relate to my empty feeling are the lonely. (artist: Roy Orbison)

- *1960*—"The Twist" (Hank Ballard): Let's move our bodies around and do that dance called "the twist." (artist: Chubby Checker)

- *1960*—"Chain Gang" (Sam Cooke): I'm in the chain gang sounding out moans, thinking about seeing my woman when I go home. (artist: Sam Cooke)

- *1960*—"You're Sixteen" (Richard Sherman, Robert Sherman): You're my dream at sixteen. (artists: Johnny Burnette, Ringo Starr)

- *1960*—"Poetry in Motion" (Paul Kaufman, Mike Anthony): My baby walks and dances elegantly like a moving poem. (artist: Johnny Tillotson)

- *1960*—"Sway" (Pablo Beltrán Ruiz, Norman Gimbel): When we glide across the room to that Calypso music and bend, I am oblivious to everything but you. (artist: Bobby Rydell)
- *1960*—"Wild One" (Kal Mann, Dave Appell, Bernie Lowe): You may be quite flirty and amorous but my kisses will light you up and quell you. (artist: Bobby Rydell)
- *1961*—"Will You Love Me Tomorrow" (Carole King, Gerry Goffin): We're lovers tonight, but will we be lovers tomorrow? (artist: The Shirelles)
- *1961*—"Shop Around" (Berry Gordy, Bill "Smokey" Robinson): Don't rush into love; be selective. (artist: The Miracles)
- *1961*—"Dedicated to the One I Love" (Ralph Bass, Lowman Pauling): When we're apart, say a prayer and dedicate it to me, the one you love. (artists: The Shirelles, The Mamas and the Papas)
- *1961*—"Pony Time" (Don Covay, John Berry): On hearing this shout, it's time to do the "pony" (dance). (artist: Chubby Checker)
- *1961*—"Spanish Harlem" (Jerry Lieber, Phil Spector): There's a special flower that's been sheltered that I'm going to pluck and help come alive in my own garden. (artists: Ben E. King, Aretha Franklin)
- *1961*—"Gee Whiz (Look at His Eyes)" (Carla Thomas): He's a dream with spellbinding eyes so I'm wowed. (artist: Carla Thomas)
- *1961*—"Mother-in-Law" (Allen Toussaint): If only my mother-in-law would leave our home, I'd be happy again. (artist: Ernie K-Doe)
- *1961*—"Rain Drops" (Dee Clark): I've been crying so much since you left me that my tears flow out like raindrops. (artist: Dee Clark)
- *1961*—"Stand by Me" (Ben E. King, Glick): I shall know no fear as long as you stand with me. (artist: Ben E. King)
- *1961*—"Tossin' and Turnin'" (Ritchie Adams, Malou Rene): Our difficulties kept me awake all last night. (artist: Bobby Lewis)
- *1961*—"Those Oldies but Goodies (Remind Me of You)" (Paul Politi, Nick Curinga): Whenever I hear songs from our past, I think of you, and I hope you'll remember me, too, when you hear those good old songs. (artist: Little Caesar and the Romans)

- *1961*—"Hit the Road Jack" (Percy Mayfield): My woman's not been treating me right, so it's time to get out—and stay away. (artist: Ray Charles)
- *1961*—"Goodbye Cruel World" (Gloria Shayne): My heart is broken, so I am going to become a crying clown in a circus where I can hide my sorrow. (artist: James Darren)
- *1962*—"Duke of Earl" (Eugene Dixon, Earl Edwards, Bernice Williams): I'm royal and you're my royal girl, and in our kingdom I will protect you. (artist: Gene Chandler)
- *1962*—"Twist and Shout" (Phil Medley, Bert Berns): Shake your body close to mine, and I'll know I'm yours. (artists: The Isley Brothers, The Beatles)
- *1962*—"The Wanderer" (Ernie Maresca): I go from girl to girl because I like to bum around. (artist: Dion)
- *1962*—"Town without Pity" (Dimitri Tiomkin, Ned Washington): People not in love don't understand young lovers with their problems and needs, and young lovers must not let those who don't have empathy break them apart. (artist: Gene Pitney)
- *1962*—"Johnny Angel" (Lee Pockriss, Lyn Duddy): I pray that Johnny Angel, the boy I love, will one day notice me and love me back. (artist: Shelley Fabares)
- *1962*—"Good Luck Charm" (Aaron Schroeder, Wally Gold): My love brings me good luck, so I want her always in my life. (artist: Elvis Presley)
- *1962*—"Soldier Boy" (Florence Greenberg, Luther Dixon): No matter where you go, I will always be faithful to you. (artist: The Shirelles)
- *1962*—"She Cried" (Greg Richards, Ted Daryll): My girlfriend wept when I let her know I found someone else and was no longer in love with her. (artist: Jay and the Americans)
- *1962*—"Let Me In" (Yvonne Baker): There's a party going on inside, and you're supposed to be my friend, so don't close me out. (artist: The Sensations)
- *1962*—"I Can't Stop Loving You" (Don Gibson): I'll live in the past with my memories of you because those were my happy times. (artist: Ray Charles)
- *1962*—"Roses Are Red (My Love)" (Paul Evans, Al Byron): Now that you're settled in life with a little girl and a husband, maybe

one day a boy will write in her graduation book the same poem I used to write to you. (artist: Bobby Vinton)

- *1962*—"Sealed with a Kiss" (Peter Udell, Gary Geld): I'll miss you when we're apart over the summer, but every day I will write you and fasten the envelope with a kiss. (artist: Brian Hyland)
- *1962*—"Big Girls Don't Cry" (Bob Crewe, Bob Gaudio): I threatened my girl we had to split, but she surprised me and didn't cry. (artist: The 4 Seasons)
- *1962*—"Return to Sender" (Otis Blackwell, Winfield Scott): I wrote my love a letter after we had a fight, and it was returned to me with a statement in her writing that there's no such address. (artist: Elvis Presley)
- *1963*—"Go Away Little Girl" (Carole King, Gerry Goffin): I can hardly hold myself back from you, but since I have to be faithful to somebody else, I'm asking you to leave me. (artists: Steve Lawrence, Mark Wynter, Donny Osmond)
- *1963*—"Tell Him" (Bert Russell): If you'd like that guy to be yours, let him know, and kiss him and hold his hand. (artist: The Exciters)
- *1963*—"Hey! Paula" (Ray Hildebrand): Paul and Paula have been waiting to finish school, so now they can get married. (artist: Paul and Paula)
- *1963*—"Bobby's Girl" (Henry Hoffman, Gary Klein): Even though he has another girl, all I want is to be his girl. (artist: Marci Blane)
- *1963*—"Walk Like a Man" (Bob Crewe, Bob Gaudio): You bad-mouthed me and put me down, and my father told me not to beg for you back but to carry on like a man. (artist: The 4 Seasons)
- *1963*—"Our Day Will Come" (Bob Hilliard, Mort Garson): We may be young now, but in the future we'll be together. (artist: Ruby and the Romantics)
- *1963*—"Baby Workout" (Jackie Wilson, Alonzo Tucker): Step on the dance floor and move your body! (artist: Jackie Wilson)
- *1963*—"He's So Fine" (Ronnie Mack): I'm going to find a way to get that guy because he's got a lot going for him. (artist: The Chiffons)

- *1963*—"Can't Get Used to Losing You" (Mort Shuman, Doc Pomus): I'll never get over that we're together no more. (artist: Andy Williams)
- *1963*—"On Broadway" (Cynthia Weil, Barry Mann, Jerry Leiber, Mike Stoller): Broadway's the place to be when you've got something going. (artist: The Drifters, George Benson)
- *1963*—"Rhythm of the Rain" (John Gummoe): My tears won't let me forget her—if only her heart felt my tears, it might kindle the love we once had. (artist: The Cascades)
- *1963*—"Mecca" (Neval Nader, John Gluck Jr.): We may live on opposite sides of the street, but each day I look out to her side and long that we can be together because her home is heavenly to me. (artist: Gene Pitney)
- *1963*—"I Will Follow Him" (Arthur Altman, Norman Gimbel, J. Stole, Del Roma): There is nothing on earth that can keep me from being with him. (artist: Little Peggy March)
- *1963*—"Puff the Magic Dragon" (Peter Yarrow, Leonard Lipton): Children get older and outgrow their toys, and while those toys may get lost, they live on in our imagination. (artist: Peter, Paul and Mary)
- *1963*—"Surfin' U.S.A." (Brian Wilson, Chuck Berry): If you could cruise across the country, then you should do it. (artist: Beach Boys)
- *1963*—"It's My Party" (Herb Weiner, John Gluck Jr., Wally Gold): The boy I want left my party with my friend only to return with his ring on her finger, and now I'm crying. (artist: Lesley Gore)
- *1963*—"Easier Said Than Done" (William Linton): Everybody's giving me advice on what to say to him, but I'm shy, so it's not so easy. (artist: The Essex)
- *1963*—"Blowin' in the Wind" (Bob Dylan): There are many deep questions in life, and the answers are right before you if you look hard enough. (artists: Peter, Paul and Mary, Stevie Wonder)
- *1963*—"If I Had a Hammer" (Lee Hays, Pete Seeger): I can do anything if I take the initiative. (artists: Trini Lopez, Peter, Paul and Mary)
- *1963*—"Then He Kissed Me" (Phil Spector, Ellie Greenwich, Jeff Barry): First he asked me to dance, and then he escorted me

home, and then he gave me a kiss, just like after I later told him I love him and he said it back. (artist: The Crystals)

- *1963*—"Blue Velvet" (Bernie Wayne, Lee Morris): She left me and broke my heart, but I'll always remember the soft blue velvet she wore. (artists: Bobby Vinton, Lana Del Rey)
- *1963*—"My Boyfriend's Back" (Bob Feldman, Gerald Goldstein, Richard Gottehrer): You hit on me when my boyfriend went away and lied to others that I was unfaithful, but now he's back, so beware! (artist: The Angels)
- *1963*—"Mockingbird" (Charlie and Inez Foxx): He's going to try to do the right thing by me, but if things don't work out, then I'll have to find my own way or just accept the situation. (artists: Inez and Charlie Foxx, Carly Simon, and James Taylor)
- *1963*—"Be My Baby" (Phil Spector, Ellie Greenwich, Jeff Barry): I want you to be mine, and only mine. (artist: The Ronettes)
- *1963*—"Donna the Prima Donna" (Dion Di Muci, Ernie Maresca): She's a high-class girl, so if you don't have money (like me), then she's going to break your heart and roam around. (artist: Dion Di Muci)
- *1963*—"Popsicles and Icicles" (David Gates): The things he loves are a part of him, and even if they're silly, I still love him because he's what I dream of. (artist: The Murmaids)
- *1963*—"Wildwood Days" (Kal Mann, Dave Appell): School will be over soon and we'll be partying like crazy on the sands of Wildwood. (artist: Bobby Rydell)
- *1964*—"There! I've Said It Again" (Redd Evans, David Mann): I can't keep it to myself, so I'm going to say it over and over: I love you. (artist: Bobby Vinton)
- *1964*—"I Want to Hold Your Hand" (John Lennon, Paul McCartney): I want to be yours and for you to say to me I can hold your hand. (artist: The Beatles)
- *1964*—"You Don't Own Me" (John Madara, David White): I can do as I please and you don't have dibs on me. (artist: Lesley Gore)
- *1964*—"Hey Little Cobra" (Carol Connors, M. H. Connors): My little sports car is going to beat all the fancier models when we race. (artist: The Rip Chords)
- *1964*—"She Loves You" (John Lennon, Paul McCartney): You hurt her badly, but don't worry—I ran into her and she told me to

tell you she knows you didn't mean it and that she still loves you. (artist: The Beatles)

- *1964*—"Hello, Dolly!" (Jerry Herman). Welcome home, the natural place where you should be, and you've still got your old gusto and beam so I don't think you'll ever want to leave here again. (artist: Louis Armstrong and The All-Stars)
- *1964*—"Dawn (Go Away)" (Bob Gaudio, Sandy Linzer): I really would like you to be mine, but I'm poor, so you'll be better off with him—even though I want you to be mine. (artist: The Four Seasons)
- *1964*—"Fun, Fun Fun" (Brian Wilson, Mike Love): You were having a blast driving your father's car, but now that he took the keys back, you can still have a blast by coming with me. (artist: The Beach Boys)
- *1964*—"Can't Buy Me Love" (John Lennon, Paul McCartney): I'll give you everything I have, but I hope the thing you'll want is nothing that can be purchased. (artist: The Beatles)
- *1964*—"Suspicion" (Doc Pomus, Mort Shuman): You kiss me and hold me, but my instincts tell me you're unfaithful, and it tears me apart. (artist: Terry Stafford)
- *1964*—"Do You Want to Know a Secret?" (John Lennon, Paul McCartney): Don't tell anyone, but I love you. (artist: Paul McCartney)
- *1964*—"My Guy" (Smokey Robinson): Nothing anyone says or does could change a thing—I'm true-blue to my man. (artist: Mary Wells)
- *1964*—"Chapel of Love" (Jeff Barry, Ellie Greenwich, Phil Spector): We're going to hear wedding bells today in the chapel of love. (artist: The Dixie Cups)
- *1964*—"Walk on By" (Burt Bacharach, Hal David): I haven't gotten over you, so don't stop if you see me on the street; just keep walking. (artist: Dionne Warwick)
- *1964*—"Don't Let the Sun Catch You Crying" (Gerrard Marsden): Save your tears for the nighttime because they'll be gone in the morning when it's time to find happiness. (artist: Gerry and the Pacemakers)

- *1964*—"A World Without Love" (John Lennon, Paul McCartney): I want to hide from the world until I find love. (artist: Peter and Gordon)
- *1964*—"I Get Around" (Brian Wilson): I've got money and a fast car, and with my friends I find the cool places to go. (artist: The Beach Boys)
- *1964*—"It's in His Kiss (The Shoop Shoop Song)" (Rudy Clark): If you want to know if a person loves you, you don't go by his eyes or face or embrace; go by his kiss. (artist: Betty Everett)
- *1964*—"Where Did Our Love Go" (Brian Holland, Lamont Dozier, Eddie Holland): You came on strong to me, and I gave you my love, but now you want to cut out and I don't know what happened to our love. (artist: The Supremes)
- *1964*—"The House of the Rising Sun" (traditional, arranged by Alan Price): A man can be ruined in that sinful house in New Orleans. (artist: The Animals)
- *1964*—"Because" (Dave Clark): I do everything I can for you because I love you. (artist: The Dave Clark Five)
- *1964*—"Bread and Butter" (Larry Parks, Jay Turnbow): My girl always fed me what I like to eat until one day I found her eating with another man, and now she doesn't feed me anymore. (artist: The Newbeats)
- *1964*—"Remember (Walking in the Rain)" (George Morton): A couple years ago my baby left me, and now this letter came from him saying it was over, so all I can do now is remember our holding hands and kissing as we walked in the sand. (artist: The Shangri-Las)
- *1964*—"Under the Boardwalk" (Arthur Resnick, Kenny Young): On a hot sunny day, the place you want to be with your baby is "under the boardwalk." (artist: The Drifters)
- *1964*—"Do Wah Diddy Diddy" (Jeff Barry, Ellie Greenwich): I saw her on the street singing this tune and went crazy for her, and the next thing I knew we were walking together and holding hands and singing that tune, and now we're going to get married. (artist: Manfred Mann)
- *1964*—"Oh, Pretty Woman" (Roy Orbison, Bill Dees): As I'm walking down the street, I spot a pretty woman who's just my type, and I wish she would stop and talk with me, but it's late, and

I start home until I turn around and see her heading over to me. (artist: Roy Orbison)

- *1964*—"We'll Sing in the Sunshine" (Gale Garnett): Love's too painful for a long relationship, but we can have a year together and find happiness on bright, sunny days. (artist: Gale Garnett)
- *1964*—"Baby Love" (Brian Holland, Lamont Dozier, Eddie Holland): You hurt me, but I want you anyway because you're my "baby love." (artist: The Supremes)
- *1964*—"You Really Got Me" (Ray Davies): I'm insane over my girl; she really has me in her clutches. (artist: The Kinks)
- *1964*—"Little Honda" (Brian Wilson, Mike Love): Get up! We're going for a ride on my little Honda motorbike. (artist: The Hondells)
- *1965*—"Come See about Me" (Brian Holland, Lamont Dozier, Eddie Holland): A spurned lover who has no friends or peace of mind and who keeps crying out of loneliness pleads for her ex to come check in on her. (artist: The Supremes)
- *1965*—"Downtown" (Tony Hatch): If you're lonely or troubled, you can put all your anxieties out of your mind by going downtown where there are bright lights and pretty neon signs. (artist: Petula Clark)
- *1965*—"You've Lost That Lovin' Feelin'" (Barry Mann, Cynthia Weil, Phil Spector): I can tell by the way you act when we're together that you don't love me anymore. (artist: The Righteous Brothers)
- *1965*—"The Name Game" (Shirley Ellis, Lincoln Chase): A "game song" in which first names are rhymed using specified rules. (artist: Shirley Ellis)
- *1965*—"The Jolly Green Giant" (Lynn Easton): A big, mean fellow leaves his home in the valley, encounters and touches someone who in turn slaps him silly, and then returns home to his valley. (artist: The Kingsmen)
- *1965*—"The Jerk" (Don Julian): A girl is asked to teach the moves of the new dance fad, the Jerk. (artist: The Larks)
- *1965*—"Let's Lock the Door (and Throw Away the Key)" (Wes Farrell, Roy Alfred): Having just met at a party last week, an anxious lover is waiting to get behind closed doors and kiss. (artist: Jay and the Americans)

- *1965*—"My Girl" (Smokey Robinson, Ronald White): Life's great! Cloudy days are bright days, and I don't need fame or fortune, because I've got a girl. (artist: The Temptations)
- *1965*—"The Boy from New York City" (John Taylor): I've been swept off my feet by this cool boy from New York City who I hope will be mine. (artist: The Ad Libs)
- *1965*—"The 'In' Crowd" (Billy Page): He's in with the "in" crowd, and if she comes with him, she will be, too. (artist: Dobie Gray)
- *1965*—"How Sweet It Is to Be Loved By You" (Holland-Dozier-Holland): Needing someone to hug him and to understand his highs and lows, it's blissful to have her love. (artist: Marvin Gaye)
- *1965*—"Eight Days a Week" (John Lennon, Paul McCartney): I need my baby to love me more than the normal week. (artist: The Beatles)
- *1965*—"This Diamond Ring" (Al Kooper, Irwin Levine, Bob Brass): He's selling the engagement ring that she returned to him, which still symbolizes the beauty and dreams of love. (artist: Gary Lewis and the Playboys)
- *1965*—"Stop! In the Name of Love" (Holland-Dozier-Holland): She asks her lover, who she knows when he leaves her home is going to meet his other love, to stop and think over what he's doing before he breaks her heart. (artist: The Supremes)
- *1965*—"Can't You Hear My Heartbeat?" (Ken Lewis, John Carter): When she looks at him or moves closer to him, his heart pounds, and he asks if she can hear that thumping beat. (artist: Herman's Hermits)
- *1965*—"Goldfinger" (John Barry, Anthony Newley, Leslie Bricusse): He's a man with the golden touch, but he's also got the touch of a spider, a cold finger, a cold heart, and he only cares about gold, so don't kiss him because it'll kill you. (artist: Shirley Bassey)
- *1965*—"Red Roses for a Blue Lady" (Sid Tepper, R. C. Bennett): After a "silly quarrel" with his girlfriend, the guy asks a florist for some pretty flowers for his sad lover, and if they do the trick he'll come back for the florist's "best white orchid" to pin on her wedding dress. (artist: Bert Kaempfert)
- *1965*—"Hurt So Bad" (Teddy Randazzo, Bobby Weinstein, B. Harshman): Knowing that his ex loves somebody else, he tells her

she can't imagine what he's going through, that it's so painful, and pleads for her to let him make it up to her and love him again like she used to. (artist: Little Anthony and the Imperials)

- *1965*—"Tell Her No" (Rod Argent): She threw his love away, so if she entices him with her charms or even professes love, "tell her no." (artist: The Zombies)
- *1965*—"I'm Telling You Now" (Freddie Garrity, Mitch Murray): It's been said before, but he wants her to believe him; he's in love with her now and he's going to be staying. (artist: Freddie and the Dreamers)
- *1965*—"The Game of Love" (C. Ballard Jr.): With the meaning of a man to be loving a woman, and vice versa, a man asks a woman to start engaging in the pursuit of romance (which originated in the Garden of Eden with Adam and Eve). (artist: Wayne Fontana and the Mindbenders)
- *1965*—"The Birds and the Bees" (Barry Stuart): The facts of life are taught using the popular expression for sex and mentioning other areas of nature for rhymes and imagery. (artist: Jewel Akens)
- *1965*—"Mrs. Brown You've Got a Lovely Daughter" (Trevor Peacock): He tells the mother of the girl who broke his heart to tell her he's doing well even though he'd get down on bended knee to get her back. (artist: Herman's Hermits)
- *1965*—"Crying in the Chapel" (Artie Glenn): Solace and happiness come from praying in a place of worship. (artist: Elvis Presley)
- *1965*—"Wooly Bully" (Samudio): Matty informed Hatty about a two-horned wooly jawed thing she saw, and Hatty tells Matty not to risk anything and to learn to dance the wooly bully. (artist: Sam the Sham and the Pharaohs)
- *1965*—"Help Me, Rhonda" (Brian Wilson): After his intended wife falls for another guy, he pleads for Rhonda to help him get her out of his mind. (artist: The Beach Boys)
- *1965*—"(I Can't Get No) Satisfaction" (Mick Jagger, Keith Richards): On a losing streak from trying to get a girl, no matter what he does he can't get any satisfaction. (artist: The Rolling Stones)

- *1965*—"Cara Mia" (Tulio Trapani, Lee Lange): Each time they part, a piece of him dies, so he asks his love to hear his prayer that he wants to be her love forever. (artist: Jay and the Americans)
- *1965*—"For Your Love" (Graham Gouldham): There's nothing I wouldn't do to have you love me. (artist: The Yardbirds)
- *1965*—"Mr. Tambourine Man" (Bob Dylan): Having been stripped of all of his senses and with no place to go, he asks Mr. Tambourine Man to play a song for him. (artist: The Byrds)
- *1965*—"I'm Henry VIII, I Am" (Fred Murray, Robert Weston): His name is Henry and his wife, a widow, was married to seven previous Henrys, so that makes him Henry the eighth. (artist: Herman's Hermits)
- *1965*—"I Got You Babe" (Sonny Bono): Even though they say we're too young to know what love is or to pay the rent, it doesn't matter because we both got each other. (artist: Sonny and Cher)
- *1965*—"California Girls" (Brian Wilson): East Coast, Midwest, southern and northern girls all have great qualities, now if only they could be in California. (artist: The Beach Boys)
- *1965*—"What's New Pussycat?" (Burt Bacharach, Hal David): He professes adoration for his love, whom he affectionately refers to as "pussycat" as well as her "pussycat" nose, eyes, and lips. (artist: Tom Jones)
- *1965*—"Baby, I'm Yours" (Van McCoy): She pledges love forever, till the stars fall out of the sky, the rivers run dry, and the sun shines no more. (artist: Barbara Lewis)
- *1965*—"Down in the Boondocks" (Joe South): They love each other, but he was born in the poor side of town and people put him down, so he can't knock on her door and he just has to be happy to see her whenever he can. (artist: Billy Joe Royal)
- *1965*—"Papa's Got a Brand New Bag" (James Brown): Papa ain't hip or fancy, but he's no drag because he can do the Jerk, the Fly, and those other cool dances. (artist: James Brown)
- *1965*—"Eve of Destruction" (P. F. Sloan): Violence is exploding in the eastern world, and you're not old enough to vote, but you're old enough to kill, and you don't believe in war, but bodies are floating in the Jordan River, so why don't you believe we're on the brink of final doom? (artist: Barry McGuire)

- *1965*—"Unchained Melody" (Hy Zaret, Alex North): Having been away from home for a while and lonely and the time going slowly, I wonder if you still belong to me. (artist: The Righteous Brothers)
- *1965*—"Yesterday" (John Lennon, Paul McCartney): I yearn for the past, when she made my worries feel distant, unlike now, where they're close at hand and I feel diminished, because she left me. (artist: The Beatles)
- *1965*—"Hang on Sloopy" (Wes Farrell, Bert Russell): Sloopy lives in a bad part of town, but her guy doesn't care what her father does because he's in love with her. (artist: The McCoys)
- *1965*—"A Lover's Concerto" (Sandy Linzer, Denny Randell): A gentle rain, singing birds, a bright colored rainbow—all these things make the day magic for us to fall in love. (artist: The Toys)
- *1965*—"Do You Believe in Magic?" (John Sebastian): Groovy music can free you and make you feel happy if you believe in magic. (artist: Lovin' Spoonful)
- *1965*—"I Hear a Symphony" (Holland-Dozier-Holland): With the love you've given me, whenever you come close, music fills the air. (artist: The Supremes)
- *1965*—"Turn! Turn! Turn!" (Pete Seeger): A lyrical adaptation from the Book of Ecclesiastes relating there is a season and purpose for everything under heaven. (artist: The Byrds)
- *1965*—"Keep on Dancing" (Allen Jones, Willie David Young): On the dance floor, stay in motion and groove. (artist: The Gentrys)
- *1965*—"1-2-3" (John Madara, David White, Leonard Borisoff): Falling in love with you is so easy it's like counting. (artist: Len Barry)
- *1965*—"Let's Hang On!" (Bob Crewe, Denny Randell, Sandy Linzer): We've had much happen between us, but let's not say goodbye; we need to hang in there. (artist: The Four Seasons)
- *1965*—"Over and Over" (Robert Byrd): Repeatedly thinking a social event (a dance) is going to be a boring affair but then spotting a pretty girl and getting excited (and rejected). (artist: The Dave Clark Five)
- *1965*—"England Swings" (Roger Miller): A paean to England with its bicycle-riding bobbies, Westminster Abbey, and Big Ben. (artist: Roger Miller)

- *1965*—"Rescue Me" (Carl Smith, Raynard Miner): I'm lonely and blue, so capture my heart and "rescue me." (artist: Fontella Bass)
- *1965*—"The Sounds of Silence" (Paul Simon): Walking alone in restless dreams, I was thrust by a neon light that can be found in the sound in the absence of sound. (artist: Simon and Garfunkle)
- *1965*—"We Can Work It Out" (John Lennon, Paul McCartney): We have our differences, but try to see it my way and perhaps we can find a way to make it work. (artist: The Beatles)
- *1966*—"Day Tripper" (John Lennon, Paul McCartney) That one-night stand was a big teaser, and it took a while to find out what she really was about. (artist: The Beatles)
- *1966*—"She's Just My Style" (Gary Lewis, Leon Russell, Thomas Lesslie, Al Capps): While other guys may not be struck by her, every time I see her, her hair, clothes, and everything else about her drives me wild because she's exactly my type. (Gary Lewis and the Playboys)
- *1966*—"As Tears Go By" (Mick Jagger, Andrew Loog Oldham, Keith Richards): At night when the children play and sing, wealth doesn't mean a thing, as I can only watch and cry. (artist: The Rolling Stones)
- *1966*—"Five O'Clock World" (Allen Reynolds): Every day is a grind getting up and getting to the job, but when it's over at five o'clock, I come to life when I fall into the arms of my "long-haired girl." (artist: The Vogues)
- *1966*—"Flowers on the Wall" (Lewis Dewitt): Don't worry about my happiness, because it's probably just your conscience; so please, don't worry about me because I've got plenty to do playing cards, smoking cigarettes, watching TV, and "counting flowers on the wall." (artist: The Statler Brothers)
- *1966*—"Barbara Ann" (Fred Fassert): At a dance, I tried lots of girls, but only Barbara Ann got me "rockin' and a reelin'." (artist: The Beach Boys)
- *1966*—"My World Is Empty without You" (Holland-Dozier-Holland): Now that I'm alone, I struggle to go on, missing you, needing you, without you my life is hollow. (artist: The Supremes)
- *1966*—"Lightnin' Strikes" (Lou Christie, Twyla Herbert): Stick with me because when I settle down I want it to be with you;

when I see your lips or you give me a sign, I feel like I'm struck by lightning. (artist: Lou Christie)

- *1966*—"My Love" (Tony Hatch): My love for you has no bounds. (artist Petula Clark)
- *1966*—"Uptight (Everything's Alright)" (Stevie Wonder, Sylvia Moy, Henry Cosby): She's rich, and I'm poor, but my baby cares for me and she knows I genuinely care for her when I'm not around. (artist: Stevie Wonder)
- *1966*—"Don't Mess with Bill" (William "Smokey" Robinson): He's made me cry over and over, but when he apologized I love him even more, so listen up, girls: stay away from my man. (artist: The Marvelettes)
- *1966*—"The Ballad of the Green Berets" (Barry Sadler, Robin Moore): Of the many brave men who will be tested today, only three will earn the Green Beret, and one who will die made a last request of his young wife: to have his son one day earn the coveted cap. (artist: Sgt. Barry Sadler)
- *1966*—"A Well Respected Man" (Ray Davies): He's fine and healthy and stands to inherit a bundle, and as his parents go about their business, he's cautious and around town is admired. (artist: The Kinks)
- *1966*—"California Dreamin'" (John Phillips): It's a dreary, cold day, and I enter a church where I fake praying, but my reverie is really to be where it's sunny and out of harm's way, in LA. (artist: The Mamas and the Papas)
- *1966*—"These Boots Are Made for Walkin'" (Lee Hazlewood): You may say you're going to love me, but I know you've been cheating, so there will come a time when I'm going to walk away from you. (artist: Nancy Sinatra)
- *1966*—"I Fought the Law" (Sonny Curtis): I was splitting rocks in the beating sun and had no money, so I turned to robbing people, and the cops—they got me. (artist: Bobby Fuller Four)
- *1966*—"Daydream" (John Sebastian): Even if, as you say, I have obligations to fulfill and time is passing me by, today's a beautiful day for a walk, and I'm going to continue sweet dreaming about the one who brings me happiness. (artist: Lovin' Spoonful)
- *1966*—"Bang Bang My Baby Shot Me Down" (Sonny Bono): When we played as kids, he used to shoot me and win the fight,

and I would fall to the ground, but he died without saying good-bye, and it's like he shot me again and I hit the ground. (artist: Cher)

- *1966*—"Secret Agent Man" (P. F. Sloan, Steve Barri): In the crowd of people you see lurks someone with a brutish mind, so don't reveal yourself, or you won't live beyond tomorrow. (artist: Johnny Rivers)
- *1966*—"19th Nervous Breakdown" (Mick Jagger, Keith Richard): You seem to be the center of attention where you go, but underneath is a sadness you can't hide, so beware your next nervous breakdown. (artist: The Rolling Stones)
- *1966*—"Nowhere Man" (John Lennon, Paul McCartney): Don't withdraw yourself and be blind to the world—get some perspective on the world. (artist: The Beatles)
- *1966*—"Sloop John B" (folk tune arranged by Brian Wilson): I'm on a boat with my grandfather with whom I fought, the first mate who drank too much, and the cook who had a tantrum, and I just want to get out of here. (artist: The Beach Boys)
- *1966*—"I Am a Rock" (Paul Simon): At home on a cold, snowy day, I've built myself in not needing friends or love because they cause pain. (artist: Simon and Garfunkle)
- *1966*—"Did You Ever Have to Make Up Your Mind?" (John Sebastian): Decisions are hard to make—especially when there are lots of girls to choose from. (artist: Lovin' Spoonful)
- *1966*—"When a Man Loves a Woman" (Calvin Lewis, Andrew Wright): Love is blind to all the faults the person you love may have. (artist: Percy Sledge)
- *1966*—"Strangers in the Night" (Charles Singleton, Eddie Snyder, Bert Kaempfert): Finding love can be a happenstance, but I knew I must have you when I saw something inviting in your eyes and smile that fateful evening. (artist: Frank Sinatra)
- *1966*—"Cool Jerk" (Donald Storball): When I stroll down the street and people see me, they know I'm cool because I can do the "cool jerk" (dance). (artist: The Capitols)
- *1966*—"Red Rubber Ball" (Paul Simon, Bruce Woodly): I never really meant much to you, but I'm over you now, and the sun above is like a glimmering rubber ball. (artist: The Cyrkle)

- *1966*—"Paperback Writer" (John Lennon, Paul McCartney): I'm a struggling writer—just like a character I'm writing about—and I hope I can get a break and get my book published because I need a gig and I want to be an author. (artist: The Beatles)
- *1966*—"You Don't Have to Say You Love Me" (Vicki Wickham, Simon Napler-Bell, Pino Donaggio, Vito Pallavicini): You broke your word that you would stay with me and you left me all alone, but if you come back, you don't have to stay with me forever or say you love me. (artist: Dusty Springfield)
- *1966*—"The More I See You" (Harry Warren, Mack Gordon): You grow on me the more we're together. (artist: Chris Montez)
- *1966*—"Hanky Panky" (Jeff Barry, Ellie Greenwich): I saw this pretty girl and asked her to come home with me, but she didn't—she danced the "hanky panky." (artist: Tommy James and the Shondells)
- *1966*—"Wild Thing" (Chip Taylor): My lover thrills me, but she's untamed, so I need to know she loves me, which I'll know if she holds "me tight." (artist: The Troggs)
- *1966*—"Lil' Red Riding Hood" (Ronald Blackwell): She's luscious and the kind that drives guys wild, so I'll walk with her a while so she's safe; but then I myself would like to hold her, but I won't because then she'd think I was like all the other guys, although I have a big heart and could love her (but maybe by the time we get to her destination, she'll see things my way). (artist: Sam the Sham and the Pharoahs)
- *1966*—"Along Comes Mary" (Tandyn Almer): When I'm lonely I write poetry about my faults, and then this girl (Mary) comes along, and I'm unaware of what's going on, so I'm alone again. (artist: The Association)
- *1966*—"See You in September" (Sid Wayne, Sherman Edwards): Summer's coming and we have to part, but with summer romances I hope I don't lose you to another guy; no, I hope to "see you in September." (artist: The Happenings)
- *1966*—"Summer in the City" (John Sebastian, Mark Sebastian, Steve Boone): A city can be brutally hot in the summer, but at night the heat can turn to coolness if you find someone and dance the night away. (artist: Lovin' Spoonful)

- *1966*—"Yellow Submarine" (John Lennon, Paul McCartney): We heard about this great place to live, so we all went out there, and with friends "near by" and music playing, everyone dwells in this underwater vessel. (artist: The Beatles)
- *1966*—"Bus Stop" (Graham Gouldman): That summer I'd see her by the bus stop, and when it rained I invited her to stay under my umbrella; a few months later she was my girl. (artist: The Hollies)
- *1966*—"96 Tears" (The Mysterians): I've cried over and over since you abandoned me, but we'll reunite temporarily, and then I'll leave you, and you'll cry just like me. (artist: ? [Question Mark] & the Mysterians)
- *1966*—"Cherish" (Terry Kirkman): I want to cherish you, but I know I'll never have you; if only there was a word that could make you understand how crazy I am about you. (artist: The Association)
- *1966*—"Sunny" (Bobby Hebb): My life was torn apart, but you shine on me your smile and your love, so now my life is bright. (artist: Bobby Hebb)
- *1966*—"What Becomes of the Brokenhearted?" (William Weatherspoon, Paul Riser, James Dean): I dwell in a land of broken hearts, looking for love and peace of mind, but I don't know what will be. (artist: Jimmy Ruffin)
- *1966*—"Cherry Cherry" (Neil Diamond): You turn me on, so tell your mother we gotta get going so we can get grooving. (artist: Neil Diamond)
- *1966*—"If I Were a Carpenter" (Tim Hardin): Would you marry me if I were a common laborer and you were a woman of high social position? (artist: Bobby Darin)
- *1966*—"Last Train to Clarksville" (Tommy Boyce, Bobby Hart): I'm leaving on the morning train, so meet me at the station for a last night together before I have to leave. (artist: The Monkees)
- *1966*—"Winchester Cathedral" (Geoff Stephens): If only Winchester Cathedral rang her chimes, my girl wouldn't have abandoned me. (artist: The New Vaudeville Band)
- *1966*—"Born Free" (John Barry, Don Black): When you're free to follow your passions, the world is beautiful. (artist: Roger Williams)

- *1966*—"Lady Godiva" (Charles Mills, Mike Leander): She was a beauty who could go places, but she took the wrong opportunity (she was fooled by a movie director who put her in a striptease show), and now she's broke, and her long blond hair is gone. (artist: Peter and Gordon)
- *1966*—"Walk Away Renee" (Mike Brown, Bob Calilli, Tony Sansone): It's not your fault, Renee, and I'm feeling pain, but when you see where we used to stroll by, just go on. (artist: The Left Banke)
- *1966*—"Good Vibrations" (Brian Wilson, Mike Love): She gives off a good vibe, and that excites me. (artist: The Beach Boys)
- *1966*—"A Place in the Sun" (Ron Miller, Bryan Wells): Everyone's dreams can come true, but you've got to keep moving to find the place where you can shine. (artist: Stevie Wonder)
- *1966*—"Tell It Like It Is" (George Davis, Lee Diamond): My time is precious, so don't play games; just let me know how you honestly feel. (artist: Aaron Neville)
- *1966*—"Working My Way Back to You" (Sandy Linzer, Denny Randell): With my wild ways I may have sabotaged our love, but now I am going to try to make you love me again. (artists: The 4 Seasons, Spinners)
- *1966*—"Opus 17 (Don't You Worry 'Bout Me)" (Sandy Linzer, Denny Randell): If you have somebody else it may tear me apart, but I want you to be happy so go on and don't concern yourself about me. (artist: The 4 Seasons)
- *1967*—"I'm a Believer" (Neil Diamond): I lost my faith in love thinking it was only for others, but then I saw her, and my faith has been restored. (artist: The Monkees)
- *1967*—"Jimmy Mack" (Brian Holland, Lamont Dozier, Eddie Holland): This sweet-talking guy keeps calling me, and I'm trying to keep faithful, but I'm lonely and he's wearing me down, so Jimmy, hurry back. (artist: Martha and the Vandellas)
- *1967*—"Kind of a Drag" (Jim Holvay): When you love somebody and they don't love you back, it's a bummer. (artist: The Buckinghams)
- *1967*—"Ruby Tuesday" (Mick Jagger, Keith Richards): She's a free spirit, changing all the time, and there's no name for her, so adieu "Ruby Tuesday." (artist: The Rolling Stones)

- *1967*—"98.6" (George Fischoff, Tony Powers): Her kiss got me back to normal—it was the best medicine I could have. (artist: Keith)
- *1967*—"Baby I Need Your Lovin'" (Brian Holland, Lamont Dozier, Eddie Holland): I'm lonely and losing sleep, so I don't care if I have to beg you to love me because I'm suffering without you. (artist: Johnny Rivers)
- *1967*—"Happy Together" (Garry Bonner, Alan Gordon): Thinking about you all the time, I know the world would be great, because we were made for each other, and bliss would be ours if we were together. (artist: The Turtles)
- *1967*—"Sock It to Me Baby!" (Bob Crewe, Larry Brown): Your kisses knock me out, so just smack me one more time! (artist: Mitch Ryder and the Detroit Wheels)
- *1967*—"This Is My Song" (Charles Chaplin): With you everything in the world is right, so for you I sing a song, a paean to you. (artist: Petula Clark)
- *1967*—"The 59th Street Bridge Song (Feelin' Groovy)" (Paul Simon): Life is marvelous when you take it slow and seek out diversion. (artist: Harpers Bizarre)
- *1967*—"The Happening" (Brian Holland, Lamont Dozier, Eddie Holland, Frank De Vol): One day you lose a love and you wake up to reality, so be careful. (artist: The Supremes)
- *1967*—"Groovin'" (Felix Cavaliere, Eddie Brigati): Get away with the one you love, and no matter where you are or what you do, you're "groovin'" (artist: The Young Rascals)
- *1967*—"Release Me (and Let Me Love Again)" (Robert Yount, Eddie Miller, James Pebworth): I no longer love you, so let me be free. (artist: Engelbert Humperdinck)
- *1967*—"Respect" (Otis Redding): I've got what you want and even money to give you, but all I'm asking is that when you come home, treat me with some admiration. (artist: Aretha Franklin)
- *1967*—"San Francisco (Be Sure to Wear Flowers in Your Hair)" (John Phillips): People across the country are hustling around, but there's love in San Francisco, so if you're going there, adorn your hair with flowers. (artist: Scott McKenzie)

- *1967*—"Light My Fire" (The Doors): We can get higher if we engage in some sexual acts, so don't wait; let's get going. (artist: The Doors)
- *1967*—"Society's Child (Baby I've Been Thinking)" (Janis Ian). We'll have to wait for our forbidden love, because right now I'm just a young person in our prejudiced world. (artist: Janis Ian)
- *1967*—"All You Need Is Love" (John Lennon, Paul McCartney): You can do anything when you have love. (artist: The Beatles)
- *1967*—"The Letter" (Wayne Carson): Just got a letter from my baby; she wants me back, and I've got to get to her fast no matter what the cost; I've got to get a plane ticket. (artist: The Box Tops)
- *1967*—"Apple Peaches Pumpkin Pie" (Maurice Irby): We used to have fun playing hide and seek when we were young, but now that we're older I'm going to find you and marry you, so you won't play around anymore. (artist: Jay and the Techniques)
- *1967*—"A Natural Woman (You Make Me Feel Like)" (Gerry Goffin, Carole King, Jerry Wexler): I felt indifferent and lost until I met you, and now I feel like a woman was made to feel. (artist: Aretha Franklin)
- *1967*—"I Can See for Miles" (Peter Townshend): You may try to fool me, but I can see past the games you play. (artist: The Who)
- *1967*—"How Can I Be Sure?" (Felix Cavaliere, Eddie Brigati): With the world always shifting when I'm not near you, how can I know how you feel about me? (artist: The Young Rascals)
- *1967*—"The Rain, the Park and Other Things" (Artie Kornfeld, Steve Duboff): It was raining when a lovely girl drew my attention; after an enchanting walk, the sun came out and she disappeared—was she real or a figment of my imagination? (artist: The Cowsills)
- *1967*—"Hello Goodbye" (John Lennon, Paul McCartney): We say opposite things, but if you bid me farewell, I'll greet you. (artist: The Beatles)
- *1967*—"(The Lights Went out in) Massachusetts" (Barry Gibb, Maurice Gibb, Robin Gibb): After I left her, the lights went out at home; I tried to get away to do what I thought I needed to do, but the lights brought me back to her. (artist: The Bee Gees)

- *1967*—"Bend Me, Shape Me" (Larry Weiss, Scott English): I need you so much that you can mold me any way you want as long as you love me. (artist: The American Breed)
- *1967*—"Keep the Ball Rollin' (Sandy Linzer, Denny Randell): Start kissing me and don't stop—just keep on going. (artist: Jay and the Techniques)
- *1968*—"Chain of Fools" (Don Covay): I may just be another dolt on your long list of lovers, but one day this dolt is going to break free. (artist: Aretha Franklin)
- *1968*—"I Heard It through the Grapevine" (Norman Whitfield, Barrett Strong): I was surprised to hear you're going to break up with me, but if you're wondering how I found out, I got wind of the chatter about it. (artist: Gladys Knight and the Pips)
- *1968*—"Spooky" (M. Sharpe, Harry Middlebrooks, Buddy Buie, James Cobb): I never know what to expect with you, never know what you're going to say or do; you're "a spooky little girl." (artist: The Classics IV)
- *1968*—"(Sittin' on) The Dock of the Bay" (Steve Cropper, Otis Redding): Having nothing to live for, I left home for the Frisco bay, where I waste my time watching boats and the tide at my home on the waterfront. (artist: Otis Redding)
- *1968*—"Dance to the Music" (Sylvester Stewart): We're going to make a little music, and when you hear it, get on your feet and dance. (Artist: Sly and the Family Stone)
- *1968*—"Honey" (Bobby Russell): She was a kid at heart when she planted a tree, and I loved her; I gave her a puppy and she cried, and I loved her; she cried over a late show, and I loved her; when she wrecked the car and cried, I loved her; and now she's passed on, and a cloud cries onto the field that my honey loved. (artist: Bobby Goldsboro)
- *1968*—"I Say a Little Prayer" (Burt Bacharach, Hal David): When I arise, ride in a bus, take a coffee break at work, for you, I make a small prayer. (artist: Aretha Franklin)
- *1968*—"Mony Mony" (Bobby Bloom, Ritchie Cordell, Bo Gentry, Tommy James): Get rid of them and come, Mony Mony, and make me feel good. (artist: Tommy James and the Shondells)

- *1968*—"Cowboys to Girls" (Kenny Gamble, Leon Huff): I played a cowboy when I was a kid, but now I'm grown up and chasing girls. (artist: The Intruders)
- *1968*—"Lady Willpower" (Jerry Fuller): Don't be afraid; surrender your love to me, and I'll give you all the tender love you need. (artist: Gary Puckett and the Union Gap)
- *1968*—"Stoned Soul Picnic" (Laura Nyro): Lots of liquor, sassafras, and honey, so come on "down to a stoned soul picnic." (artist: The Fifth Dimension)
- *1968*—"Harper Valley P.T.A." (Tom T. Hall): When her teenaged daughter came home one day with a note from school accusing the mother, a widow, of wearing short dresses, boozing, and carousing with men, mama let loose on the PTA's hypocrites. (artist: Jeannie C. Riley)
- *1968*—"The Fool on the Hill" (John Lennon, Paul McCartney): Listen to the people you think are unwise; they may see things you don't and give you a surprise. (artist: Sergio Mendes & Brasil '66)
- *1968*—"I've Gotta Get a Message to You" (Maurice, Robin, and Barry Gibb): My life will be over soon, and I don't have a dime to phone, but I asked the preacher to tell you I'm sorry for breaking your heart. (artist: The Bee Gees)
- *1968*—"Abraham, Martin and John" (Dick Holler), An ode to three distinguished men who were cut down in the prime of their professional lives: Abraham Lincoln, John F. Kennedy, and Martin Luther King Jr. (artist: Dion)
- *1968*—"Chewy Chewy" (Joey Levine, Kris Resnick): My sweetheart always says sweet things. (artist: The Ohio Express)
- *1969*—"Build Me up Buttercup" (Tony Macaulay, Mike D'Abo): You give me confidence that you care about me, but then you disappoint me, not calling me or coming over when you say you will. (artist: The Foundations)
- *1969*—"This Magic Moment" (Doc Pomus, Mort Shuman): That special feeling we had when we first kissed will always be with us. (artist: Jay and the Americans)
- *1969*—"Time of the Season" (Rod Argent): It's that special time for living and loving. (artist: The Zombies)

- *1969*—"Hair" (James Rado, Gerome Ragni, Galt MacDermot): Don't know why I want so much hair, but it's beautiful and splendid, and I want to grow it as long as it'll go. (artist: The Cowsills)
- *1969*—"These Eyes" (Randy Bachman, Burton Cummings): After you broke your promise to me, my eyes will always shed tears for you. (artist: Guess Who)
- *1969*—"Spinning Wheel" (David Clayton-Thomas): What goes around comes around. (artist: Blood Sweat and Tears)
- *1969*—"More Today Than Yesterday" (Patrick Upton): Every day I love you more than the day before. (artist: The Spiral Staircase)
- *1969*—"Crystal Blue Persuasion" (Tommy James, Mike Vale): The world is changing, so search your soul to find love and feel that new vibe. (artist: Tommy James and the Shondells)
- *1969*—"One" (Harry Nilsson): Now that you're gone and I'm all alone, I realize that "one" is a lonely number. (artist: Three Dog Night)
- *1969*—"My Cherie Amour" (Henry Cosby, Stevie Wonder, Sylvia Moy): My darling love, pretty but distant, I hope you'll notice me one day. (artist: Stevie Wonder)
- *1969*—"Baby I Love You" (Jeff Barry, Ellie Greenwich, Phil Spector): When I hold you or you touch me, I have to tell you I'm in love with you. (artist: Andy Kim)
- *1969*—"Ruby, Don't Take Your Love to Town" (Mel Tillis): I got mangled in the war, so I'm not who I used to be, but baby, please don't cheat on me. (artist: Kenny Rogers and the First Edition)
- *1969*—"Honky Tonk Women" (Mick Jagger, Keith Richards): A certain kind of woman—the disreputable kind—gives me a certain kind of feeling. (artist: The Rolling Stones)
- *1969*—"A Boy Named Sue" (Shel Silverstein): For giving me a girl's name, I vowed revenge on my father, but after I hunted him down, he told me he did it to make me tough, so I put down my gun and embraced him. (artist: Johnny Cash)
- *1969*—"Put a Little Love in Your Heart" (Jackie DeShannon, Randy Myers, Jimmy Holiday): You can make the world better if you put some "love in your heart." (artist: Jackie DeShannon)
- *1969*—"Polk Salad Annie" (Tony Joe White): Story about a girl with a mean mama, a lazy daddy, and thieving brothers who goes

down to the fields to pick a plant that people called "polk salad," which is served for the family dinner. (artist: Tony Joe White)

- *1969*—"Hot Fun in the Summertime" (Sylvester Stewart): School's out, and there are outdoor celebrations—wow!—there's nothing like the summertime. (artist: Sly and the Family Stone)
- *1969*—"Wedding Bell Blues" (Laura Nyro): I've stuck by your side and have always been faithful to you, so I'm feeling down in the dumps because when are you going to marry me? (artist: The Fifth Dimension)
- *1969*—"Take a Letter Maria" (R. B. Greaves): After seeing his wife with another man, he dictates a letter to his secretary in which he tells his wife he's leaving her. (artist: R. B. Greaves)
- *1969*—"Yester-Me, Yester-You, Yesterday" (Ron Miller, B. Wells): When we were young, we had dreams, but now they're just cruel memories—what happened to our world? (artist: Stevie Wonder)
- *1969*—"Smile a Little Smile for Me" (Tony Macaulay, Geoff Stephens): He left you, so I know you're sad, but there'll be lots of other guys in your life, so give me a little smile. (artist: Flying Machine)
- *1969*—"Raindrops Keep Fallin' on My Head" (Burt Bacharach, Hal David): Life may be hitting me over and over, but looking on the brighter side of things, I'm not going to let it defeat me. (artist: B. J. Thomas)
- *1970*—"He Ain't Heavy, He's My Brother" (Bob Russell, Bobby Scott): When someone is down and out, I'm there to help, only wishing all people could be there for our downtrodden brothers and sisters. (artist: The Hollies)
- *1970*—"ABC" (The Corporation): You might have attended school, but I'm the teacher now, and I'm going to teach you the ABCs of love. (artist: The Jackson Five)
- *1970*—"Easy Come, Easy Go" (Diane Hildebrand, Jack Keller): I lost my heart to her even though she wasn't very nice, but I've learned from the experience, so I can move on now. (artist: Bobby Sherman)
- *1970*—"Let It Be" (Paul McCartney, John Lennon): There are many problems in the world, but stay calm; they will straighten themselves out naturally. (artist: The Beatles)

- *1970*—"Spirit in the Sky" (Norman Greenbaum): I've lived a clean life, so when I breathe my last here, I'm going up to heaven. (artist: Norman Greenbaum)
- *1970*—"Love Grows (Where My Rosemary Goes)" (Barry Mason, Tony Macaulay): My girl is broke, dresses weirdly, and has crazy hair, but she's got a magic charm that makes me helplessly love her. (artist: Edison Lighthouse)
- *1970*—"The Long and Winding Road" (John Lennon, Paul McCartney): No matter how often I've been hurt, I will always want to take the path to your door. (artist: The Beatles)
- *1970*—"Band of Gold" (Ron Dunbar, Edyth Wayne): You left me, and now all I have is my wedding ring, leaving me with fond remembrances of what could have been. (artist: Freda Payne)
- *1970*—"(They Long to Be) Close to You" (Hal David, Burt Bacharach): You're a living dream that creatures on earth and stars in the sky, just like me, want to be near you (artist: Carpenters)
- *1970*—"War" (Norman Whitfield, Barret Strong): War serves no purpose but ruins lives. (artist: Edwin Starr)
- *1970*—"Candida" (Toni Wine, Irwin Levine): Even though I'm just an ordinary fellow, we could have a wonderful life together if you let me take you away from here. (artist: Dawn)
- *1970*—"Fire and Rain" (James Taylor): For all the hardships I've been through, I never thought you'd disappoint me, but you've left, and we may not see each other again. (artist: James Taylor)
- *1970*—"Snowbird" (Gene MacLellan): I listened to my heart when I was young and had it broken because you were unfaithful, and now I'd like to follow the tiny snowbird to that tranquil place where the winds are soft and the waters are calm. (artist: Anne Murray)
- *1970*—"We've Only Just Begun" (Paul Williams, Roger Nichols): There's so much ahead of us and we'll grow together, sharing and talking things over as we move along. (artist: Carpenters)
- *1970*—"The Tears of a Clown" (Hank Cosby, William Robinson Jr., Stevie Wonder): Don't go by the happy expression on my face because underneath I am sad and cry when I'm alone even though I may not show that face in public. (artist: Smokey Robinson & the Miracles)

- *1970*—"I Think I Love You" (Tony Romeo): I have this unshakeable feeling that I love you, but it scares me because I don't know what it means, and it won't go away. (artist: The Partridge Family)
- *1970*—"Out in the Country" (Paul Williams, Roger Nichols): The country is my comforting get-away place. (artist: Three Dog Night)
- *1970*—"One Less Bell to Answer" (Burt Bacharach, Hal David): Since you left there's once less of everything for me to do, and it makes me very sad. (artist: The 5th Dimension)
- *1970*—"Knock Three Times" (Larry Russell Brown, Irwin Levine): We're neighbors, but I don't know if you know how I adore you, so send me a signal if you're interested. (artist: Dawn)
- *1971*—"It's Impossible" (Sid Wayne, Armando Manzanero): Certain things in life are impossible, and living without you loving me would be one of them. (artist: Perry Como)
- *1971*—"Rose Garden" (Joe South): Life isn't always perfect, so I'm not going to tell you things that may not come true, but let's just be together and try to enjoy ourselves. (artist: Lynn Anderson)
- *1971*—"I Hear You Knocking" (Pearl King, Dave Bartholomew): When you abandoned me, you lost your chance to come back into my life, so stop bothering me and go away. (artist: Dave Edmunds)
- *1971*—"Me and Bobby McGee" (Kris Kristofferson, Fred Foster): My lover left me in search of a home, but I hope he returns to me. (artist: Janis Joplin)
- *1971*—"Just My Imagination (Running Away with Me)" (Norman Whitfield, Barrett Strong): She's all mine—but only in my dreams. (artist: The Temptations)
- *1971*—"Help Me Make It through the Night" (Kris Kristofferson): I'm all alone and need you next to me as I try to fall asleep tonight. (artist: Sammi Smith)
- *1971*—"If You Could Read My Mind" (Gordon Lightfoot): I don't know what broke us apart, but if you knew my thoughts, you'd know I no longer care. (artist: Gordon Lightfoot)
- *1971*—"What's Going On" (Alfred Cleveland, Marvin Gaye, Renaldo Benson): We need love, not hate, and I'll explain it to you so that you understand what's happening. (artist: Marvin Gaye)

- *1971*—"Joy to the World" (Hoyt Axton): The world would be a better place if we all sang of joy. (artist: Three Dog Night)
- *1971*—"She's a Lady" (Paul Anka): My woman is faithful, modest, and understands me—everything I want. (artist: Tom Jones)
- *1971*—"Never Can Say Goodbye" (Clifton Davis): We may have our problems, but I can't leave you. (artist: The Jackson 5)
- *1971*—"If" (David Gates): Life has a lot of possibilities, but all I want is to be with you. (artist: Bread)
- *1971*—"Rainy Days and Mondays" (Paul Williams, Roger Nichols): Some things bum me out, but your love always makes me feel better. (artist: Carpenters)
- *1971*—"It Don't Come Easy" (Richard Starkey): My love for you grows, but it can at times be difficult. (artist: Ringo Starr)
- *1971*—"How Can You Mend a Broken Heart? (Barry Gibb, Robin Gibb): When I was young I embraced life, but no one ever taught me how to deal with having your heart broken. (artist: The Bee Gees)
- *1971*—"You've Got a Friend" (Carole King): If life is being hard on you and you need someone who cares, just let me know. (artists: Carole King, James Taylor)
- *1971*—"Family Affair" (Sylvester Stewart): Children may turn out differently, but they're all part of the same mold, and Mom loves them just the same. (artist: Sly and the Family Stone)
- *1971*—"Brand New Key" (Melanie Safka): We may not be together now, but I still think we could be a pair, and you've got the key to make it happen (artist: Melanie)
- *1971*—"An Old-Fashioned Love Song" (Paul Williams): That old familiar love song you hear on the radio fits us perfectly. (artist: Three Dog Night)
- *1972*—"American Pie (Pts. 1 and 2)" (Don McLean): When that icon of rock and roll went down, the music of America stopped. (artist: Don McLean)
- *1972*—"Without You" (Tom Evans, Peter Ham): When you left tonight, I could see the sadness in your eyes, but now that I know I made a mistake in letting you go, I can't go on with you not there. (artist: Nilsson)

- *1972*—"A Horse with No Name" (Dewey Bunnell): In our journey through life, strangers can lead us to good (if not unexpected) places. (artist: America)
- *1972*—"The First Time Ever I Saw Your Face" (Ewan MacColl): All my "firsts" with you were wonderfully, beautifully life changing. (artist: Roberta Flack)
- *1972*—"Sylvia's Mother" (Shel Silverstein): I need to talk to my girl before she goes off and gets married, but her mother won't put her on the phone. (artist: Dr. Hook and the Medicine Show)
- *1972*—"Morning Has Broken" (Eleanor Farjeon): Morning is like the renewal of life. (artist: Cat Stevens)
- *1972*—"Rocket Man" (Elton John, Bernie Taupin): When you're away for a long while and alone, you may not return the same person. (artist: Elton John)
- *1972*—"Alone Again (Naturally)" (Gilbert O'Sullivan): In our journey through life, from our parents to our loves, we all end up in our natural state, which is alone. (artist: Gilbert O'Sullivan)
- *1972*—"Brandy (You're a Fine Girl)" (Elliot Lurie): All the sailors who come to port praise Brandy the barmaid, but she only wants the sailor who keeps returning to the sea. (artist: Looking Glass)
- *1972*—"Baby Don't Get Hooked on Me" (Mac Davis): I'm not ready to settle down, so don't get taken in by me, or I'll have to move on. (artist: Mac Davis)
- *1972*—"Black and White" (David Arkin, Earl Robinson): Black . . . white . . . we all need to come together and dance as one. (artist: Three Dog Night)
- *1972*—"Long Cool Woman (In a Black Dress)" (Roger Cook, Alan Clarke, Roger Greenaway): Life can get messy, but it just takes one (right) person to straighten it out. (artist: The Hollies)
- *1972*—"Goodbye to Love" (Richard Carpenter, John Bettis): No one's ever really loved me, so I will look for love no more. (artist: Carpenters)
- *1972*—"Everybody Plays the Fool" (Rudy Clark, J. R. Bailey, Ken Williams): Don't kick yourself for your mistakes; we all do foolish things sometimes. (artist: The Main Ingredient)
- *1972*—"I Can See Clearly Now" (Johnny Nash): Now that I'm over my heartbreak, my head is clear and bright days are ahead. (artist: Johnny Nash)

- *1972*—"I Am Woman" (Helen Reddy, Ray Burton): I've learned the hard way, and now I'm embracing my womanhood and know there's nothing I can't do. (artist: Helen Reddy)
- *1972*—"Papa Was a Rollin' Stone" (Norman Whitfield, Barrett Strong): My father was a drifter who I never got to know, and while people gossiped about him, he's gone now and we're all alone. (artist: The Temptations)
- *1972*—"Me and Mrs. Jones" (Kenny Gamble, Leon Huff, Carey Gilbert): I'm having an affair with a married woman, and while we both know it's not the right thing to do, we can't help ourselves. (artist: Billy Paul)
- *1972*—"It Never Rains in California" (Albert Hammond, Mike Hazelwood): California is supposed to be the land of opportunity, but it can disappoint. (artist: Albert Hammond)
- *1972*—"Summer Breeze" (James Seals, Darrell Crofts): Summer is a relaxing time, and its breezes are soothing. (artist: Seals and Crofts)
- *1973*—"Crocodile Rock" (Elton John, Bernie Taupin): Young love may not last, but the music you danced to will bring back great memories. (artist: Elton John)
- *1973*—"Killing Me Softly with His Song" (Norman Gimble, Charles Fox): I went to hear this stranger sing, and it was like he knew my life story, and I felt pain as he played and sang. (artist: Roberta Flack)
- *1973*—"Neither One of Us (Wants to Be the First to Say Good-bye)" (James Weatherly): Even though we know it's not working, we continue on because neither you or I can find a way to end it. (artist: Gladys Knight & the Pips)
- *1973*—"Tie a Yellow Ribbon Round the Ole Oak Tree" (Irwin Levine, L. Russell Brown): I'll be taking a bus home after being away in prison for three years, and as I wrote in my letters, I'll know if you still love me if you affix a yellow ribbon to that old oak tree. (artist: Dawn featuring Tony Orlando)
- *1973*—"Will It Go Round in Circles" (Billy Preston, Bruce Fisher): When there's no substance to something, try to make the best of it and even soar high. (artist: Billy Preston)
- *1973*—"Loves Me Like a Rock" (Paul Simon): Maternal love is unshakable (artist: Paul Simon)

- *1973*—"Midnight Train to Georgia" (Jim Weatherly): If your dreams of making it don't work out, you can always return to the place you left from, and if that happens to somebody you love and you want to be in their life, you follow along with them. (artist: Gladys Knight and the Pips)
- *1973*—"The Most Beautiful Girl" (Norro Wilson, Rory Bourke, Billy Sherrill): I don't know what got into me, but I made a big mistake in saying what I did to my girl, so if you run into her let her know I'm sorry and love her. (artist: Charlie Rich)
- *1973*—"Heartbeat It's a Love Beat" (Greg Williams, Mike Kennedy): When we're together my heartbeat makes a wonderful vibrating sound that's really a love beat. (artist: The DeFranco Family featuring Tony DeFranco)
- *1973*—"Say, Has Anybody Seen My Sweet Gypsy Rose" (Irwin Levine, L. Russell Brown): My wife left me to become a stripteaser but I miss her and love her and hope she'll come to her senses and come home. (artist: Dawn featuring Tony Orlando)
- *1974*—"You and Me against the World" (Paul Williams, Kenny Ascher): Whenever it seems like others are giving either of us a hard time, don't worry—we've got each other. (artist: Helen Reddy)
- *1974*—"Time in a Bottle" (Jim Croce): I wish I could save time so I could spend every day with you. (artist: Jim Croce)
- *1974*—"The Way We Were" (Marvin Hamlisch, Alan and Marilyn Bergman): Remember the happy times of our past, and forget the difficult times. (artist: Barbra Streisand)
- *1974*—"Seasons in the Sun" (Jacques Brel, Rod McKuen): Enjoy life while you can, because eventually it comes to an end. (artist: Terry Jacks)
- *1974*—"Hooked on a Feeling" (Mark James): I'm captivated by the idea that you love me. (artist: Blue Swede)
- *1974*—"Come and Get Your Love" (Lolly Vegas): I'm here to give you love. (artist: Redbone)
- *1974*—"Oh My My" (Richard Starkey, Vincent Poncia Jr.): Moving is the way to stay healthy, and to boogie is a fun way to do it. (artist: Ringo Starr)

- *1974*—"You Make Me Feel Brand New" (Thom Bell, Linda Creed): I was down but you brought me back to life again. (artist: The Stylistics)
- *1974*—"Billy, Don't Be a Hero" (Mitch Murray, Peter Callander): When he went off to war, she warned him not to be a hero, but he died that way, and she discarded the report of his death. (artist: Bo Donaldson and the Heywoods)
- *1974*—"Rock Me Gently" (Andy Kim): Embrace me and move tenderly. (artist: Andy Kim)
- *1974*—"Nothing from Nothing" (Billy Preston, Bruce Fisher): If you want to be my partner, you can't be doing nothing. (artist: Billy Preston)
- *1974*—"My Melody of Love" (Henry Mayer, Georg Buschor, Bobby Vinton): I need to get away from wherever music plays that brings back memories of us, because I still love you. (artist: Bobby Vinton)
- *1974*—"When Will I See You Again" (Kenny Gamble, Leon Huff): I don't know whether our relationship is romantic or platonic, but I can't wait until we're together again. (artist: The Three Degrees)
- *1974*—"You're the First, the Last, My Everything" (Barry White, Tony Sepe, Peter Radcliffe): You're everything to me. (artist: Barry White)
- *1974*—"Fire" (James Williams, Leroy Bonner, Clarence Satchell, Marshall Jones, Ralph Middlebrooks, Marvin Pierce, William Beck): Everything about you lights me up. (artist: Ohio Players)
- *1975*—"Laughter in the Rain" (Neil Sedaka, Phil Cody): You could be getting soaked in the rain, but if you're walking with your love, you can find it exhilarating. (artist: Neil Sedaka)
- *1975*—"My Eyes Adored You" (Bob Crewe, Kenny Nolan): From school days till now, you never knew it, but I always loved you. (artist: Frankie Valli)
- *1975*—"Lady Marmalade (Voulez-Vous Coucher Avec Moi Ce Soir?)" (Bob Crewe, Kenny Nolan): Some women will play you and cost you big, but when you go back to your regular life, you'll be thinking about them and the love they gave you. (artist: Labelle)

- *1975*—"Lovin' You" (Minnie Riperton, Richard Rudolph): All I want to do is love you, and that's easy (artist: Minnie Riperton)
- *1975*—"Philadelphia Freedom" (Elton John, Bernie Taupin): Being a free spirit is the way to live. (artist: The Elton John Band)
- *1975*—"Love Will Keep Us Together" (Neil Sedaka, Howard Greenfield): We may face temptations, but love is our glue. (artist: The Captain & Tennille)
- *1975*—"Rhinestone Cowboy" (Larry Weiss): It's a hard road to fame, but dreams can get you there. (artist: Glen Campbell)
- *1975*—"At Seventeen" (Janis Ian). Long ago, when I was a teenager, I learned that the world was made for beautiful people, and unsightly people like me had to find our own ways to cope. (artist: Janis Ian
- *1975*—"Fame" (David Bowie, John Lennon, Carlos Alomar): Fame is power, but it's hollow. (artist: David Bowie)
- *1975*—"Wasted Days and Wasted Nights" (B. Huerta, D. Duncan): You left me, so I'm not going to waste my time loving you. (artist: Freddie Fender)
- *1975*—"Feelings" (Morris Albert): I will always have feelings for you, even if you're not in my life. (artist: Morris Albert)
- *1975*—"I Write the Songs" (Bruce Johnston): Music is part of your soul forever, and it can affect others who you share it with. (artist: Barry Manilow)
- *1975*—"Love Rollercoaster" (James Williams, Leroy Bonner, Clarence Satchell, Marshall Jones, Ralph Middlebrooks, Marvin Pierce, William Beck): Being drawn to you is like being on a crazy amusement park ride. (artist: Ohio Players)
- *1976*—"Bohemian Rhapsody" (Freddie Mercury): I just murdered someone, and I'm done. (artist: Queen)
- *1976*—"I'd Really Love to See You Tonight" (Parker McGee): Yeah, it's been some time, but can we just meet up for a little while later? (artist: England Dan and John Ford Coley)
- *1976*—"Play That Funky Music" (Robert Parissi): People don't want to hear that old outdated music; they want to hear the new funky sounds. (artist: Wild Cherry)
- *1977*—"You Make Me Feel Like Dancing" (Leo Sayer, Vincent Poncia Jr.): You excite me so much I just want to dance. (artist: Leo Sayer)

- *1977*—"After the Lovin'" (Alan Bernstein, Ritchie Adams): As you go to sleep after we make love, I want to sing to you how much I love you. (artist: Engelbert Humperdinck)
- *1977*—"Dancing Queen" (Benny Andersson, Stig Anderson, Björn Ulvaeus): You're young and charming, and on that dance floor the guys come looking for you and you're the queen. (artist: Abba)
- *1977*—"Evergreen (Love Theme from *A Star Is Born*)" (Barbra Streisand, Paul Williams): Our love will always be fresh and will remain forever. (artist: Barbra Streisand)
- *1977*—"Southern Nights" (Alan Tousaint): Evenings in the south are heavenly. (artist: Glen Campbell)
- *1977*—"When I Need You" (Carole Bayer Sager, Albert Hammond): You're there whenever I need you because all I have to do is shut my eyes and you're there for me. (artist: Leo Sayer)
- *1977*—"Sir Duke" (Stevie Wonder): Music is a universal language, and we should never forget its pioneers, especially Duke Ellington. (artist: Stevie Wonder)
- *1977*—"You Light Up My Life" (Joe Brooks): I was alone and feeling blue, but you've brightened my life. (artist: Debby Boone)
- *1977*—"Native New Yorker" (Sandy Linzer, Denny Randell): Having been born and bred in New York you've got street smarts so you should know what's going on. (artist: Odyssey)
- *1978*—"We Are the Champions" (Freddie Mercury): I've traveled a hard road to get here, but I'm not going to lose because I'm a winner. (artist: Queen)
- *1978*—"Just the Way You Are" (Billy Joel): There's no need to be anyone else than who you are because that's the person I love. (artist: Billy Joel)
- *1978*—"You Needed Me" (Randy Goodrum): You've always been there for me in my times of need, because you felt the same need for me. (artist: Anne Murray)
- *1979*—"I Will Survive" (Dino Fekaris, Freddie Perren): I don't need you to survive, I can thrive on my own. (artist: Gloria Gaynor)
- *1979*—"Y.M.C.A." (Jacques Morali, Henri Belolo, Victor Willis): If you're new in town, and down, go to the place that can cheer you up, the Y.M.C.A. (artist: Village People)

- *1979*—"Makin' It" (Dino Fekaris, Freddie Perren): I've got what it takes to make it, and I'm going to make it. (artist: David Naughton)
- *1979*—"We Are Family" (Nile Rodgers, Bernard Edwards): We stick together because we're a loving family (artist: Sister Sledge)
- *1980*—"Another One Bites the Dust" (John Richard Deacon): With bullets ripping out of doorways, someone falls, and then another, and another, and so on. (artist: Queen)
- *1982*—"Maneater" (Daryl Hall, John Oates, Sara Allen): You may be in it for love, but she's in it for money, so watch out because she will devour you. (artist: Hall and Oates)
- *1983*—"Girls Just Want to Have Fun" (Robert Hazard): Sorry Mom, sorry Dad, but after work I can stay out all night because having fun is what girls want. (artist: Cyndi Lauper)
- *1983*—"Sweet Dreams (Are Made of This)" (Annie Lennox, David Stewart). The world over people are trying to find themselves, maybe getting hurt along the way, but searching is what makes wonderful reveries so I journey around also and keep going. (artist: Eurythmics)
- *1984*—"Wake Me up Before You Go-Go" (George Michael): You turn me on and are everything I want, but you can be cruel, so when you leave, awake me so I'm not left hanging on and "take me dancing tonight." (artist: Wham!)
- *1984*—"Like a Virgin" (Billy Steinberg, Tom Kelly): Before I met you I was lost, incomplete, and sad, but you made me feel brand new, like I was starting over. (artist: Madonna)
- *1985*—"We Are the World" (Michael Jackson, Lionel Richie): People are dying, and we can't pretend we can't make a difference, so as children of the world who can brighten days of the people who need help, we need to start giving. (artist: USA for Africa)
- *1988*—"Simply Irresistible" (Robert Palmer): She's an addiction, a force, a law of nature, and she can't be resisted. (artist: Robert Palmer)
- *1989*—"She Drives Me Crazy" (Roland Gift, David Steele): I can't help how I feel; I might be obsessed, but I can't escape you, and you lie, so you drive me crazy. (Artist: Fine Young Cannibals)

- *1989*—"We Didn't Start the Fire" (Billy Joel): There may be problems in the world today, but we're not responsible for them; there's always been a fire. (artist: Billy Joel)
- *1990*—"From a Distance" (Julie Gold). If we could separate ourselves from our penchants for conflict and our prejudices, we could see how the world would look with peace, harmony and hope, just as God sees it, from far away. (artist: Bette Midler)
- *1993*—"Freak Me" (Keith Sweat, Roy Murray, Anthony Johnson): A lover's outpouring of all the (freaky) things he'd like to do to his lover's body. (artist: Silk)
- *1999*—"What a Girl Wants" (Guy Roche, Shelley Peiken): For waiting patiently and giving this girl space—what she wanted and needed—she got herself together and showed you care about her, and that makes her happy. (artist: Christina Aguilera)
- *1999*—"No Scrubs" (Lisa Lopes, Kevin Briggs, Tameka Cottle, Kandi Burress). Broke guys who chase after me won't score with me. (artist: TLC).
- *2000*—"Oops! . . . I Did It Again" (Max Martin, Rami Yacoub): She led him on to think it was more serious than it was; she played with his heart, and he thought she was a gift from heaven, but she's not really innocent, and it was another mistake on her part. (artist: Britney Spears)
- *2007*—"Before He Cheats" (Chris Tompkins, Josh Kear): Suspecting he's cheating on her with another woman, she wreaks havoc on his four-wheel drive so he'll think about what he's doing the next time before he becomes unfaithful. (artist: Carrie Underwood)
- *2007*—"No One" (Alicia Keys, George Harry, Kerry Brothers Jr.): I have no worries about us—everything will be fine—because no one can spoil my feelings for you. (artist: Alicia Keys)
- *2009*—"Tik Tok" (Kesha Sebert, Benny Blanco, Dr. Luke): I'm broke and don't have any cares, but let's party all night like it doesn't matter. (artist: Kesha)
- *2013*—"Roar" (Katy Perry, Max Martin, Bonnie McKee, Cirkut, Dr. Luke): You may push me, but I am no longer going to be scared to speak up for myself—you are going to hear me roar. (artist: Katy Perry)

- *2013*—"Just Give Me a Reason" (Pink, Nate Ruess, Jeff Bhasker): I showed you all my rough parts, and you helped me, but now you're saying in your dream that you've had enough, but "just give me a reason." (artist: Pink)
- *2014*—"Happy" (Pharrell Williams): I'm happy, and if you know what happiness is, too, clap along. (artist: Pharrell Williams)
- *2015*—"Uptown Funk!" (Mark Ronson, Nicholas Williams, Jeff Bhasker, Peter Hernandez, Lonnie Simmons, Phillip Lawrence, Charles Wilson, Devon Gallaspy, Rudolph Taylor, Ronnie Wilson, Robert Wilson): I'm really hot, damn hot, and if you don't believe me, just wait and see, because uptown funk is going to "give it to you." (artist: Mark Ronson ft. Bruno Mars)
- *2016*—"Hello" (Adele Adkins, Greg Kurstin): After all these years, time hasn't healed my feelings for you, and I've called you about a thousand times to say I'm sorry for breaking your heart, but you never seem around to pick up. (artist: Adele)
- *2017*—"Believer" (Daniel Platzman, Wayne Sermon, Justin Tranter, Dan Reynolds, Ben McKee, Mattias Larsson, Robin Fredriksson): From the time I was young, I was broken, singing from pain, but you built me up and made me a believer. (artist: Imagine Dragons)
- *2017*—"Havana" (Camila Cabello, Adam King "Frank Dukes" Feeny, A. Wotman, P. L. Williams, A. Tamposi, J. L. Williams, B. Lee, K. Gunesberk, B. T. Hazzard, L. Bell, R. L. Ayala Rodriguez): He approached me in the right way, and he had the right manner, so I feel like I really knew him, but after taking me back to his home, I had to leave even though I loved him because Havana is where my heart is. (artist: Camila Cabello ft. Young Thug)
- *2018*—"I Like It" (Belcalis Almanzar, Benito Antonio Martinez Ocasio, Luian Malave, Pardison Fontaine, Edgar Machuca, Xavier Alexis Semper Vargas, Tony Pabon, Edgar Wilmer Semper Vargas, Vincent Marcellus Watson, Craig Richard Kallman, Jose Alvaro Osorio Balvin, Manny Rodriguez, Noah K Assad, Jermaine White): I like money, jewelry, million-dollar deals, fancy footwear, diamonds in my watch, messages from my exes asking for a second chance; that's how I like it. (artist: Cardi B, Bad Bunny, and J Balvin)

APPENDIX B

Rock and Roll Labels of the 1950s, 1960s, and 1970s and Some of Their Major Artists

- *ABC-Paramount*—Paul Anka, Lloyd Price, Ray Charles, Brian Hyland, Danny and the Juniors, Tommy Roe, Della Reese, Barry Mann, The Elegants, Eydie Gormé, The Poni-Tails, Maxine Brown, B. B. King, Tommy Sands, Tammy Grimes, The Impressions
- *Monument*—Roy Orbison, Boots Randolph and His Combo, Billy Grammer, Kathy Linden, Norris Wilson, Curtis & Del
- *Columbia*—Mitch Miller, Johnny Horton, Guy Mitchell, Jimmie Dean, Marty Robbins, Percy Faith, Steve Lawrence, Barbra Streisand, The Byrds, The Union Gap, Simon and Garfunkel, Janis Joplin, Mac Davis, Bruce Springsteen, Johnny Mathis, Bobby Vinton, Herbie Hancock, Paul Simon, The O'Jays, The Isley Brothers, Boots Randolph, Kansas, Kris Kristofferson, Albert Hammond, Billy Paul, Chicago, The Animals, Bob Dylan, Billy Joel, Loggins and Messina, The Trammps
- *Mercury*—The Platters, Lesley Gore, Sarah Vaughan, Rod Stewart, Lee Hazlewood, Dinah Washington, The Chad Mitchell Trio
- *Tollie*—The Beatles, Barrett Strong, The Clinger Sisters, Jimmy Velvet, Terry Black
- *Atco*—The Beatles, Bobby Darin, Nino Tempo and April Stevens, Bobby Darin, Mr. Acker Bilk, Sonny and Cher, The Bee Gees

- *Capitol*—Nat King Cole, The Beatles, Tennessee Ernie Ford, The Kingston Trio, The Beach Boys, Peter and Gordon, Glen Campbell, Anne Murray, Helen Reddy, Grand Funk, Bobby Gentry, Steve Miller Band, Tavares
- *Dunhill*—The Mamas & the Papas, Barry McGuire, The Grass Roots, Three Dog Night, Steppenwolf, Jimmy Buffett
- *Valiant*—Barry and the Tamerlanes, The Association
- *Asylum*— Linda Ronstadt, The Eagles, Joni Mitchell, Jo Jo Gunne, Andrew Gold, Randy Meisner
- *A&M*—Joe Cocker, The Captain & Tennille, The Carpenters, Herb Alpert and the Tijuana Brass, Burt Bacharach, Supertramp, Sergio Mendes and Brasil '66, Styx, Cat Stevens, The Police, Joan Armatrading, Rick Wakeman
- *Kapp*—The Searchers, Louis Armstrong, Roger Williams, Ruby and the Romantics, Cher, Jack Jones, Brian Hyland, Shirley Ellis, The Good Rats
- *Liberty*—David Seville, Jan & Dean, Gary Lewis and the Playboys, Canned Heat, Ike & Tina Turner, The Nitty Gritty Dirt Band
- *Casablanca*—The Village People, Donna Summer, Kiss, Cher
- *Cameo-Parkway*—The Orlons, Bobby Rydell, Dee Dee Sharp, Mark Dinning, The Applejacks, Chubby Checker, The Tymes
- *MGM*—Sheb Wooly, Conway Twitty, Tommy Edwards, Connie Francis, Mark Dinning, Herman's Hermits, The Animals, Lou Christie, The Osmonds, Sammy Davis Jr.
- *Philles*—The Crystals, The Righteous Brothers, Bob B. Soxx and the Blue Jeans, The Ronettes, Darlene Love
- *Jubilee*—Sonny Til and the Orioles, The Cadillacs, Della Reese, The Raindrops, Don Rondo, Betty Ann Grove, The Four Tunes, Bobby Freeman
- *Polydor*—Gloria Gaynor, Peaches & Herb, Alicia Bridges
- *Tamla*—The Marvelettes, The Miracles, Stevie Wonder, Marvin Gaye, Thelma Houston, Eddie Kendricks
- *RCA*—Elvis Presley, Ed Ames, Perez "Prez" Prado and His Orchestra, Kay Starr, Perry Como, The Tokens, Little Peggy March, Lorne Greene, Guess Who, Henry Mancini, Nilsson, Zager and Evans, Taco, David Bowie
- *RSO*—The Bee Gees, Andy Gibb, Suzi Quatro and Chris Norman, Yvonne Elliman

- *Epic*—The Dave Clark Five, Bobby Vinton, Donovan, Looking Glass, Sly and the Family Stone, Charlie Rich, Johnny Nash
- *Vanguard*—The Rooftop Singers, Country Joe and the Fish, Buffy Sainte-Marie, Joan Baez, Tom Paxton
- *Arista*—Raydio, Barry Manilow, The Bay City Rollers, The Alan Parsons Project, Melissa Manchester, Eric Carmen, Tony Orlando & Dawn, Heart Williams, Patti Smith Group
- *Reprise*—Frank Sinatra, Nancy Sinatra, Norman Greenbaum, Neil Young, Gordon Lightfoot
- *MCA*—Elton John, Olivia Newton-John, Electric Light Orchestra, Hoyt Axton, Marvin Hamlisch, Jimmy Buffett, Steely Dan, Freddy Fender, Brenda Lee
- *De-Lite*—Kool and the Gang, Crown Heights Affair
- *Warner Bros.*—Peter, Paul and Mary, Allan Sherman, Everly Brothers, Petula Clark, James Taylor, America, Leo Sayer, Freddie Cannon, Faces
- *Chrysalis*—Blondie, Jethro Tull, Pat Benatar, Leo Sayer, Gentle Giant, Ten Years After, Robin Trower, Laurie Styvers, Steeleye Span
- *Swan*—The Beatles, Freddie Cannon, Dickie Doo and the Don'ts, Rockin' Rebels
- *Scepter*—The Shirelles, The Shangri-Las, Joey Dee & The Starlighters, B. J. Thomas, Dionne Warwick, The Guess Who, The Soldier Boys, Judy Clay, Tommy Hunt, Lori Rogers
- *Philips*—Paul and Paula, The 4 Seasons, Paul Mauriat and His Orchestra, The Singing Nun
- *Hickory*—The Newbeats, Don Gibson, Ernie Ashworth, Donovan, Leona Williams
- *Malaco*—Dorothy Moore, Eddie Floyd, The Williams Family, Jewel Bass, Natural High
- *Musicor*—Gene Pitney, Hot Butter, Eartha Kitt, Melba Montgomery, Don Adams, Inez and Charlie Foxx, George Jones, Judy Lynn, Floyd Tillman, Jimmy Radcliffe, Rex Allen
- *Garpax*—Bobby "Boris" Pickett and the Crypt-Kickers, The Five Superiors, Gary Paxton, Don Wyatt, The Rev-Lons
- *Vee Jay*—Gene Chandler, The Four Seasons, John Lee Hooker, Betty Everett, The Beatles

- *Motown*—The Four Tops, The Supremes, Stevie Wonder, Mary Wells, The Jackson Five, Bonnie Pointer, The Miracles, The Contours
- *United Artists*—Bobby Goldsboro, Don McLean, Electric Light Orchestra, Jay and the Americans, Ferrante & Teicher, Gerry Mulligan, Johnny Rivers, Steve Lawrence and Eydie Gormé, The Exciters
- *Dark Horse*—George Harrison, Ravi Shankar Family & Friends, Splinters
- *Decca*—Fred Waring and His Pennsylvanians, Bill Haley and His Comets, Bert Kaempfert, the Four Aces, Brenda Lee
- *Mala*—The Box Tops, The Hully Gully Boys, The Young Sisters, Ray Rapa, The Majestics, The Hi Boy, Bunker Hill, David Gates, J. R. Bailey
- *Cotillion*—Brook Benton, Emerson, Lake & Palmer, The Dynamics, Freddie King, Otis Clay, Delorise Berry, Darrell Banks, Chris Towns & the Townsmen
- *T.K.*—George McCrae, KC & The Sunshine Band, Betty Wright, Foxy, T-Connection, Bobby Caldwell, Anita Ward
- *Imperial*—Ricky Nelson, Johnny Rivers, Classics IV
- *Dimension*—Little Eva, Big Dee Irwin, The Cookies, The Spandells, Sonny Curtis, Ron Winters
- *Brunswick*—The Crickets, The Chi-Lites, Jackie Wilson, Brenda Lee, The Surfaris, Burl Ives, Patsy Cline, The Kingston Trio, Billie Holiday, The Kalin Twins, Ella Fitzgerald, Bing Crosby, The Four Aces, The Rhymettes, Louis Armstrong and His Orchestra, Benny Goodman and His Orchestra, Coleman Hawkins, Bill Haley and His Comets, Peter Duchin, Leroy Anderson, Kitty Wells, Sammy Davis Jr.
- *Roulette*—Jimmie Rodgers, Buddy Knox, Joey Dee and the Starliters, The Essex, Tommy James and the Shondells, The Exciters, The Three Degrees
- *Apt*—The Elegants, Johnny Maestro, Joe South, Dee Mize, Vince Castro, The Dozier Boys, The Twisters, Caney Creek Reunion, Bobby Brown, Bobby Guy, The Click-Clacks, The Youngsters
- *Keen*—Sam Cooke, Johnny "Guitar" Watson
- *Fontana*—Wayne Fontana and the Mindbenders, The Troggs, The New Vaudeville Band
- *Buddah*—Lemon Pipers, Gladys Knight and the Pips, Ohio Express

- *London*—The Rolling Stones, Moody Blues, The Tornadoes, The Zombies, Luciano Pavarotti, Engelbert Humperdinck, Tom Jones, Hazel Dean
- *Colpix*—The Marcels, Shelley Fabares, Paul Petersen, The Virginians, The Barry Sisters, Nina Simone, Zoot Sims and His Orchestra
- *Elektra*—The Doors, Bread, Carly Simon, The Cars, Tony Orlando & Dawn, Judy Collins, Harry Chapin, Mel Tillis, Neil Sedaka, Eddie Rabbit, Sergio Mendes Brasil "88"
- *Atlantic*—Percy Sledge, The Drifters, Aretha Franklin, The Young Rascals, Roberta Flack, The Manhattan Transfer, ABBA
- *Apple*—The Beatles, George Harrison, Mary Hopkin, John Lennon, Ringo Starr, The Plastic Ono Band, Wings
- *Philadelphia International*—The O'Jays, Billy Paul, Edwin Birdsong, MFSB, Teddy Pendergrass, Lou Rawls, Harold Melvin & the Blue Notes, Patti LaBelle, The Three Degrees, Archie Bell & the Drells
- *Mam*—Gilbert O'Sullivan, Dave Edmunds, Tom Paxton, Engelbert Humperdinck, Tom Jones, Lynsey de Paul
- *Laurie*—The Chiffons, Dion & the Belmonts, The Royal Guardsmen, Gerry & the Pacemakers, Cathy Carr, The Mystics, The Del-Satins, The Jarmels, The Velveteens
- *Plantation*—Jeannie C. Riley, Skip Gibbs, Linda Martell, Jimmie Dale and the Flatlanders, Sonny Hall, Ray Pillow, Dee Mullins, Melvin Nash
- *Bell*—The Partridge Family, Tony Orlando & Dawn, Terry Jacks, Vicki Lawrence, The 5th Dimension, The Bay City Rollers, David Cassidy, Solomon Burke, Michel Legrand, Showaddywaddy, Gary Glitter, Mountain, Leslie West, The Box Tops, Crazy Elephant, The Drifters
- *Parrot*—Engelbert Humperdinck, Clarence "Frogman" Henry, Tom Jones, The Ides of March, The Zombies, Lulu
- *Kama Sutra*—The Lovin' Spoonful, The Charlie Daniels Band, Brewer and Shipley, Buzzy Linhart, Sha Na Na
- *Red Bird*—The Dixie Cups, The Shangri-Las, Eva Sands, The Jelly Beans, Ellie Greenwich
- *Verve*—Stan Getz, Buddy Rich, The Righteous Brothers, The Oscar Peterson Trio, Ella Fitzgerald, Kenny Burrell, The Velvet Underground, Bobby Hatfield, Dizzy Gillespie, Anita O'Day, Astrud Gilberto, Buddy Rich, Wes Montgomery, Bill Evans

- *Hi*—Al Green, Ann Peebles, Syl Johnson, The Duncan Sisters, Heinsight
- *Ode*—Carole King, Scott McKenzie, Merry Clayton, Peggy Lipton, Gene McDaniels
- *Soul City*—The Fifth Dimension, Al Wilson, Johnny Rivers, George McCrae
- *Dot*—Pat Boone, Andy Kim, Donna Fargo, Jimmie Rodgers, Freddy Fender, The Anita Kerr Singers, The American Breed, Mia Farrow, Lawrence Welk, Jimmy Gilmore, Eddie Fisher, Billy Vaughn and His Orchestra, Leonard Nimoy
- *Volt*—Otis Redding, The Bar-Kays, The Emotions, Mavis Staples, Inez Foxx, Eddie Purrell, Bobby Wilson
- *Chancellor*—Frankie Avalon, Fabian Forte, Jimmy Wisner Trio
- *Herald*—Maurice Williams and the Zodiacs, The Mello Kings, The Nutmegs, The Mint Juleps
- *Gordy*—The Temptations, Edwin Starr, Martha and the Vandellas, Rick James, DeBarge, The Contours
- *Ascot*—Manfred Mann, The James Gang, Morgana King, Billy Bishop, Bobby Comstock
- *Legrand*—Gary U.S. Bonds, The Concertones, Daddy "G" and the Church Street, Five, Lenis Guess, Elsie Strong, Tommy Facenda
- *Leader*—Brian Hyland, Johnny Duncan, The Palisades, The Lane Brothers
- *Tower*—Freddie and the Dreamers, Ian Whitcomb, The Chocolate Watchband
- *Barnaby*—Ray Stevens, The Everly Brothers, Johnny Tillotson, The Chordettes
- *Lute*—The Hollywood Argyles, The Uptones, Gary Paxton, Danny the Dreamer, The Starr Sisters, Ty Terrell, Darlene Paul
- *USA*—The Buckinghams, Willie Mabon, The Tempos, The Echoes, The Great Society, Elmore James, The Nobelmen, The Mod Singers, The Deltones, Carole Waller, Perk Lee, Oscar & Anita, Frankie Gem
- *White Whale*—The Turtles, The Everpresent, The Odyssey, Harper & Rowe, Nino Tempo & April Stevens, Rene & Rene, Bobby Lile, Jan Davis, The Malibu's
- *Stax*—The Staple Singers, Isaac Hayes, Booker T. and the MGs, The Emotions, Carla Thomas, Johnny Taylor

- *Uni*—Neil Diamond, Hugh Masekela, Strawberry Alarm Clock, Steve Earle, The Rainy Daze, The Shy Guys, The Foundations, The Hippy Dippys
- *Dolton*—The Fleetwoods, The Ventures, Vic Dana, Dodie Stevens
- *Cadence*—Everly Brothers, The Chordettes, Andy Williams, Lennie Welch, Johnny Tillotson, Julius La Rosa
- *Coral*—Debby Reynolds, Teresa Brewer, The Crickets, Buddy Holly, The Treniers, The McGuire Sisters, Jackie Wilson, Steve Lawrence, Liberace
- *Dore*—The Teddy Bears, Jan and Dean, Deanne Hawley, John and Judy, The Zanies, The Tides, The Debonaires, Jim Eddy, Vic Granton, The Choppers, The Raindrops, Carole Winters
- *Chess*—Chuck Berry, Howlin' Wolf, Bo Diddley, Muddy Waters, The Coronets, Jimmie Rogers, Al Hibbler, Johnny Lee Hooker, J. B. and His Bayou Boys, Eddie Ware, Doctor Ross and His Jump and Jive Boys, Washboard Sam, Jackie Brenston and His Delta Cats

BIBLIOGRAPHY

General reference sources used in writing this book were *Billboard* magazine and the digital news subscription services *Music Business Worldwide* and *Digital Music News*.

"A History of Rock Music in 500 Songs." Podcast, Episode 27: "Tweedle Dee," by LaVern Baker, April 8, 2019.

Alden-Rochelle Inc. v. American Soc. Of Composers, Authors and Publishers, et al. U.S. District Court for the Southern District of New York. 80 F. Supp. 888, July 19, 1948.

American Society of Composers, Authors & Publishers. *ASCAP Hit Songs*. New York: Author, n.d. (Source for many of the song titles in chapters 2 and 3 as well as the song titles and writers in appendix A.)

Associated Press. "Eagles' *Greatest Hits* Overtakes Michael Jackson's *Thriller* as Best-Selling Album of All Time in the U.S." August, 20, 2018.

Auerbach, Brad. "Pat Boone: What You Don't Know about the Entrepreneur, Recording Artist and Friend of Fats Domino." *Forbes*, November 1, 2017.

The Beatles: A Pocket Reference Guide to More Than 100 Songs! Milwaukee: Hal Leonard Corporation, 1995.

Bergerac, Cyrano de. *Voyages to the Moon and the Sun*. Translated by Richard Adlington. New York: Orion Press, 1962.

Billboard Staff. "Head of WMG's Playlist Brand Topsify and Streaming Label Leaves Company." *Billboard Online*, October 23, 2017.

Bronson, Fred. *The Billboard Book of Number One Hits*. New York: Billboard Publications, 1985.

"Build the Edison Tin-Foil Phonograph." Sheets. West Orange, NJ: Edison National Historic Site, n.d.

Burton, Jack. *The Blue Book of Tin Pan Alley: A Human Interest Anthology of American Popular Music*. Watkins Glen, NY: Century House, 1951.

Christman, Ed. "Going for a Song." *Billboard*, March 30, 2013.

Cobo, Leila. "Sony's Secret Sessions." *Billboard*, December 8, 2018.

Denisoff, R. Serge. *Solid Gold: The Popular Record Industry*. New Brunswick, NJ: Transaction Books, 1975.

Elson, Louis C. *The National Music of America and Its Sources*. Boston: L. C. Page, 1924.

Ergo, Richard W. "ASCAP and the Antitrust Laws: The Story of a Reasonable Compromise." 1958. Reprinted in Duke Law Scholarship Repository.

Ewen, David. *All the Years of American Popular Music*. Englewood Cliffs, NJ: Prentice-Hall, 1977. (An excellent book on the history of popular music up to 1977, and an important source for British lyrics recast for American songs, William Billings and "Chester," and an important source for chapter 2—including information on music publishers, jazz, origin of the Tin Pan Alley name, and "Happy Birthday to You"—and for radio shows and *Rhapsody in Blue* for chapter 3.)

Feist, Leonard. *An Introduction to Popular Music Publishing in America*. New York: National Music Publishers' Association, 1980. (Another important source for chapter 2.)

The Frank Sinatra Timex Special: Welcome Home Elvis. Broadcast on May 12, 1960, on the ABC-TV network. Note: I made considerable effort to find and contact the copyright owners for dialogue from this show that is used in chapter 5 of this book. Should the copyright owners step forward, I would be happy to secure the appropriate permissions.

Gelatt, Roland. *The Fabulous Phonograph: From Tin Foil to High Fidelity*. Philadelphia: J.B. Lippincott, 1955.

Geller, James J. *Famous Songs and Their Stories*. New York: Garden City, 1940. (Source for some of the song stories in chapter 2.)

Goldberg, Isaac. *Tin Pan Alley: A Chronicle of the American Popular Music Racket*. New York: The John Day Company, 1930. (Source for the cost of sheet music in chapter 2.)

"Great Welcome for New Opera." New York Times, December 11, 1910. A source of information for the premier of *The Girl of the Golden West* at the Metropolitan Opera in New York City in chapter 2.

Koenigsberg, Allen. *Edison Cylinder Records, 1889-1912, with an Illustrated History of the Phonograph*. Brooklyn: APM Press, 1987.

Levine, Robert. "The 'Despacito' Mystery." *Billboard*, December 8, 2018.

Library of Congress Historic Sheet Music Collection, Library of Congress, Music Division, Library of Congress, Washington, DC.

Lindsay, Martin. *Songwriting*. London: Teach Yourself Books, 1955. (Source for the metaphor of the home and vacation [AABA] structure of a popular song.)

The Lyn Farnol Group, compiler and ed. *The ASCAP Biographical Dictionary of Composers, Authors and Publisher*, 3rd ed. New York: The American Society of Composers, Authors and Publishers, 1966.

Marks, Craig. "How a Hit Happens Now." *Vulture*, September 18–October 1, 2017. Accessed July 13, 2019. www.vulture.com/2017/09/spotify-rapcaviar-most-influential-playlist-in-music.html.

Mather, Cotton. *Diary of Cotton Mather, 1709–1724*. Vol. 7, *Massachusetts Historical Society Collections, Seventh Series*. Boston: Massachusetts Historical Society, 1912.

McAleer, Dave. *The Book of Hit Singles: Top 20 Charts from 1954 to the Present Day*. San Francisco: Miller Freeman Books, 1999. (An excellent reference source of U.S. and UK chart hits.)

Milligan, Harold Vincent. *Stephen Collins Foster: A Biography of America's Folk-Song Composer*. New York: G. Schirmer, 1920.

Mondello, Bob. "George M. Cohan, NPR, 'The Man Who Created Broadway, Was an Anthem Machine." *NPR*, December 20, 2018. Accessed July 13, 2019. www.npr.org/2018/12/20/677552863/george-m-cohan-the-man-who-created-broadway-american-anthem.

"NARM Special." *Billboard*, March 23, 1968. (Source of the Jules Malamud and George Marek quotes in chapter 4.)

Oberndorfer, Marx, and Anne Oberndorfer. *The New American Song Book*. Minneapolis: Schmitt, Hall & McCreary, 1961. (Source of *Te Deum* reference [in which a Columbus journal is cited] and songs from foreign lands in chapters 1 and 11.)

"One Hundred Years of Sound Recording." Press release. New York: Recording Industry Association of America, 1977. Source of information on demonstrations of Edison's phonograph, the phonograph parlor, and records by Russian artists on RCA's "red label."

Rachlin, Harvey. *The Encyclopedia of the Music Business*. New York: Harper & Row, 1981. (A general source used throughout the book and for particular sections including copyright law history and the history of performing rights, ASCAP, and performing rights organizations in chapter 2, electrical transcriptions in chapter 3, and beats per minute and record pools in chapter 7.)

———. *Jumbo's Hide, Elvis's Ride, and the Tooth of Buddha*. New York: Henry Holt, 2000. (One of the sources of information about Edison's invention of the phonograph player.)

———. *The Kennedys: A Chronological History 1823–Present*. New York: World Almanac, 1986. (Source of the Kennedy introduction of chapter 6.)

———. *Lucy's Bones, Sacred Stones and Einstein's Brain*. New York: Henry Holt, 1996.

———. "Songwriter Profile—Irving Caesar." *The Songwriter's Review*. (Source of the Irving Caesar "Swanee" anecdote in chapter 3.)

———. "The Sound Recording Industry." *Songwriter's Review* 33., no. 3 (June/July 1978).

Roehl, Harvey N. *Player Piano Treasury: The Scrapbook History of the Mechanical Piano in America as Told in Story Pictures, Trade Journal Articles and Advertising*. Vestal, NY: The Vestal Press, 1961.

Rosenberg, Robert A., et al., eds. *The Papers of Thomas A. Edison, Menlo Park: The Early Years, April 1876–December 1877*. Volume 3. Baltimore: Johns Hopkins University Press, 1995.

Sanchez, Daniel. "Spotify Now Has 200 Million Monthly Active Users—But How Many Are Paying?" *Digital Music News*, January 11, 2019.

Schumach, Murray. "Willie Howard—the World's His Straight Man." *New York Times*, May 2, 1948.

Slater, Graham. "Notes." In *Greatest Hits of Rock and Roll*. New York: Charles Hansen Music & Books, n.d.

Steele, Anne. "Music Samples for Sale Are a Hit." *Wall Street Journal*, March 21, 2019.

Steele, Anne, and Tripp Mickle. "Apple Passes Spotify in U.S. Players." *Wall Street Journal*, April 6–7, 2019.

Tarr, Douglas. "Sound Recording." Sheet. West Orange, NJ: Edison National Historic Site, May 15, 1998.

Wicker, Jewell. "Managers Jump into Label Game." *Billboard*, December 8, 2018.

Wilson, Carl. "Pop's New Team." *Billboard*, December 15, 2018.

Witmark, Isadore, and Isaac Goldberg. *From Ragtime to Swingtime*. New York: Lee Furman, 1939. (Source of the New York City vaudeville theaters mentioned in chapter 2.)

INDEX

ABOUT THE AUTHOR

Harvey Rachlin runs the music business program at Manhattanville College in Purchase, New York. He is the author of thirteen books including *The Songwriter's Handbook* and *The Encyclopedia of the Music Business*. The latter title won the ASCAP Deems Taylor Award for excellence in music journalism, was named Outstanding Music Reference Book of the Year by the American Library Association, and was recommended by composer Henry Mancini on behalf of CBS Television and the Library of Congress on the 1984 internationally televised Grammy Awards. His music books have been praised by Elton John, Aaron Copland, Morton Gould, Johnny Mathis, Pat Boone, and Academy Award–winning songwriters Richard Rodgers, Burt Bacharach, Sammy Cahn, Jule Styne, Marvin Hamlisch, and Henry Mancini.

Rachlin's book *Lucy's Bones, Sacred Stones, and Einstein's Brain* was adapted for the History Channel series *History's Lost and Found*, narrated by actor Edward Herrmann and introduced on the network by the renowned television journalist Roger Mudd. He cowrote the three pilot episodes, which broke ratings records for the History Channel and won the Cine Golden Eagle Award for Best History Series.

Harvey Rachlin's books have been translated into Korean, Spanish, German, and Polish and have been selections of the Book of the Month Club, Quality Paperback Book Club, History Book Club, *Encyclopedia Britannica* Home Library, *Writer's Digest* Book Club, and the Fireside Theatre Book Club. He has written more than two hundred newspaper and magazine articles, with publication credits in the *Wall Street Journal*, the *New York Times*, and *The Times* (London), and he has ap-

peared on hundreds of radio and television shows. He lives in Larch-
mont, New York, with his significant other and her dog, Cody.